IMAGES
of America

COLUMBUS RADIO

I0807606

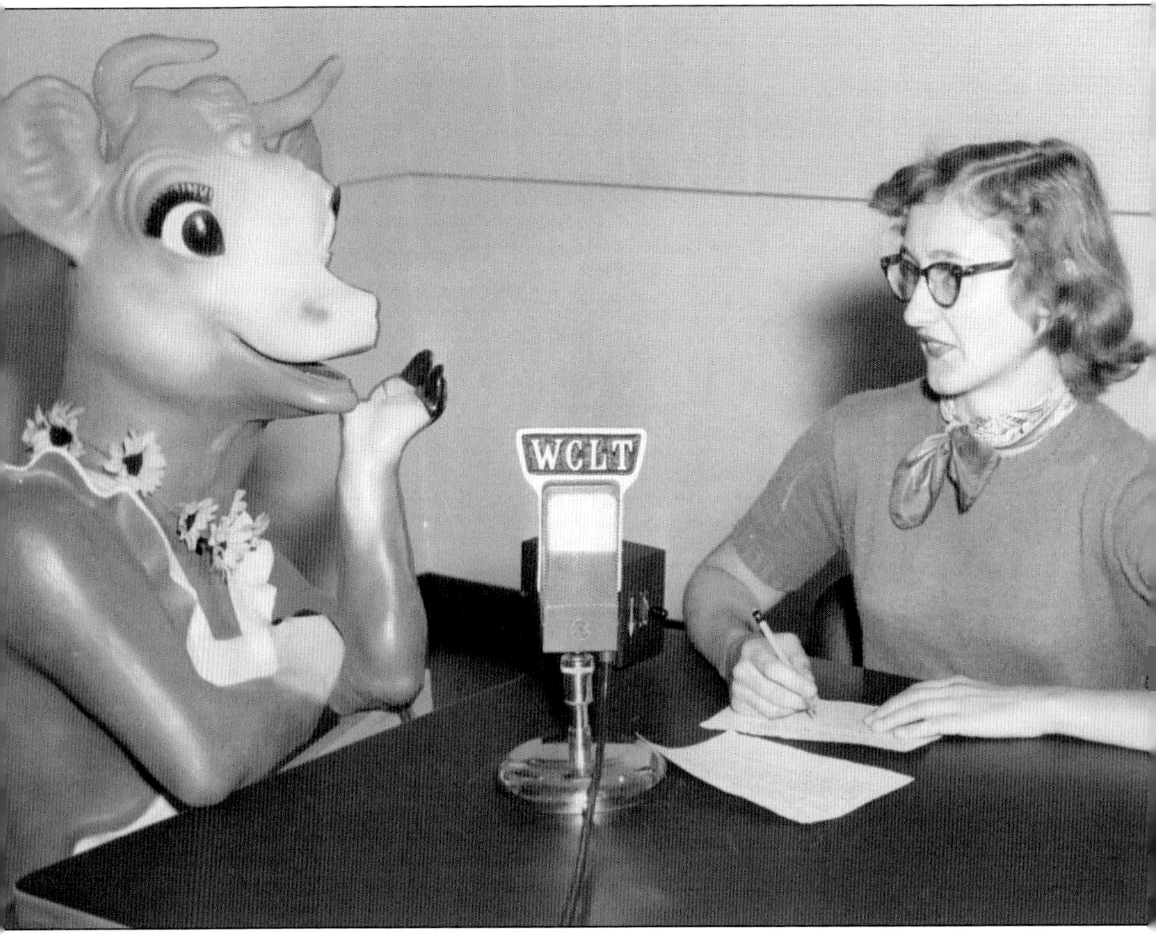

Stations were given many opportunities to interview famous people, the goal being free publicity. Here is a WCLT announcer interviewing Elsie the Cow, likely promoting one product or the udder. What could Elsie say other than, "Drink your milk, boys and girls." Or "Get me out of this hot suit!" Could this all be lost on the radio audience? (Douglas Pricer, WCLT)

On the Cover: In this 1950s photograph, three WVKO personalities are giving the audience what they expect from their radios: entertainment. Pictured on the right is Columbus radio legend Eddie Saunders with two unidentified program participants. It was an experimental time for radio as long form "programs" migrated to television, leaving radio with recorded music programs delivered by an announcer, now called a disc jockey. Saunders was prescient enough to collect many images of his time at WVKO and place them in a public archive for continued understanding of the importance of this radio station in Columbus life. His commitment demonstrates why you should save your history and make it available to those researchers that follow. (The Ohio History Connection, MSS422AV.)

IMAGES
of America

COLUMBUS RADIO

Mike Adams

ARCADIA
PUBLISHING

ISBN 978-1-4671-2440-9

Published by Arcadia Publishing
Charleston, South Carolina

Printed in the United States of America

Library of Congress Control Number: 2016945807

For all general information, please contact Arcadia Publishing:
Telephone 843-853-2070
Fax 843-853-0044
E-mail sales@arcadiapublishing.com
For customer service and orders:
Toll-Free 1-888-313-2665

Visit us on the Internet at www.arcadiapublishing.com

To all the talented people with whom I have worked and to those who came before me and made Columbus Radio special during its golden age.

Contents

Acknowledgments

Thank you, thank you, thank you.

This illustrated history of Columbus radio required the cooperation of radio stations, public libraries, and archives. But there are also many individuals who have just one story and a photograph or two of their own lives in broadcasting. All contributed an important part of a massive story of the greatest media of the 20th century—radio.

A book like this cannot be made without the help of those who have saved their personal history or that of their organization. Some were found in attics or dusty corners of a radio station's transmitter building, while other collections were organized, preserved, and catalogued for public use. Two stations, WBNS and WCLT, were owned by newspapers, and that resulted in many high-quality images from professional photographers assigned to document their stations. Conversely, some stations are underrepresented because they had not saved a bit of their history or the station was sold and its location changed, its history left behind. Some station histories are very complete: Bob Dildine's *History of WBNS since 1924* helped me caption the photo collection provided by WBNS director of engineering Greg Armstrong.

These individuals contributed their personal history or pointed me to a source: Bob Alan, Tom Burris, Tracy Beckman, Tamera Durrence, Natalie Fritz, Cathy Hackett, Lou Henry, Dennis Gibson, Johnny Hill, Dave Hull, Frank Jazzo, Chris and Diana Johnson, Bill Kirkpatrick, Art Leberman, Clay Lowe, Bryan McIntyre, Bob Masys, Daniel Moss, Jack Park, Fritz Peerenboom, Mike Perkins, John Potter, Josh Sheppard, A.V. Shirk, Bruce Sinton, Steve Sinton, John Sinton, Jay Solomon, Jeff Rehl, Dudley Taft, and Brian Wolf.

These station owners and managers understood the big picture, the greater perspective of their stations: Dan Morris from WCOL and WNCI, Jim Pidcock from WTVN, Greg Armstrong from WBNS, Mike Eiland from iHeart Media, Douglas Pricer of WCLT, Dan Mushalko of WCBE, Thomas Rieland of WOSU Public Media, and Matt Mnich of WMNI.

Fortunately, many of the high-quality images are organized and protected in libraries. Major help was provided by these individuals and their archives: Rebecca Felkner of the Photohio *Citizen-Journal* Archives at Grandview Heights Public Library; Lisa Wood, the Ohio History Connection; Colleen Goodhart, Dennison University Library; Aaron Odonovan, Columbus Metropolitan Library; and Michelle Drobik, the Ohio State University Library Special Collections.

And finally, a small group of individuals that were not only interested in this project but were able to reintroduce me to Columbus, to house me, and who were always there to make many calls on my behalf. They are Neal Shapiro, Don Gorman, and Landa Brunetto. Most important is Barbara Adams, who proofreads everything and makes many suggestions for improvement. And of course thanks to the very capable team at Arcadia Publishing: Katelyn Carter and my editor, Henry Clougherty.

Thanks to all of you for making this work possible.

INTRODUCTION

In the formative years of broadcasting, the early 1920s, Columbus was a town of 240,000 citizens. And while it was the capital of Ohio, its population was less than that of Cleveland with 800,000 and Cincinnati at 400,000. This original small size, this rural footprint, meant that unlike Cleveland and Cincinnati, Columbus radio stations were of relatively low power and would remain that way. Cleveland and Cincinnati both had 50,000-watt mega-stations serving large regional audiences. Several Columbus stations would broadcast with 5,000 watts, but none were so-called "clear channel" stations.

In the November 1922 *Radio Digest* entry of "Stations on the Air in Columbus Ohio," these were listed: WBAV, WCAH, WEAO, and WMAN. You don't recognize these stations? What about WJD? In the 1920s, all of these stations would change call letters and ownership or disappear entirely. Out of these first experimental attempts at both understanding and practicing broadcasting by radio would evolve the stations that defined the 20th century for Columbus listeners: WOSU, WBNS, WCOL, WTVN, WRFD, WVKO, and WMNI, plus the FMs that reimagined radio in the 1970s: WCOL-FM, WOSU-FM, WNCI, and WCBE. And there are suburban stations, like WCLT in Newark.

In this visual tour of Columbus radio history, three stations will emerge as the most important in the lives of listeners, all for unique reasons: first WOSU, for its very pioneering and prescient work in radio for education; then WBNS, for being the class act of local radio during its golden age; and finally WCOL, for dominating Columbus radio with rock and roll for the emerging teenage audience. During the first half of the 20th century, radio technology was invented and improved, the content of broadcasting evolved, and the radio audience was defined.

I lived the Columbus radio life. When I was a small child, my mother took me to be in the audiences of several programs. On our local station, WCLT in Newark, my mother had a Saturday morning program called *The Mothersingers*, a small choir composed of women who I assumed were all mothers during the week. She was a music teacher and choir director, so this made sense. I was in awe of the WCLT tower, looming over the parking lot and art deco–like building. It was sited just right to impress. I was also taken to WBNS to observe *The Early Worm* show with Irwin Johnson, and I remember that we were given a tiny glass worm for visiting.

My grandfather had a radio listening habit, and in his house, each room had a radio and a chair where he sat to listen. He had a dozen or so large, well-polished wood console radios with shortwave. He had medium-sized table radios, and he listened to all of them daily. This was odd, but I never questioned it. I became a radio collector myself, now owning several hundred such sets. Soon I had moved from radio listener to radio tinkerer to radio student to radio personality. At age 19, I applied to WCOL and was hired. I only had to show up a few minutes before midnight and go on the air. All the program director asked was, "Do you have a radio name?" I said, "No, go ahead and pick one for me."

It was five minutes to midnight when I pushed the night buzzer for entry into the station. The DJ on the air greeted me and said, "You must be Mike Adams." He knew that before I did because on a tape cartridge were the words "Mike Adams Show Intro." At midnight he pushed a button, and from the loudspeaker a heavy tympani drumroll and a powerful voice in heavy echo said, "From Columbus, entertainment capital of the great Midwest, it's all hit music with Mike Adams!" My radio life began. This book presents my broader perspective on Columbus radio, the important stations, and the personalities. I hope you enjoy the images of Columbus radio. This is my legacy, my gift to you.

—Mike Adams
mike.adams@sjsu.edu

One

Radio Enters the Columbus Home

In 1922, the Radio Corporation of America published a book titled *Radio Enters the Home*. It attempted to set the stage for the fast-emerging technology of radio broadcasting. This book detailed the past, present, and future of the radio. It paid homage to the wireless telegraph roots of the radio as an entertainment medium and acknowledged the role of its original use, saving lives at sea. It predicted a future when radio would educate, inform, and entertain, promote world peace, and in general be a good citizen. This book also had something for the experimenter in the form of a complete mail order parts catalogue. But its major value was that for the first time, the public could buy ready-made radios in all price ranges, from the basic crystal set to the console with a loudspeaker. Also published in 1922 were several juvenile books under the series titles of Radio Boys and Radio Girls, and there was a weekly radio column in the local newspaper. Through the printed word, Columbus families were able to learn about and participate in the new medium of radio.

Columbus was a little late to licensing. The first commercial station, KDKA in Pittsburgh, began a few hours a day of broadcasting, starting with the presidential election returns in November 1920. Other stations followed, resulting in several hundred stations on the air in 1921. And while 1920 marked the beginning of broadcasting, 1922 was its defining year. It was during that year that radio exploded in popularity. It literally moved from the attics and garages of postwar experimenters into the family living room. In 1922, Columbus had at least five licensed radio broadcasting stations, each on for a few hours a day. The teenager who would be so important as a listener of rock and roll radio in the 1960s was building radios in 1922. The kids lead the way, their parents follow.

An important international event helped to nudge radio from a two-way communication technology to a family entertainment medium. The just-concluded Great War had forced the companies that made radio devices to pool their patents together in the service of better wartime communication technology. These improvements in receivers and transmitters would be needed for the broadcasting of voice and music. And with peacetime came a collective sigh of relief and a need for something fun. Radio entertainment was just the thing. By 1922, radio had entered the Columbus home.

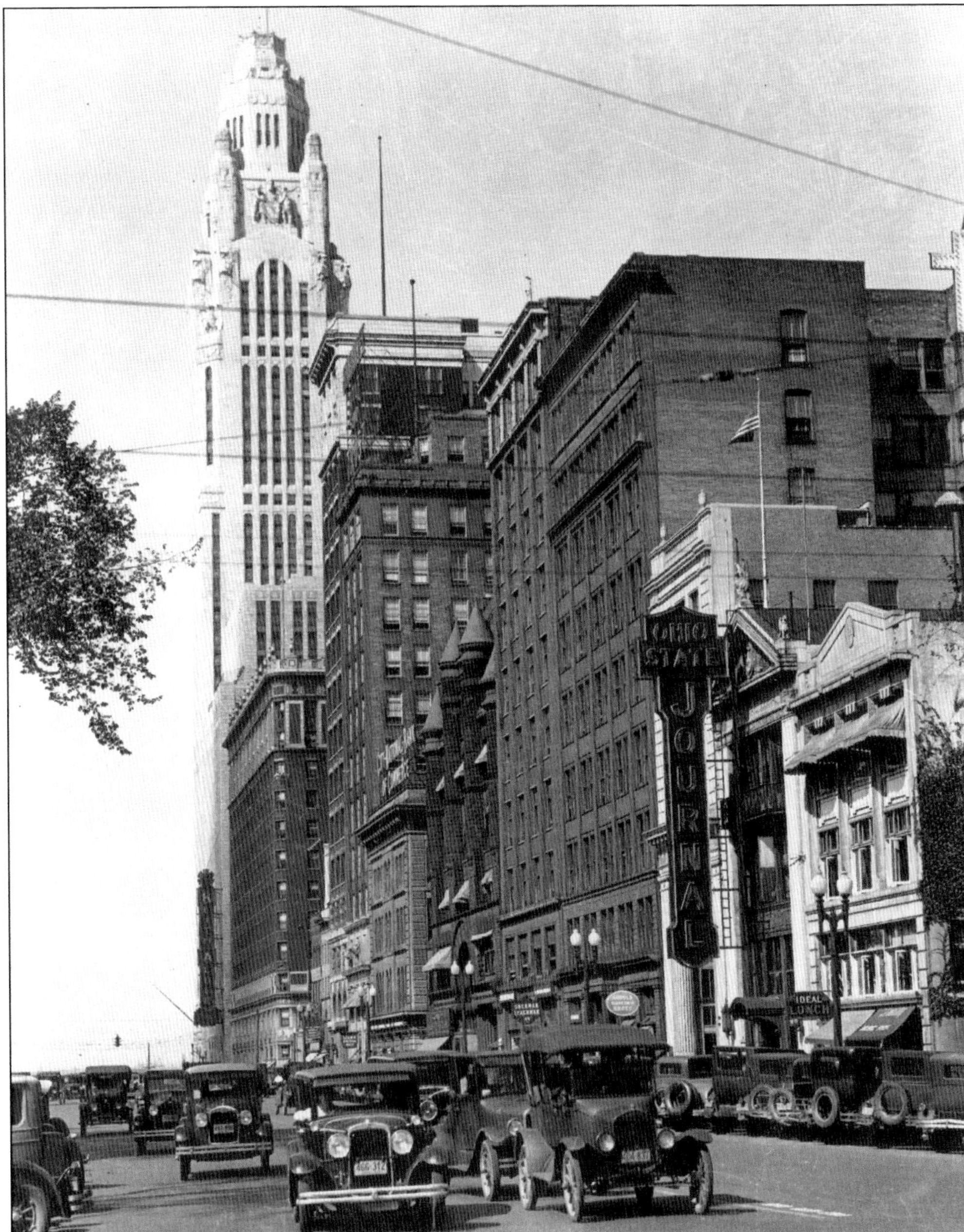

This is downtown Columbus, Broad and High Streets, about 1927. Just five years earlier, very few of these people owned a radio—not in their homes, not in their cars. They didn't think about radio, didn't understand it, and didn't realize that they even needed a radio. By the mid-1920s, almost every one of these people would have that first radio in their homes. Maybe it was built by the neighborhood high school student, or maybe it was purchased from Lazarus department store in downtown Columbus. In the background of this image is the newly constructed American Insurance Union (AIU) Citadel, known today as the Leveque-Lincoln Tower, important in local broadcasting. This view is looking west on Broad Street, the state capitol unseen on the left. (The Ohio History Connection, *Columbus Dispatch*, ALO1744.)

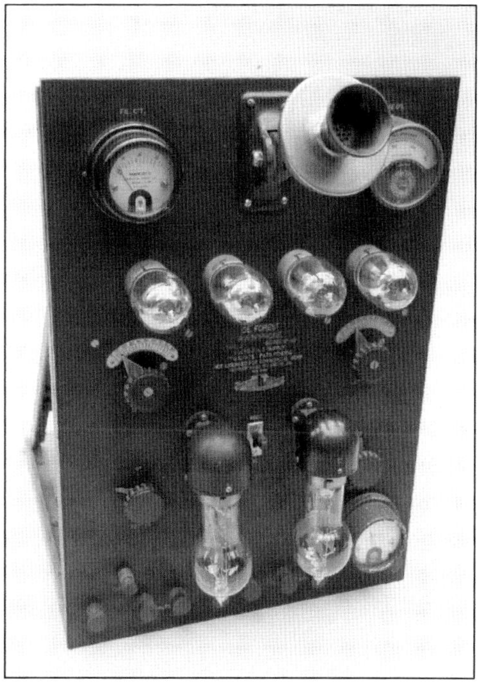

The first broadcast transmitters were called radiotelephones or wireless telephones, and this Lee de Forest device, used in 1920 by Detroit news station WJR, shows why. The most prominent feature of the device is none other than the familiar telephone transmitter itself. One might say that inventors took bits and pieces of wireless telegraph technology and the wired telephone to create radio. (Author photograph.)

The radio receiver itself began with the basic crystal set, which had to be listened to using earphones. This 1920 set has among its parts a piece of galena crystal called a detector, to which the listener touches a tiny wire called a "cat whisker" to find the most sensitive part on the crystal. Prominent are the large tuning coil for selecting stations and connectors for antenna, ground, and earphone. (Author photograph.)

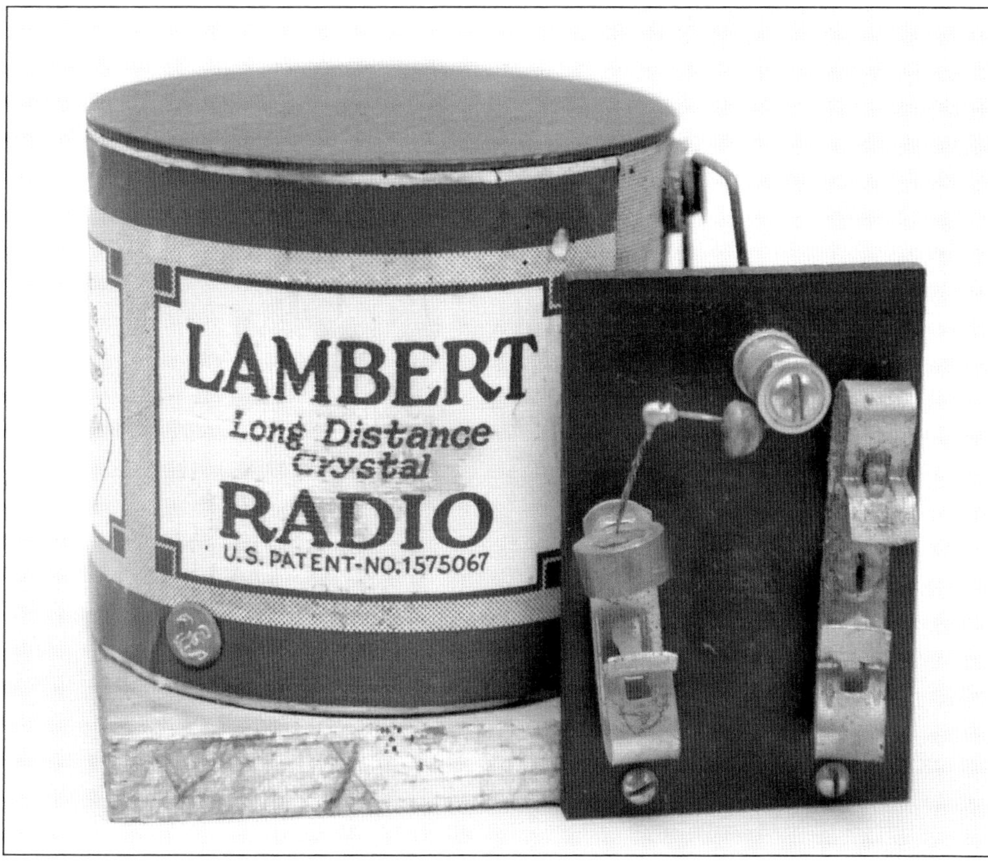

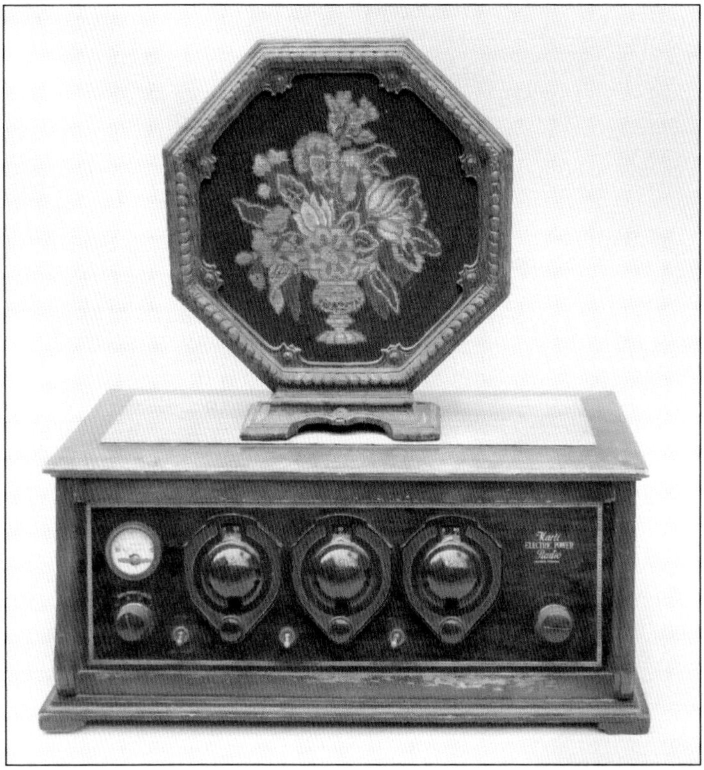

This is a 1922 radio receiver with vacuum tubes to amplify the sound for loudspeaker volume. This allowed an entire room to be filled with music and talk, leading to family listening. The loudspeaker was important, as it moved the radio from a curiosity and a child's hobby to an important source of entertainment and information that attracted everyone. (Author photograph.)

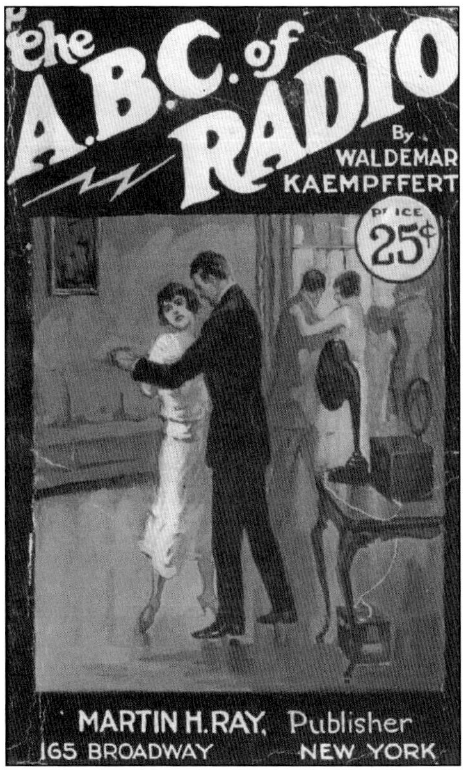

In this 1922 book, *The A.B.C. of Radio*, how did the author introduce and demystify radio? "The first question that a thinking man is sure to ask about radio is this: How does the music reach me? The windows are closed, and yet I hear"—what a simple thought. Books like this one introduced several thousand early Columbus listeners to radio. Imagine a small box that talks! (Author's collection.)

Radio magazines described the purpose of radio. On this cover from a 1920 *Radio News*, couples use the past to invent the present. Live music, but more recently the phonograph, accompanied dancing. Now it's radio, and couples invent the wireless dance. Imagine getting tangled up in all those earphone wires. (Author's collection.)

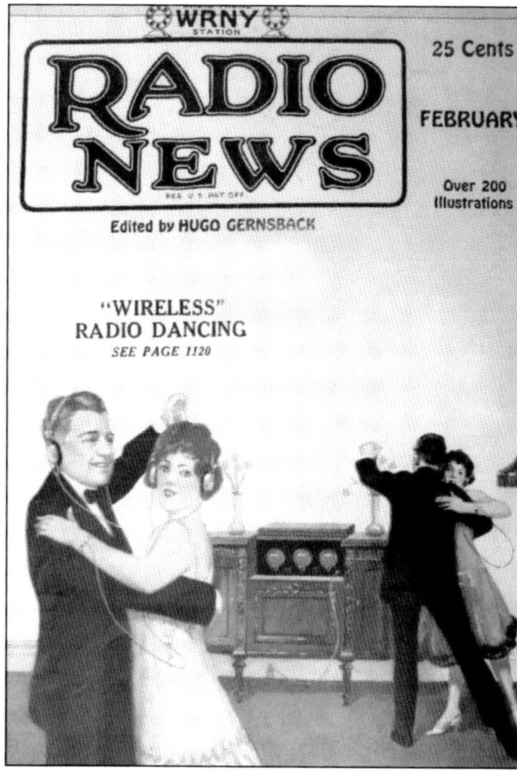

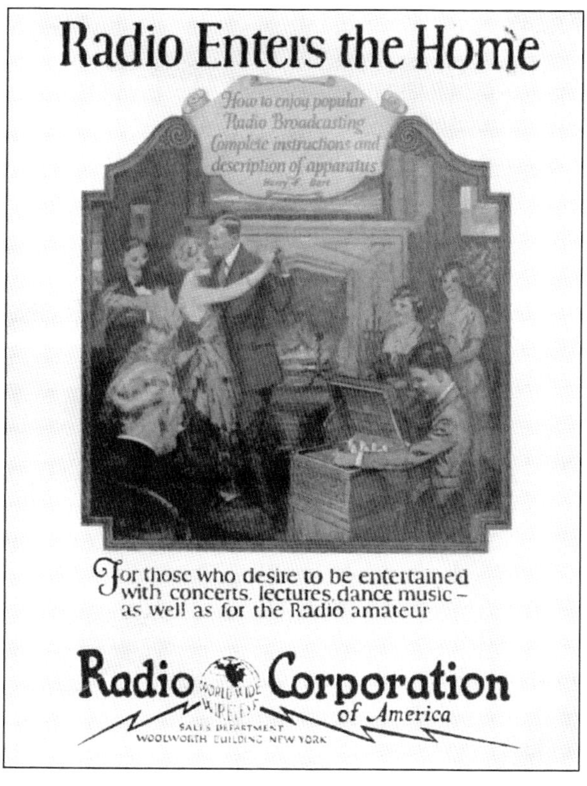

This popular 1922 book, *Radio Enters the Home*, was for those who wanted to learn about radio, how to build one, and how to buy ready-made radios sold by RCA: "For those who desire to be entertained with concerts, lectures, dance music—as well as for the radio amateur." This book detailed the transformation of radio from hobby to family media. (Author's collection.)

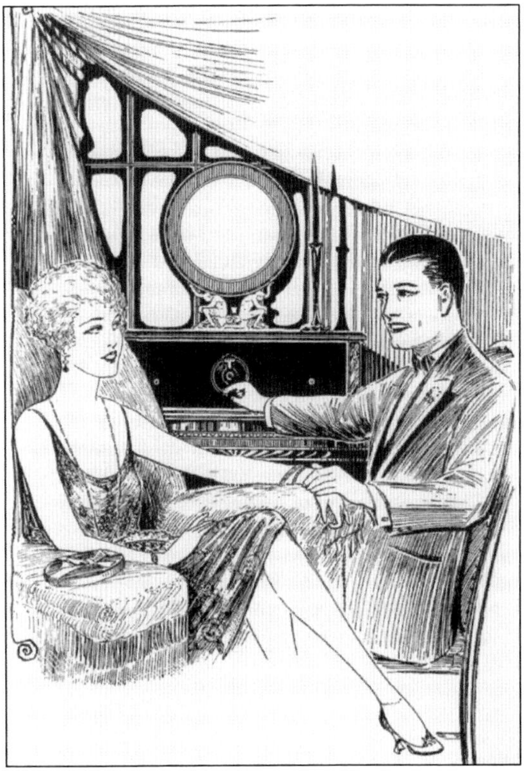

This is one way that the manufacturers were marketing their radios, an obvious appeal to a boy and girl sitting in the parlor listening to the radio. They wouldn't have to talk to each other! Decades later the radio would be replaced by television and then the smart phone. (Author's collection.)

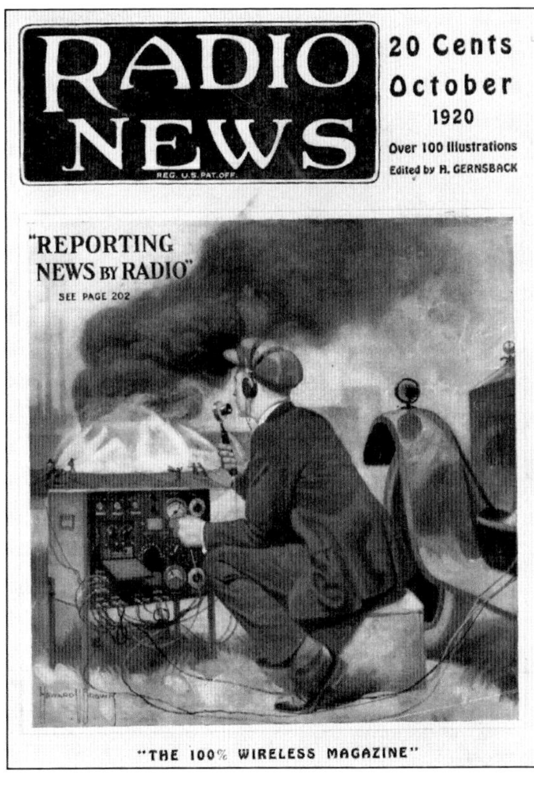
RADIO NEWS
REG. U.S. PAT. OFF.
20 Cents
October
1920
Over 100 Illustrations
Edited by H. GERNSBACK
"REPORTING NEWS BY RADIO"
SEE PAGE 202
"THE 100% WIRELESS MAGAZINE"

A 1920 *Radio News* cover depicts a reporter using shortwave radio to cover a news event: "Reporting News by Radio." One might think that the receiver of this news reporter's story is a radio station and he was quickly switched live on the air, but this is not so. What he is doing is sending back the live story to an editor of the local newspaper, who is writing a story for an "extra" edition of the print news. (Author's collection.)

Two

Professors and Preachers Invent Radio

It is no coincidence that the first radio stations evolved out of the technical curiosity of amateur experimenters and college students. Broadcasting as a business would have to prove itself, and many early licensees failed because, while they could build their own transmitters, they knew little about building an audience. No one did, so it is no wonder that the first radio broadcast stations were conceived in the classroom. Following the end of World War I and the lifting of the radio use ban, there was pent-up demand for something new and exciting. The professors and their students were there first.

Beginning before 1920, two local professors were the first to become licensed for what was then the experimental talking wireless. Columbus radio started in 1919 at Ohio State University in an engineering class and was licensed in 1922 as WEAO. Prior to World War I, Granville High School senior Richard Howe was also experimenting with the sending of messages without wires. After the war, he would graduate from Denison University, teach physics there, and obtain a license for a station, WJD, also in 1922. Shortly after Ohio State began its radio programming, a local Baptist church applied for and received a license for WMAN. It was only on for a few hours on Sunday mornings. Later it would become WCOL. Stations with entertainment programs went on the air a year later with WCAH, which by 1930 would become WBNS. Then there was WBAV, which would become WAIU, then WHKC, and finally WTVN.

This was the first decade of Columbus radio. These were the formative years for radio, both technical and programming, as licensing and regulation were clarified, advertising became the basis of support for radio, and networks were formed. By the end of the 1920s, solid radio regulation was in place. The decade that began with radio experimentation, leading to radio confusion, was now managed by a new government agency, the Federal Radio Commission, or FRC. The Radio Act of 1927 declared that radio must operate in the public interest, convenience, and necessity. But its most important contribution was to establish a permanent AM radio dial with specified power for certain stations on certain channels to reduce interference. In the 1920s, radio moved from a classroom curiosity to the most important media of the 20th century.

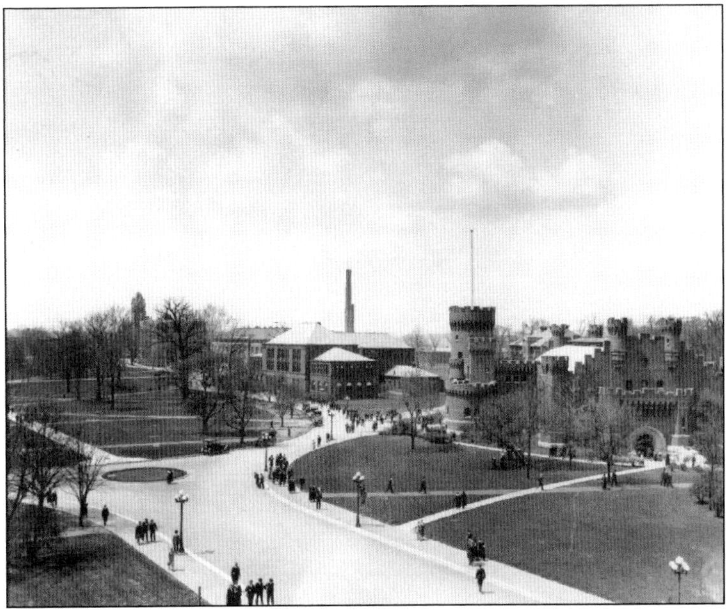

It is 1920, and this is an image of the famous OSU Oval. Because the university was much smaller then, students would likely encounter people they knew every day. It is on this campus that one of the very early radio stations, the first in Columbus, was created in an engineering class. In future decades, the station would develop a national reputation as an educational pioneer. (The Ohio State University Archives.)

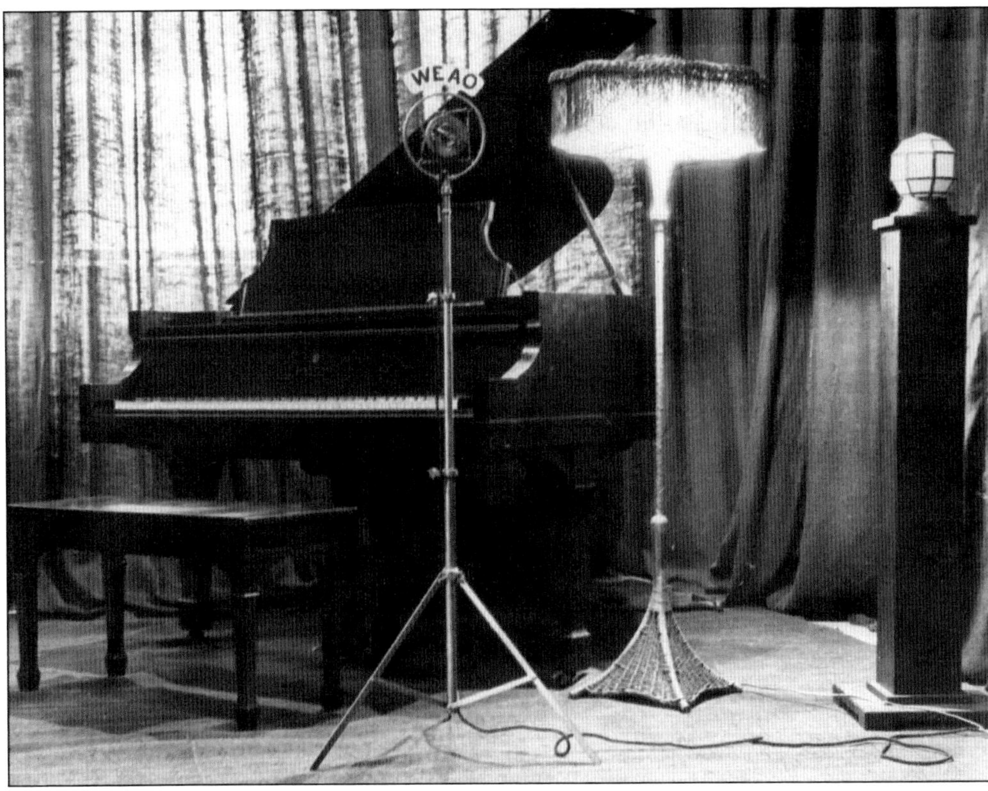

While students were attending classes, a radio station was taking shape in the engineering department. Licensed in 1922, the call letters were WEAO, to be changed in 1930 to WOSU to better reflect the brand. This is the WEAO studio in 1922. For the next 30 years, every radio studio seemed to have a grand piano, a microphone, and heavy drapes on the walls. (The Ohio State University Archives.)

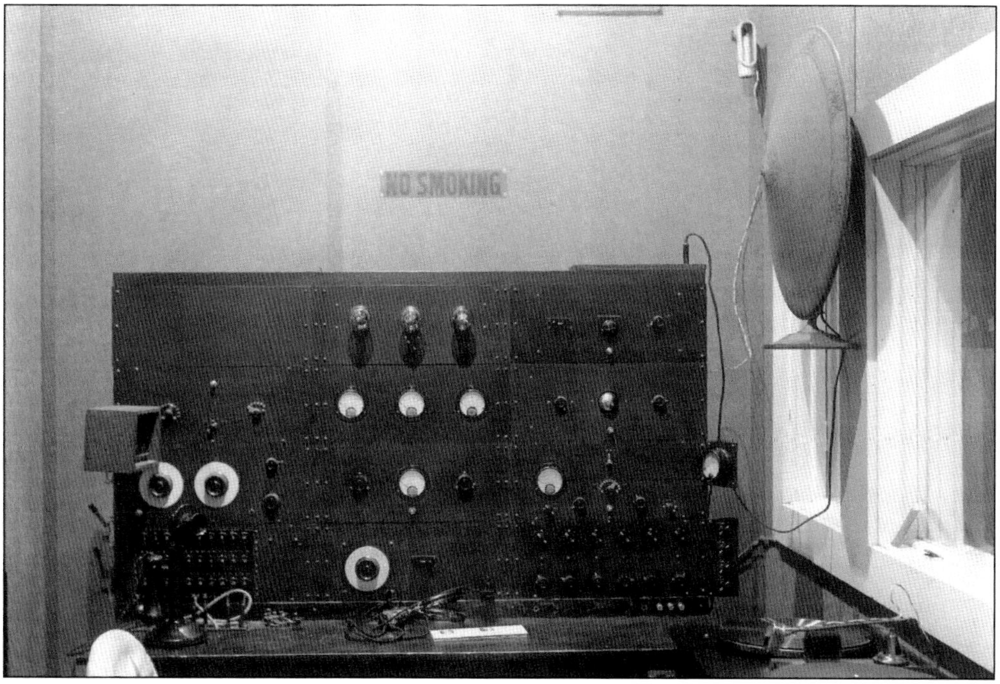

Here is the WEAO control room in 1922. Notice that there is a double-pane window on the right, looking into the studio. The control panel is a combination of familiar electrical gauges and telephone patch panels for routing audio sources from the studio to the transmitter. On the desk at lower left is a telegraph key, a throwback to radio's wireless heritage. (The Ohio State University Archives.)

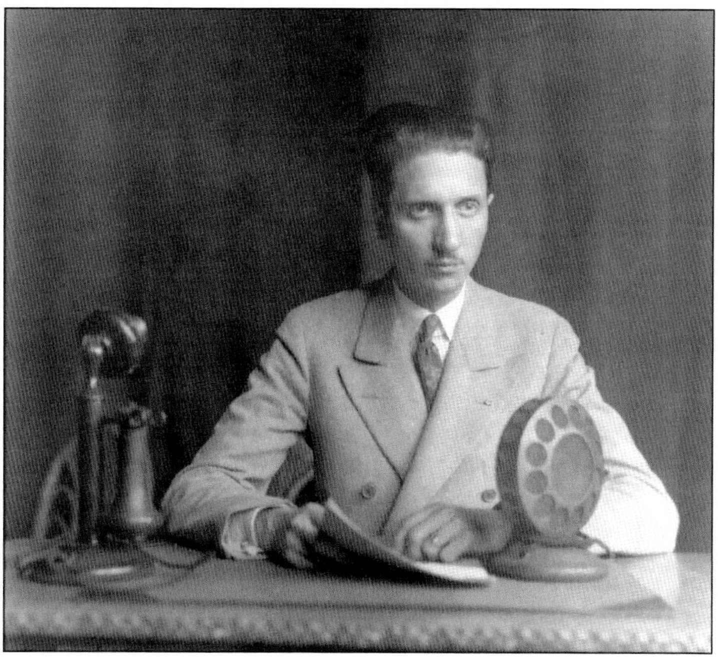

Pictured is Robert Coleman, likely one of the first Columbus radio announcers, shown in the WEAO announcer studio in the early 1920s with a crude carbon microphone at the right. The radio microphone evolved out of the carbon microphone used in the common telephone, seen on the left. He is reading a script, probably the latest sports news featuring the Ohio State Buckeyes. (The Ohio State University Archives.)

The Columbus Agreement

An Agreement Reached Between the Columbus Radio Club and Representatives of the Principal Broadcasting Stations of Columbus.

We, the undersigned, do hereby agree to observe and obey the following rules and regulations:

I. (a) All spark continuous wave and amateur radiophone sets (regular and special licensed amateur included) which are located in the city of Columbus, Ohio, or whose owners are members of the Columbus Radio Club, shall not transmit between the hours of seven (7) and ten (10) p. m. nightly except Saturday.

(b) These hours shall be known as "Quiet Hours."

(c) There shall be no Quiet Hours on Saturday nights.

II. All broadcasting stations located in the city of Columbus, Ohio, or whose owners are members of the Columbus Radio Club, mav transmit any night during the Quiet Hours, except as follows:
There shall be no local broadcasting between the hours of nine (9) and ten (10) p. m. nightly during the Quiet Hours.

III. All testing of the transmitting sets of all local amateurs and broadcasting stations shall be done between the hours of six (6) a. m. and five (5) p. m.

IV. The time used shall be Columbus City Time.

V. These rules cannot be changed without the consent of all participants of this agreement.

Signed this 27th day of October, 1922, in the belief that this will give the general public a period in which they may operate their receiving sets without local interference, and will eliminate friction between the various branches of local radio enthusiasts.

AMATEURS — (Signed) FRED W. REDDING, President, The Columbus Radio Club.

WBAV (Signed) R. C. BOHANNAN, The Erner & Hopkins Co.

WCAH (Signed) C. A. ENTREKIN, Entrekin Electric Co.

WEAO X (Signed) PROF. R. A. BROWN, Ohio State University.

WPAL (Signed) R. C. GARFINKEL, Superior Radio & Telephone Equipment Co.

This important document, "The Columbus Agreement," was basically a handshake between the newly licensed broadcasters, the original amateurs, and other experimenters and users of radio, signed in 1922. In this agreement, the allocated frequencies are to be shared by all users by time of day. Each operator can broadcast only during its agreed-upon hours. A "silent night" was one day each week that no Columbus transmitters would be on the air to allow listeners to attempt reception of distant stations. Each party signed the agreement; this copy is signed by Prof. R.A. Brown of Ohio State University. Specified in the agreement is that spark code transmissions, by amateurs or commercial communications users, shall not use their transmitters between 7:00 and 10:00 p.m. nightly except Saturdays. Broadcasting stations can transmit any night. Experimenting and testing of equipment will be allowed between 6:00 a.m. and 5:00 p.m. This was one of the first postwar attempts at self-regulation. Even as the Commerce Department under Herbert Hoover was in charge of licensing and rules, many did not understand or comply with the developing regulations. (The Ohio State University Archives.)

In the spring of 1922, OSU president William Oxley Thompson dedicates WEAO and explains how it began as a science experiment. He promises, "We are starting tonight the first of a series of programs of entertainment and instruction for the citizens of Central Ohio. These programs will be of the highest type, including music, science, and other subjects of popular interest." WEAO was said to stand for Willing, Energetic, Athletic Ohio. It was more likely a random assignment of call letters. (The Ohio State University Archives.)

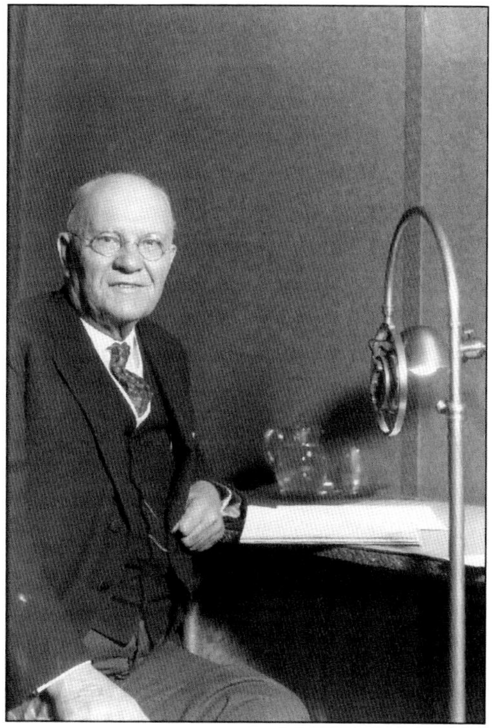

Robert Charles Higgy was the man behind the first radio station in Columbus. At first, the station operated informally and experimentally, but in 1926, Higgy was made the first full-time director. In 1925, Higgy wrote, "During the year 1924, WEAO held the distinction of broadcasting more educational lectures than any other station in the United States." (The Ohio State University Archives.)

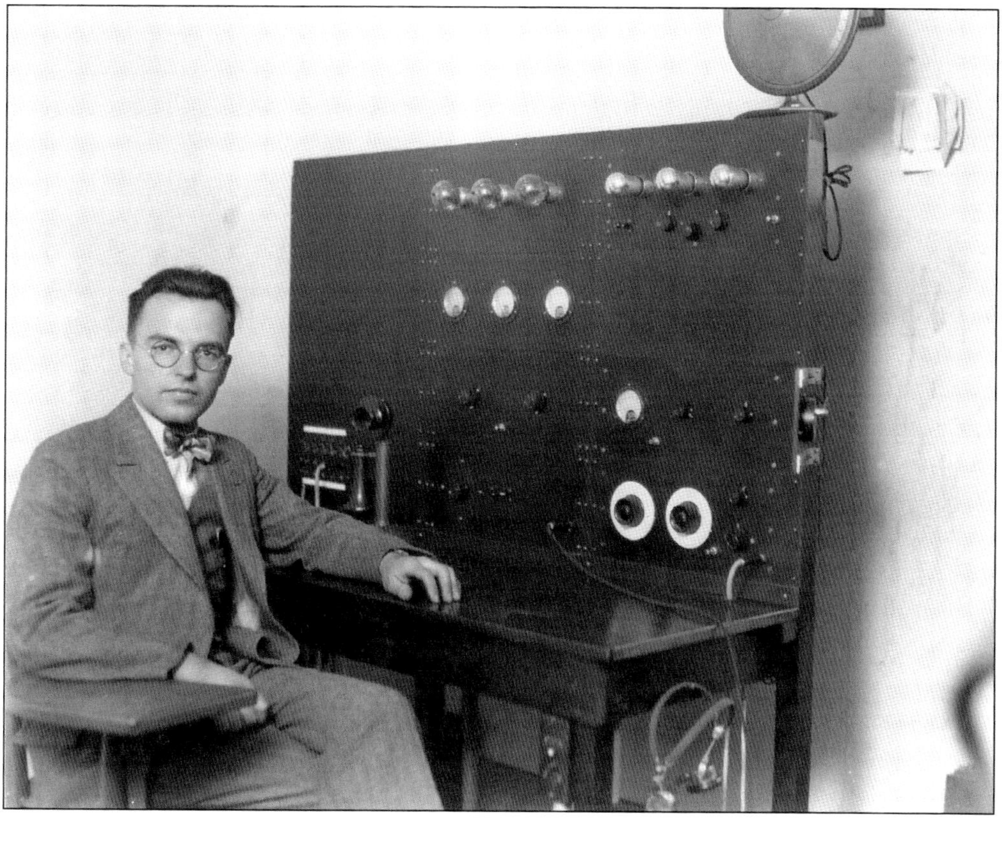

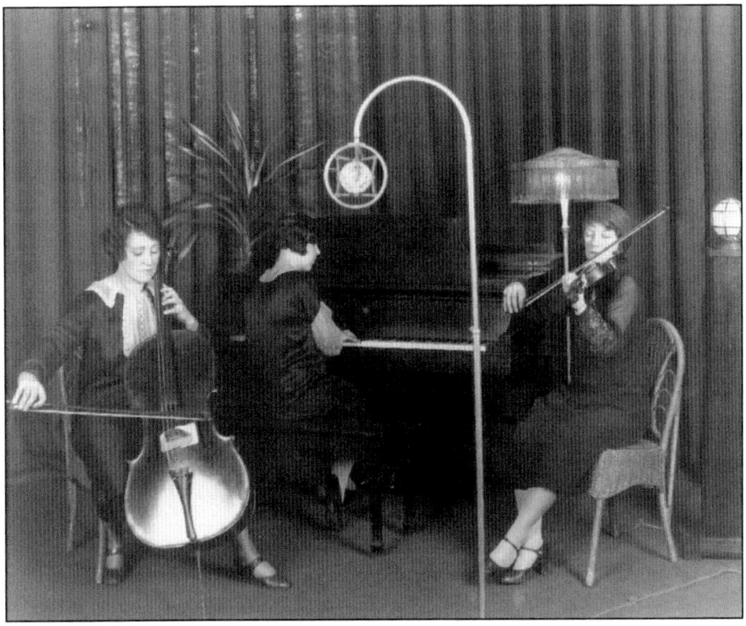

Programming on WEAO in the 1920s consisted of what President Thompson had earlier promised, that "of the highest type," such as this trio performing live in the WEAO studio. Ohio State, unlike other commercial stations, had ready-made free content for radio programs in music, theater, and lectures performed by faculty and students. (The Ohio State University Archives.)

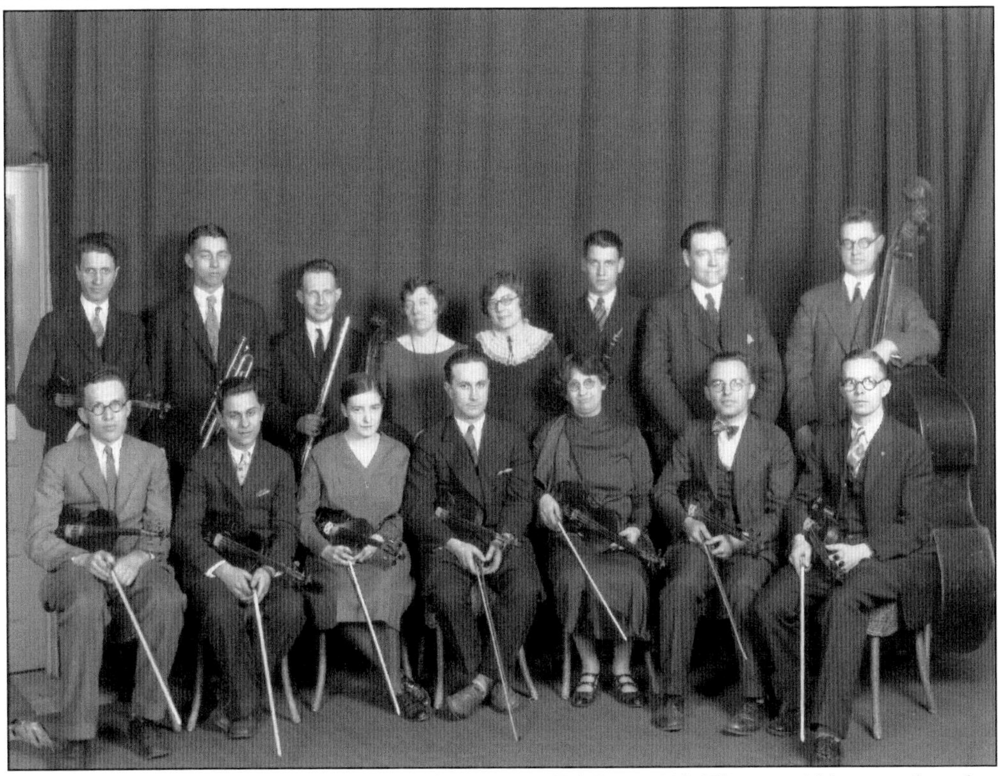

The Ohio State University orchestra performs on WEAO in 1927. This would have to be a big deal for listeners not easily able to travel to hear in-person performances. Radio originally was supposed to do this sort of thing: to get great art to the masses that do not have the ability to pay for it. This is why the early university stations were so important to the cultural life of their local audiences. (The Ohio State University Archives.)

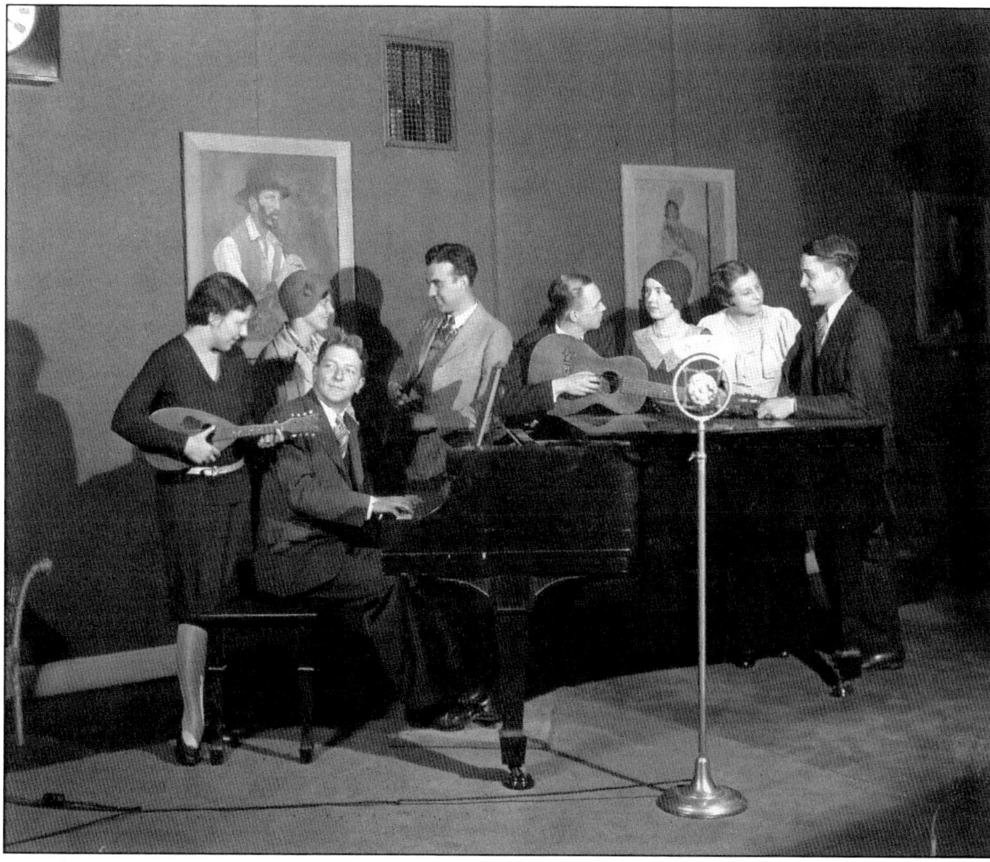

Another group from the performing arts on WEAO was the OSU Players. Their instruments indicate that they may be an eclectic folk or early music group or perhaps a troupe of actors performing with music accompaniment. Later, stations would take their microphones into the concert hall to broadcast musical performances live, called a "remote" broadcast. (The Ohio State University Archives.)

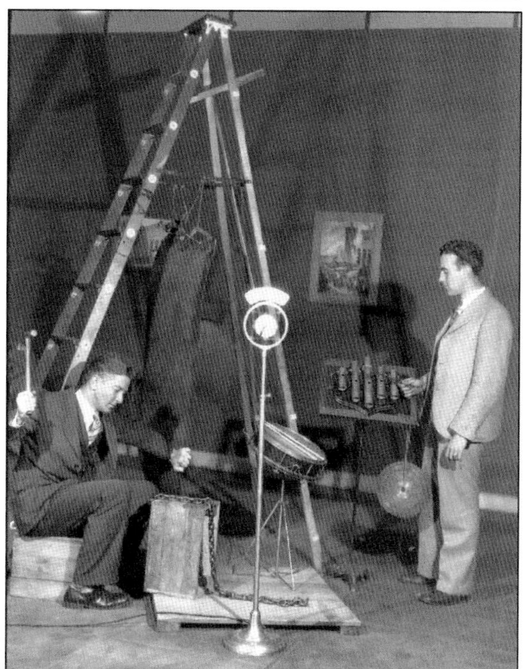

University theater groups adapted their work as radio drama in the 1920s. Here is how the sounds were made for the radio play. These two individuals are using all manner of sound effects to illustrate parts of a story. There are dozens of possibilities for sound represented here. In the very early days of radio, all content had to be performed live and often in front of a single microphone. (The Ohio State University Archives.)

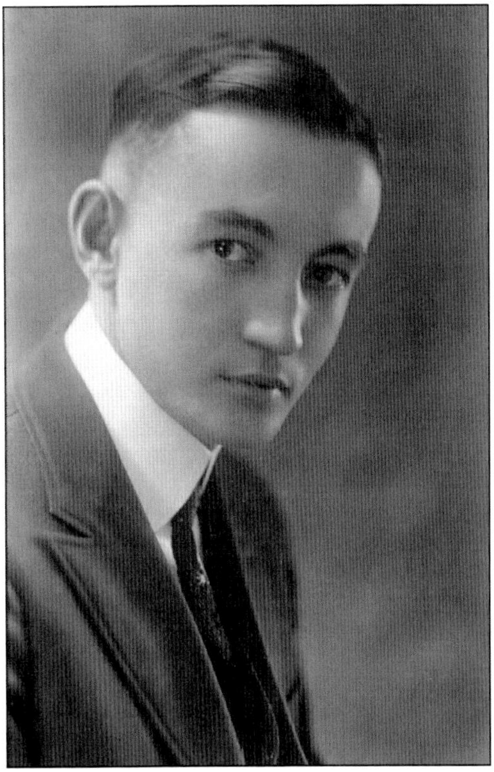

A Granville High graduate in 1916, Richard Howe was tasked with delivering the graduation speech, "The Evolution of Wireless Telegraphy," for his high school commencement. Howe believed that it "represents a golden opportunity to the scientists and experimenters, who are bent on discovering the secrets it holds." After serving in World War I, Howe graduated from Denison University and was hired as a physics instructor. (Howe Papers, Denison University Archives and Special Collections, Granville, Ohio.)

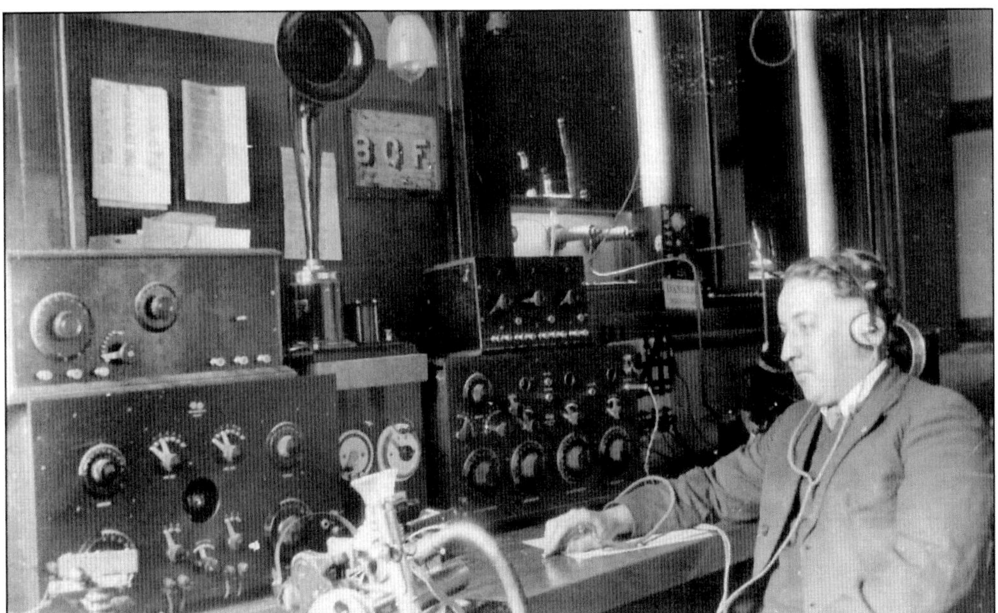

In the Denison University catalogue of 1922, the Physics Department is promoted as having "a telephone transmitting station, licensed under the call letters WJD, used for the broadcasting of music and educational matters." In these early years, the term "radio" was used interchangeably with "radiotelephone" and "wireless telephone." In this image, a student operates the experimental station 8QF. (Howe Papers, Denison University Archives and Special Collections, Granville, Ohio.)

Playing music was not allowed under his experimental license, so in February 1922, the Commerce Department sent this letter to Howe: "I have to advise you that I cannot authorize the Denison University to broadcast music or educational matter unless they first secure a 'Limited Commercial' broadcasting station license." Howe complied, and station WJD was licensed later that year. (Howe Papers, Denison University Archives and Special Collections, Granville, Ohio.)

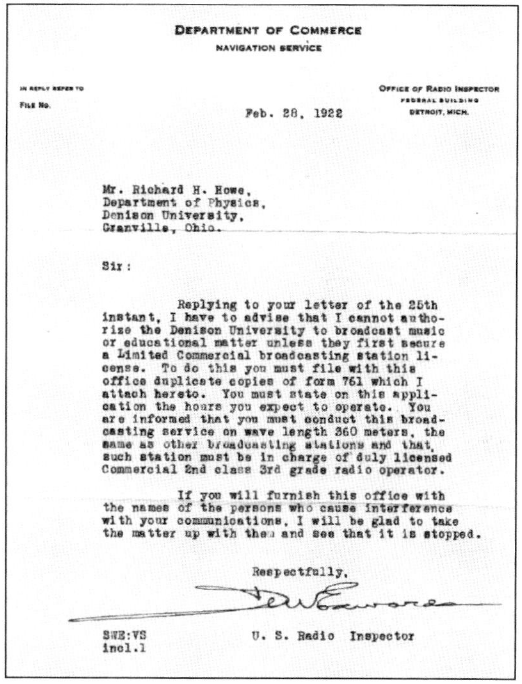

DEPARTMENT OF COMMERCE
NAVIGATION SERVICE

IN REPLY REFER TO
FILE NO.

OFFICE OF RADIO INSPECTOR
FEDERAL BUILDING
DETROIT, MICH.

Feb. 28, 1922

Mr. Richard H. Howe,
Department of Physics,
Denison University,
Granville, Ohio.

Sir:

Replying to your letter of the 25th instant, I have to advise that I cannot authorize the Denison University to broadcast music or educational matter unless they first secure a Limited Commercial broadcasting station license. To do this you must file with this office duplicate copies of form 761 which I attach hereto. You must state on this application the hours you expect to operate. You are informed that you must conduct this broadcasting service on wave length 360 meters, the same as other broadcasting stations and that, such station must be in charge of duly licensed Commercial 2nd class 3rd grade radio operator.

If you will furnish this office with the names of the persons who cause interference with your communications, I will be glad to take the matter up with them and see that it is stopped.

Respectfully,

U. S. Radio Inspector

SWE:VS
incl.1

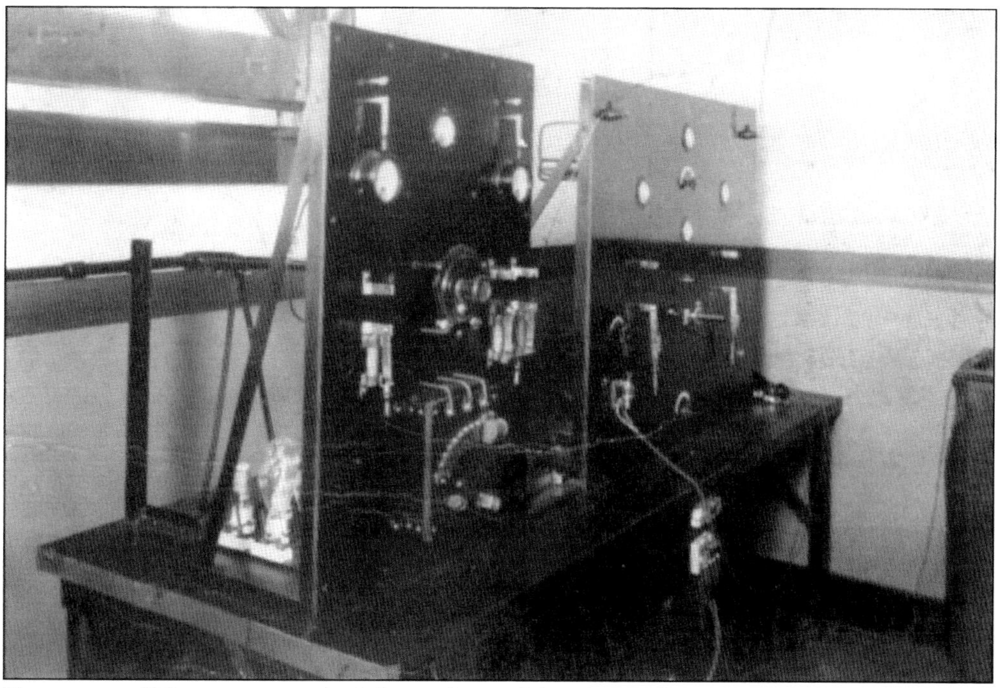

Howe wrote, "The station was built by students of the physics department and the parts for the studio and transmitter were purchased from the meager departmental budget." He went on to estimate that the power was between 10 and 20 watts and had been heard within a 70-mile radius. Howe explained that the students built and operated WJD to get practical electronics experience, but "there was no attempt made at that time to train studio announcers." (Howe Papers, Denison University Archives and Special Collections, Granville, Ohio.)

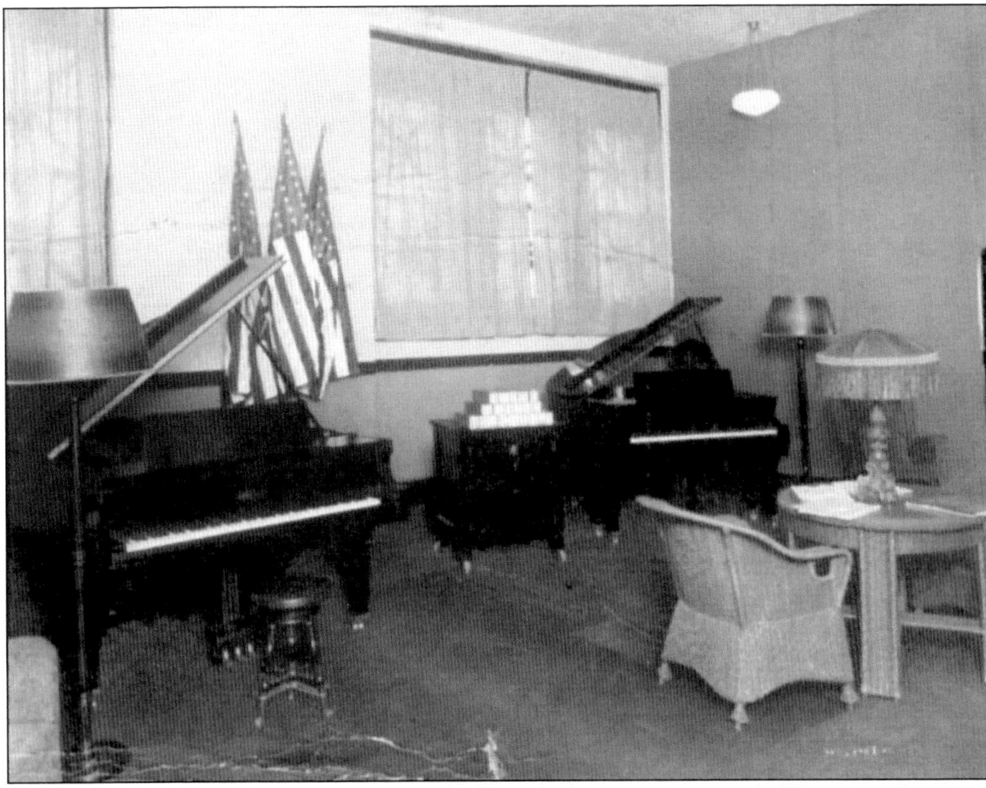

Howe wrote, "A spring wound victrola cranked out the latest victor records. The microphone was simply placed in front of the victrola horn to pick up the music. Paul Whiteman was famous at that time. The records were furnished gratis by the Wyeth Victrola store in Newark in payment for an occasional plug for the store over the air." The station also featured Denison music students performing and basketball and football play-by-play. (Howe Papers, Denison University Archives and Special Collections, Granville, Ohio.)

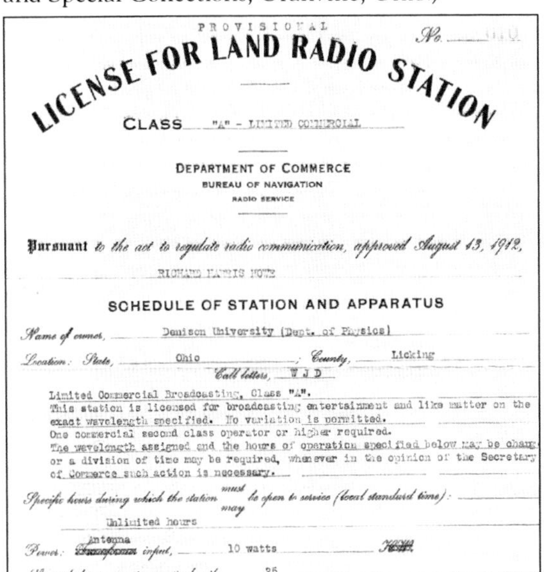

PROVISIONAL

No.

LICENSE FOR LAND RADIO STATION

CLASS "A" - LIMITED COMMERCIAL

DEPARTMENT OF COMMERCE
BUREAU OF NAVIGATION
RADIO SERVICE

Pursuant to the act to regulate radio communication, approved August 13, 1912,

RICHARD HARRIS HOWE

SCHEDULE OF STATION AND APPARATUS

Name of owner, Denison University (Dept. of Physics)

Location: State, Ohio; County, Licking

Call letters, WJD

Limited Commercial Broadcasting, Class "A".
This station is licensed for broadcasting entertainment and like matter on the exact wavelength specified. No variation is permitted.
One commercial second class operator or higher required.
The wavelength assigned and the hours of operation specified below may be chang[ed] or a division of time may be required, whenever in the opinion of the Secretary of Commerce such action is necessary.

Specific hours during which the station must/may be open to service (local standard time):

Unlimited hours

Power: Antenna input, 10 watts

Normal day range in nautical miles, 25

The license was not renewed after 1925, because in order to meet the government technical requirements, Denison would have had to invest about $10,000 ($136,000 today), and the university could not do it. After 1925, Howe and his students were satisfied with an amateur license. In this image is a portion of the five-page WJD commercial broadcasting license. (Howe Papers, Denison University Archives and Special Collections, Granville, Ohio.)

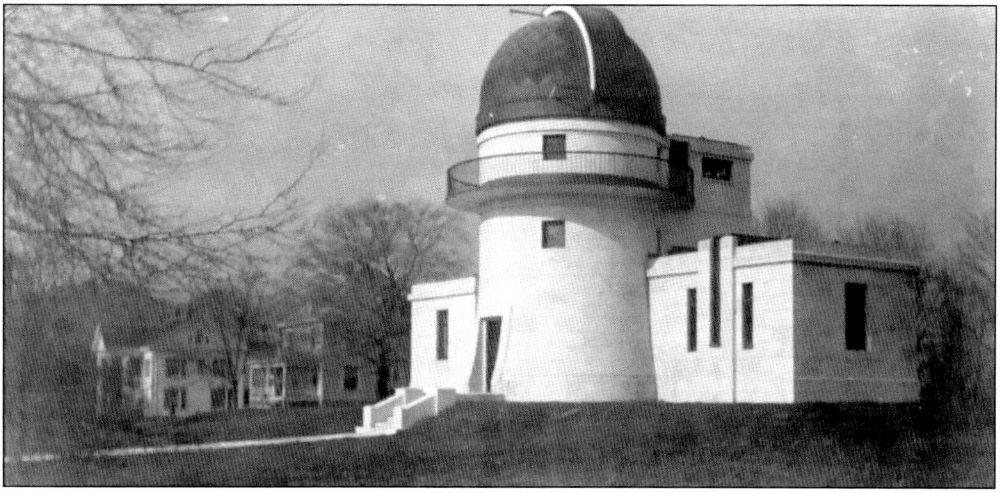

Nestled in the verdant suburbs of Columbus is Denison University, home of early radio broadcasting. Swazee Observatory on the campus is pictured around 1920. It was just a short distance away from where Richard Howe and his physics students created one of the first radio stations in the Columbus market. (Howe Papers, Denison University Archives and Special Collections, Granville, Ohio.)

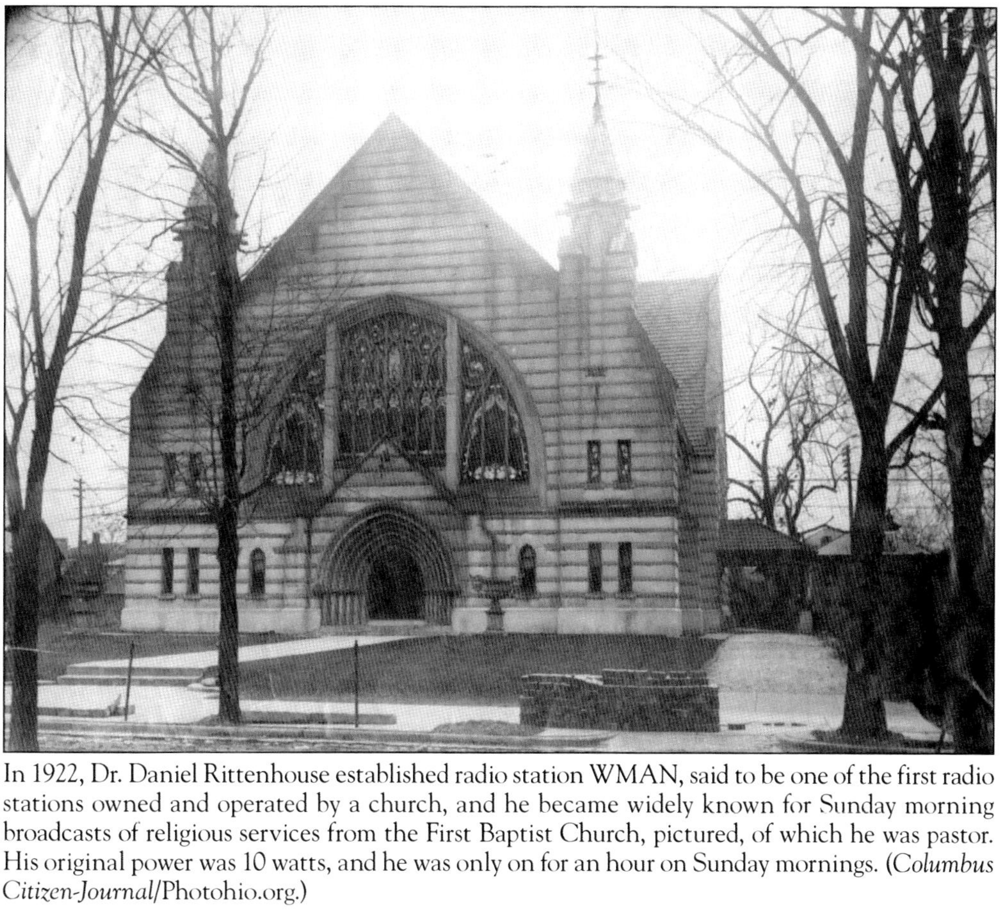

In 1922, Dr. Daniel Rittenhouse established radio station WMAN, said to be one of the first radio stations owned and operated by a church, and he became widely known for Sunday morning broadcasts of religious services from the First Baptist Church, pictured, of which he was pastor. His original power was 10 watts, and he was only on for an hour on Sunday mornings. (*Columbus Citizen-Journal*/Photohio.org.)

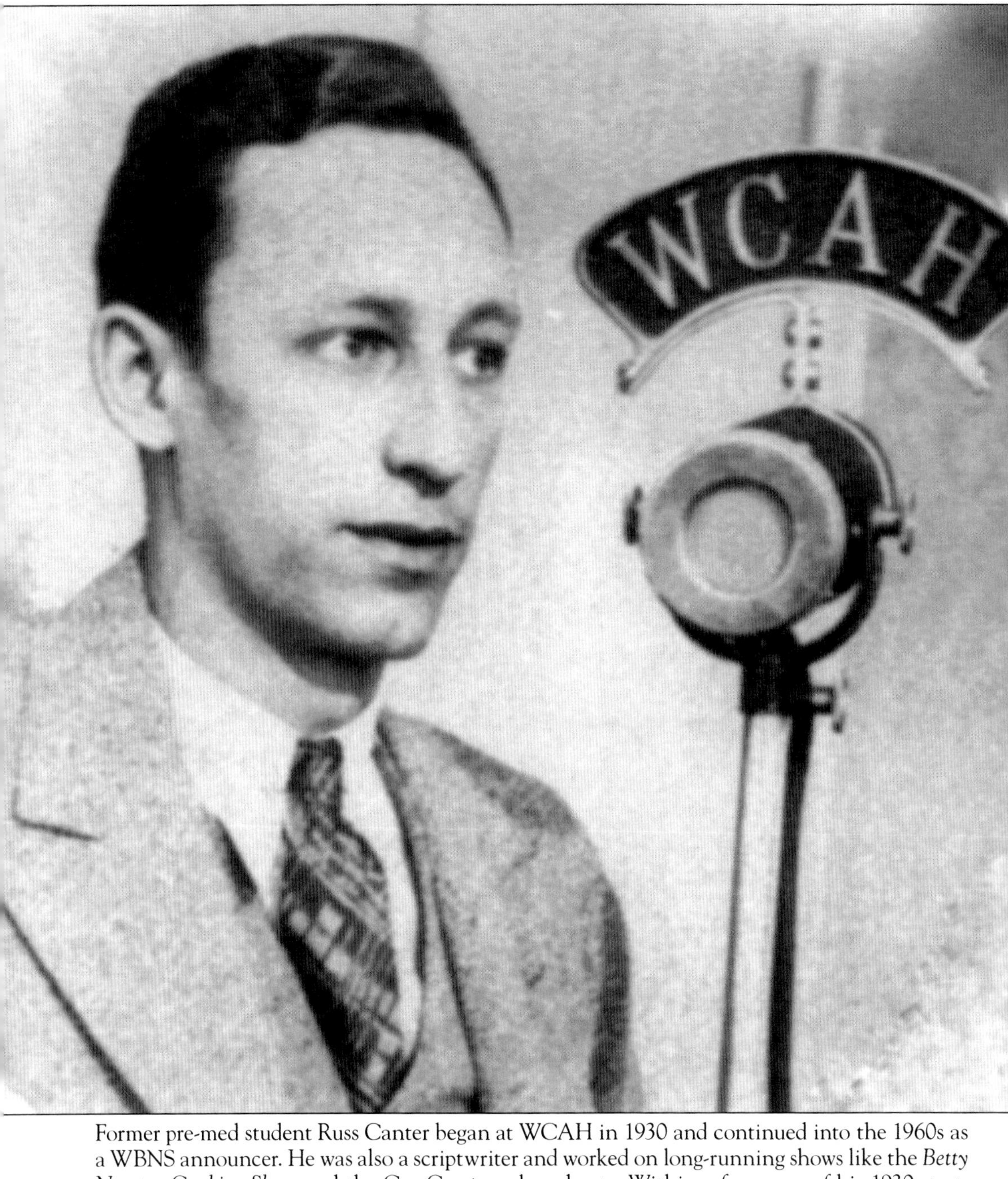

Former pre-med student Russ Canter began at WCAH in 1930 and continued into the 1960s as a WBNS announcer. He was also a scriptwriter and worked on long-running shows like the *Betty Newton Cooking Show* and the *Gas Company* broadcasts. Within a few years of his 1930 start, Canter would be the first local voice heard on the CBS radio network. (WBNS 25th Anniversary booklet, author's collection.)

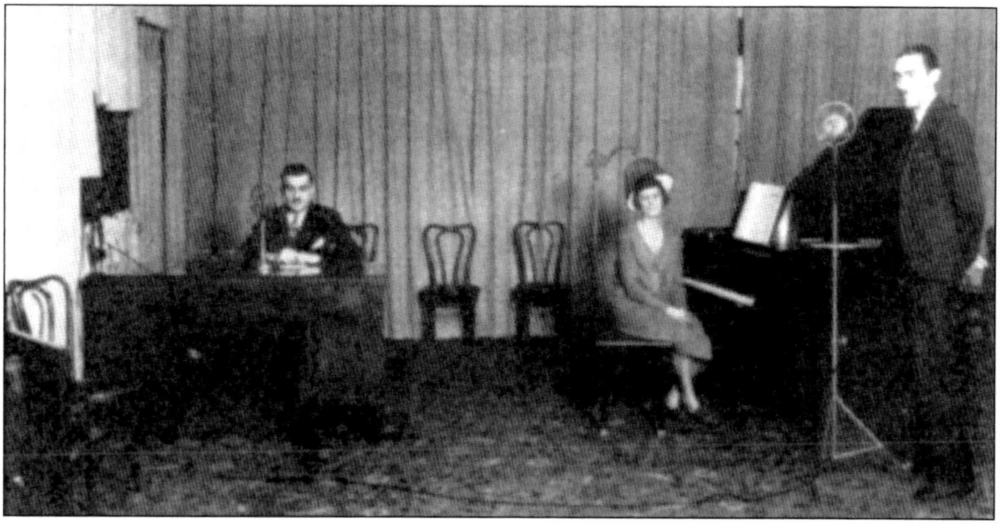

The station was owned by the Entrekin Electric Company. According to Bob Dildine in his *History of WBNS from 1924*, "Music came from a mechanical phonograph. Later the power was increased to 100 watts. The living room of his [station owner Entrekin's] home served as the studio, and the talents of Mrs. Entrekin at the piano were added to the program. A local music store supplied the records." Later in the 1920s, WCAH moved to a larger location and built the studio shown in this image. (WBNS 25th Anniversary booklet, author's collection.)

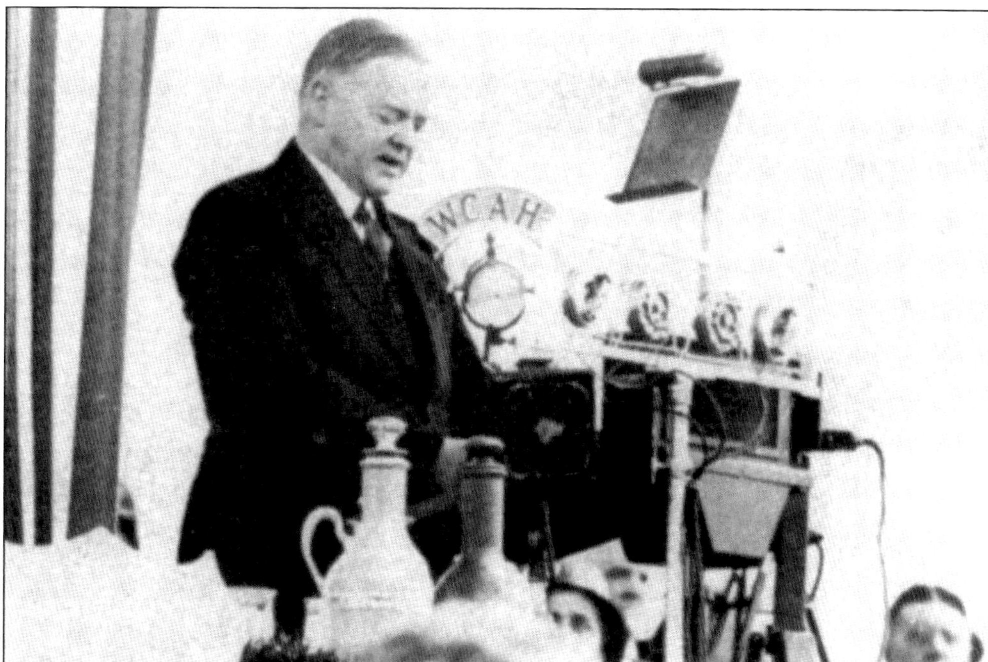

In the final days of WCAH before becoming WBNS, this was the June 1931 dedication of the memorial to the late Ohioan Pres. Warren G. Harding, carried live by what was still WCAH but broadcast to the nation over the CBS radio network. Presiding is President Hoover, who 10 years earlier had been in charge of radio licensing as secretary of commerce. (WBNS 25th Anniversary booklet, author's collection.)

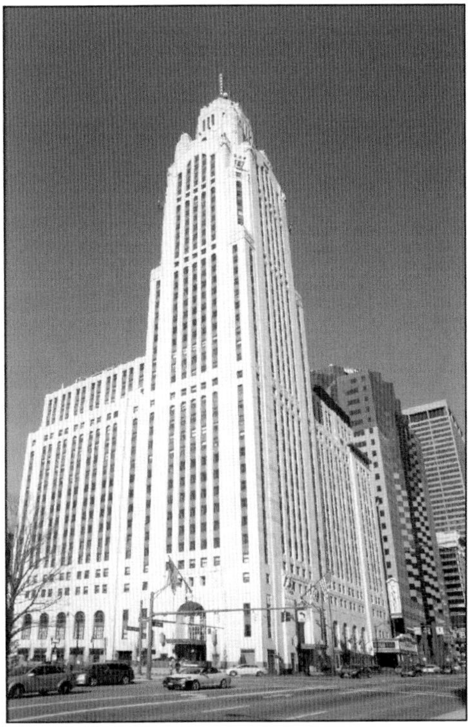

The American Insurance Union Citadel, built in 1927 and known today as the Leveque-Lincoln Tower, still stands tall in downtown Columbus. This striking structure has been home to several radio stations: WAIU, WBNS-FM, and WCBE-FM. It is an ideal height for FM broadcasting, absent any local mountains or other higher structures. This is what it looks like today. (Author photograph.)

The Hall of Mirrors is pictured in the 1940s. Pictured in the back of this room, the WAIU pipe organ was used in broadcasts from the studio in the tower above. AIU historian Mike Perkins wrote, "In 1925 the American Insurance Union purchased the station to serve as a home base for the views of its president, John J. Lentz, a progressive politician who co-founded the AIU in 1894." (Mike Perkins.)

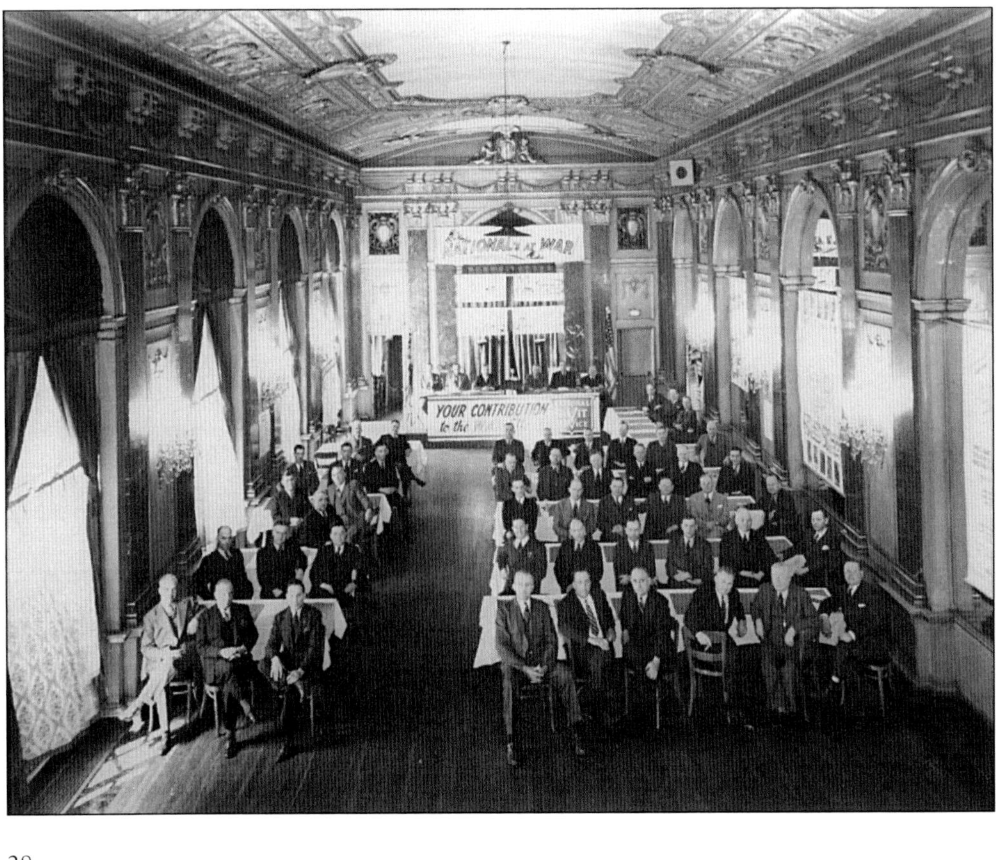

This radio script outline is for the 1927 dedication of WAIU's broadcasting power increase to 5,000 watts. Previously, the station was owned by the Erner and Hopkins Electric Company, originally at 500 watts and using the call letters WBAV. This outline shows in detail who and what the audience would hear and when, a common way to organize radio programming. (John Potter.)

American Insurance Union

PROGRAM

Celebration 5000 Watts

W A I U Studio - Deshler Hotel

Monday Evening, February 21, 1927

6:00 P. M.

6:00 P. M. Dick Fidler and his dance orchestra

7:00 P. M. Talk-Sponsored by the Telling Belle-Vernon Ice Cream Company.

7:05 P. M. Short Dedicatorial Talks, with introduction by Hon. John J. Lentz, President of the American Insurance Union. Talks interspersed by James Moorehouse, pianist
Hon. A. Vic. Donahey, Governor of Ohio
Hon. James J. Thomas, Mayor of Columbus
James A. Maddox, President of Columbus Chamber of Commerce
L. C. Wallick, President, Deshler-Wallick Hotel
Burns O'Sullivan, Manager, Keith-Albee Theater, Columbus
M. M. Carothers, Representative, Columbus Dispatch
Earl Minderman, Secretary, Columbus Radio League
Charles W. Rife, Radio Critic, Columbus Dispatch
Arthur R. Harper, Naturalist
Fred. Ostreicher, Radio Critic, Columbus Citizen

9:00 P. M. Capital City Products Company will inaugurate the first of a series of concerts, known as "Kingtaste Hour" featuring the Kingtaste Symphonette, Irene French, soprano and Vincent O'Brien, tenor.

10:00 P. M. "Melodies Immortal," a Radio Production devised and produced by Don Bernard. This Production requires the services of: Aladdin Temple Shrine Band of 165 pieces, Earl McCullough, Director.
Trinity Episcopal Boys Choir - Karl H. Hoenig, Director
Instrumental Trio
Pipe Organ
Margaret Matheny, Whistler
Ruth Basden, Soprano
Rose Graham, Contralto
Harold Voelker, Tenor

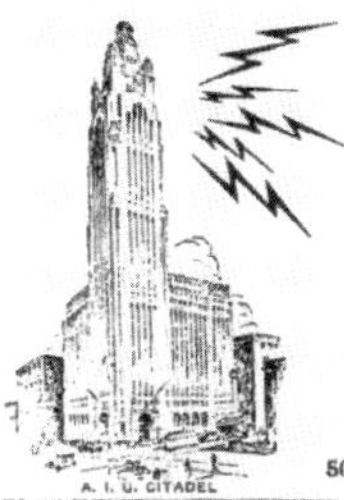

WAIU Radio Program

American Insurance Union

Columbus, Ohio

Hon. John J. Lentz, National President
Mary E. Colborn, National Secretary

Life—Health—Accident—Old Age—Child Insurance—At Cost

5000 Watts | 282.8 Meters | 1060 Kilocyles

Vol. I | AUGUST, 1927 | No. 2

Don Bernard, Talented Director, WAIU

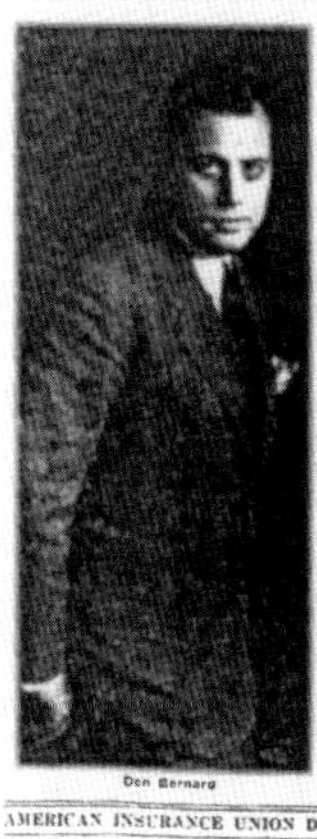

Don Bernard

Don Bernard, Director of WAIU, is not only a talented director, but he is also an excellent violinist, and possesses a very remarkable tenor voice. He is thoroughly schooled in music, having studied the violin and majored in voice at Sanbourn Hall, at Ohio Wesleyan University. He continued his musical education in Chicago, graduating from the Bush Conservatory in voice, violin, composition, and conducting. He was fortunate in having some voice tuterage under such world-known masters as Parvin Witte, Boza Oumiroff, and Vittorio Trevisan.

At the age of nineteen, Mr. Bernard sang one season with the Chicago Civic Opera Company. He later sang five seasons with the Publix Theatres Inc. In covering this circuit, Mr. Bernard sang in the largest cinema theatres of the United States and Canada. He has appeared as soloist with many of the larger symphony orchestras, and has given many concerts throughout the United States and Canada.

As a conductor of orchestras and choruses, Mr. Bernard has gained international recognition. During the past few years, he conducted many performances of Handel's "Messiah." He not only conducted these performances, but employed his personal efforts in training the chorus, numbering two hundred and fifty voices. He was conductor of the choirs at the Cathedral of the Holy Name in Chicago for three years. Mr. Bernard was one of the first artists to broadcast having sung the second night that broadcasting was attempted in Chicago, in the pioneer days of KYW. Mr. Bernard is also a noted recording artist, and many records of his splendid tenor voice have been released.

Many original ideas about broadcasting have been introduced to the radio public by Mr. Bernard. Chief of these is the "Radio Production," a new type of entertainment, which synchronizes dialogue and music in dramatic form. Most important of these productions is "Melodies Immortal," which the National Music Week Committee of New York City has asked to obtain for exclusive right of presentation. It is a rare setting for old loved tunes by famous composers. The presentation requires the services of a hundred and fifty piece band, a boys' choir, a symphony orchestra, and many soloists, both instrumental and vocal. Many other stations have used this production in commemorating special occasions.

AMERICAN INSURANCE UNION Dedicates Its Citadel, The World's Most Beautiful Building, September 21, 1927

This flyer promotes WAIU's director, Don Bernard, on the occasion of the power increase of WAIU. The flyer said this about Bernard: "Many original ideas about broadcasting have been introduced to the radio public by Mr. Bernard. Chief of these is 'the radio production,' a new type of entertainment, which synchronizes dialogue and music in dramatic form." It was also called the radio play. (Mike Perkins.)

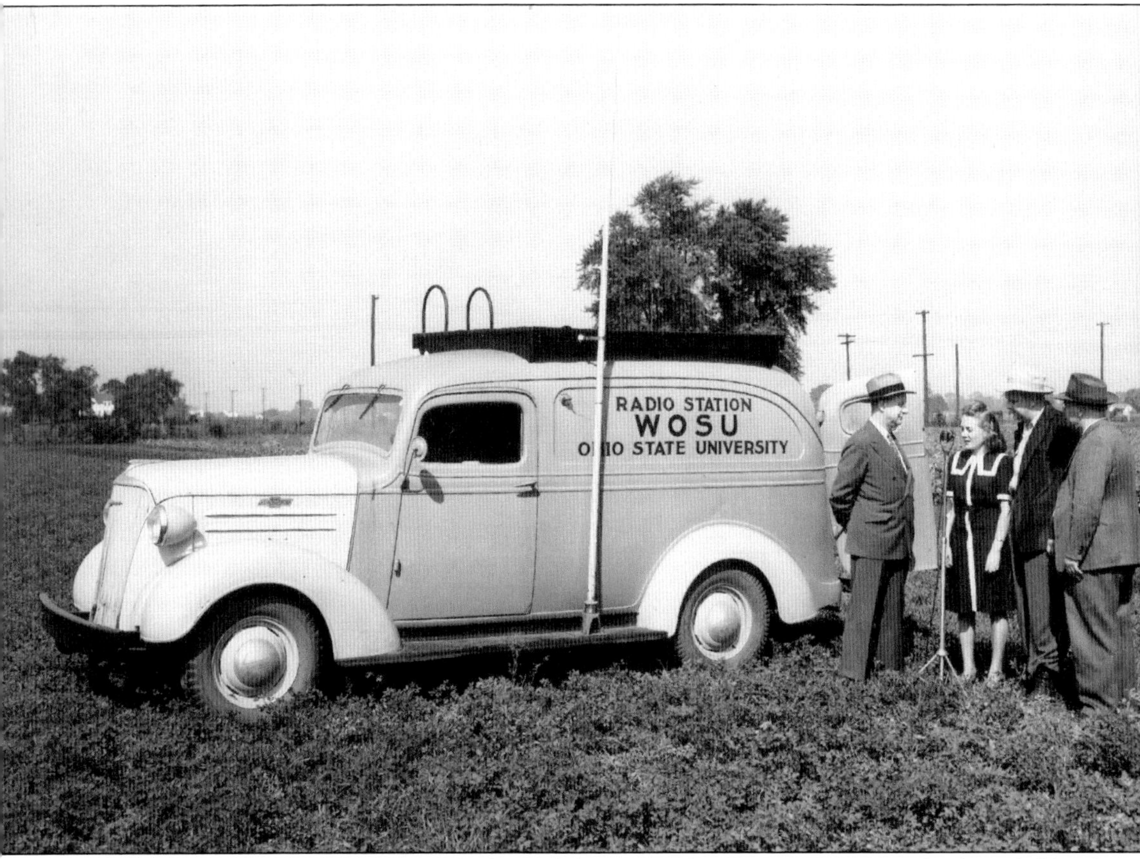

By the end of the 1930s, WOSU had a mobile unit and spent some time in the farm fields of Ohio, broadcasting the agricultural news to all of the state. Because programs were done live, this shortwave-equipped vehicle was used to send the audio of the interview back to the station control room for airing. The radio mobile unit was also used for news coverage beginning in the 1930s. Before that, radio announcers actually read the news from the local newspapers over the air. By the mid-1930s, the newspapers began to object, saying that if listeners could hear the news stories contained in the print format, they might not buy the actual paper. Stations developed their own news operations, and wire services were established for news from the nation and world. The remote unit was important for on-the-spot local coverage or breaking news. (The Ohio State University Archives.)

Three

Radio Gets Serious as Everyone Listens

The decade of the 1920s was radio's most interesting, as engineers and experimenters gave way to announcers, musicians, and news reporters. By the 1930s, radio was for real. There was now substantial regulation in place, and many of the technical mistakes of radio's first decade had been corrected. The advertisers were supportive, and performers found new audiences. Networks evolved, and it was the era of big stars, big shows, and big business.

WBNS, the class act of early Columbus radio, is one of the early CBS network affiliates, having joined the network when it was WCAH. WBNS was said to stand for Wolfe Banks, News, and Shoes. The Wolfe family owned the local newspaper and, for a while, a second and smaller radio station, WCOL. The Wolfes obviously were proud of their media empire, and they did not seem to care how much it cost, as long as it was the best. In an attempt to replicate the New York–based NBC Radio Central experience, the two WBNS stations named their studios at 33 North High Street Radio Center. This began a long reign of top-rated radio, as WBNS became the best-equipped, the best-funded, and the most secure broadcasting entity in Columbus history.

Radio was popular in Depression-era America. Like the movies, radio provided an escape from the realities of hard times. Radio made people laugh. Radio made people think. Radio was also an early example of social media, as neighbors gathered in homes to share radio programs and to discuss their content. Radio became more than just a device that was on for a few hours a day to play phonograph records or to allow a local vaudeville act to sing and dance. In the 1920s, there were birdcalls, readings of Shakespeare plays, and all the novelty acts of the live stage. But by the 1930s, radio would find its unique content in the form of live music, mystery shows, comedy, news, and soap operas.

There were more ownership and call letter changes in the 1930s. WAIU was sold to a Cleveland company and became WHKC. There was a new experiment in delivering education to classrooms using radio. WEAO at Ohio State changed its call letters to the more descriptive WOSU. The Baptist station WMAN was purchased from the church, moved to the Seneca Hotel, and aptly became WSEN. By the middle of the decade, WSEN became WCOL, finally finding its brief moment of radio glory as part of the WBNS family.

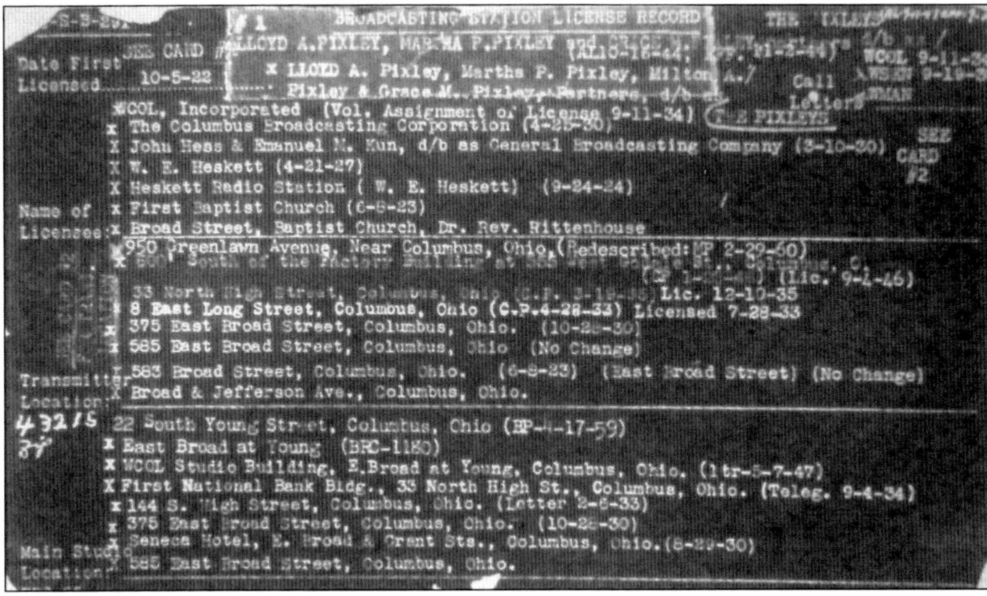
BROADCASTING STATION LICENSE RECORD

Date First Licensed 10-5-22

LLOYD A. PIXLEY, MARTHA P. PIXLEY and

x LLOYD A. Pixley, Martha P. Pixley, Milton A./ Pixley & Grace M. Pixley, Partners, d/b

Call Letters WCOL 9-11-34 WMAN

Name of Licensee:
WCOL, Incorporated (Vol. Assignment of License 9-11-34)
x The Columbus Broadcasting Corporation (4-25-30)
X John Hess & Emanuel M. Kun, d/b as General Broadcasting Company (3-10-30)
X W. E. Heskett (4-21-27)
X Heskett Radio Station (W. E. Heskett) (9-24-24)
x First Baptist Church (6-8-23)
x Broad Street, Baptist Church, Dr. Rev. Rittenhouse

SEE CARD #2

Transmitter Location:
950 Greenlawn Avenue, Near Columbus, Ohio, (Redescribed: MP 2-29-60)
(Lic. 9-4-46)
Lic. 12-10-35
8 East Long Street, Columbus, Ohio (C.P.4-28-33) Licensed 7-28-33
x 375 East Broad Street, Columbus, Ohio. (10-28-30)
x 585 East Broad Street, Columbus, Ohio (No Change)
x 583 Broad Street, Columbus, Ohio. (6-8-23) (East Broad Street) (No Change)
X Broad & Jefferson Ave., Columbus, Ohio.

Main Studio Location:
22 South Young Street, Columbus, Ohio (BP-4-17-59)
x East Broad at Young (BRC-1180)
x WCOL Studio Building, E.Broad at Young, Columbus, Ohio. (1tr-5-7-47)
X First National Bank Bldg., 33 North High St., Columbus, Ohio. (Teleg. 9-4-34)
x 144 S. High Street, Columbus, Ohio. (Letter 2-6-33)
x 375 East Broad Street, Columbus, Ohio. (10-28-30)
x Seneca Hotel, E. Broad & Grant Sts., Columbus, Ohio. (8-29-30)
X 585 East Broad Street, Columbus, Ohio.

The federal government kept radio station licensing records using three-by-five-inch index cards, and every time a facility or ownership change occurred, a notation was made on the station's card. Look closely and see the decades of WCOL, including its few years with WBNS. When the FCC ruled that a company could not own two AM stations in the same market, WBNS sold WCOL to the Pixley family in 1939. (FCC.)

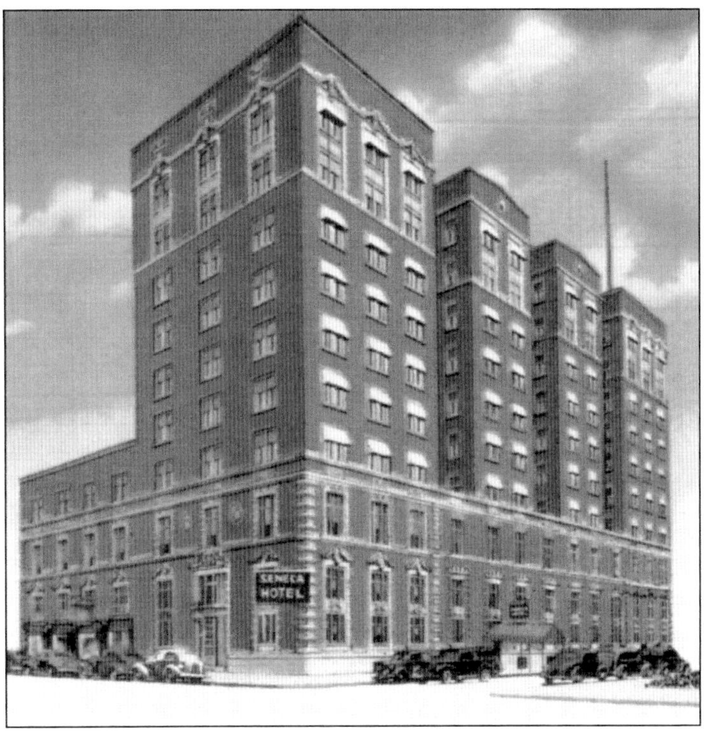

After serving the Baptists as WMAN for most of the 1920s, the church could not devote resources to a full time station. Just two hours on Sunday morning was no longer allowed. A station had to serve the community, and sermons were now carried by all local broadcasters. Next stop: the Seneca Hotel in Downtown Columbus, and a call letter change to reflect the new location, WSEN. (The Ohio History Connection, ALO5862.)

This is called a "radio stamp," a form of listener confirmation card. It displays the call letters, the channel, and the operating power. It shows that WCOL was one of the lowest-power stations in the market, a mere 100 watts, and at a frequency of 1210 kilocycles. When WBNS bought WCOL in 1936, they applied to raise the power to 250 watts. (Author's collection.)

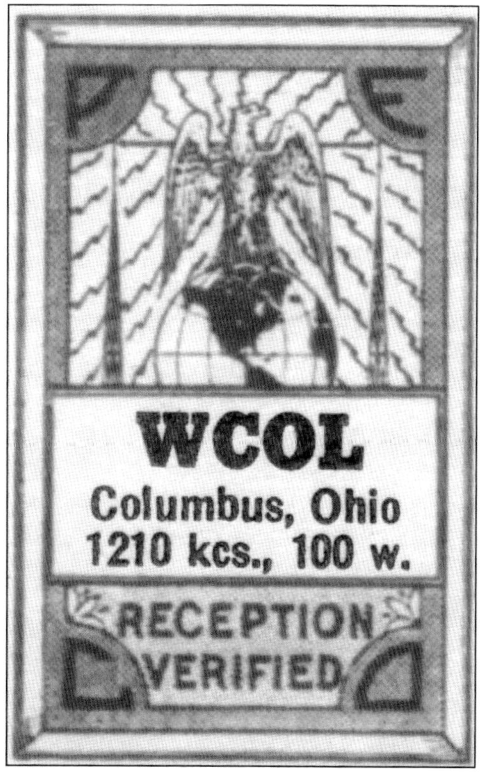

Pictured is one of the Radio Center control rooms for WCOL. Behind the engineer is an elaborate patch panel allowing audio to be routed from studio or network feed to the transmitter of one or the other station. This would be a complex arrangement requiring a perfect sense of timing and the ability to run several sources over several stations at once. (Greg Armstrong, Radio Ohio, WBNS.)

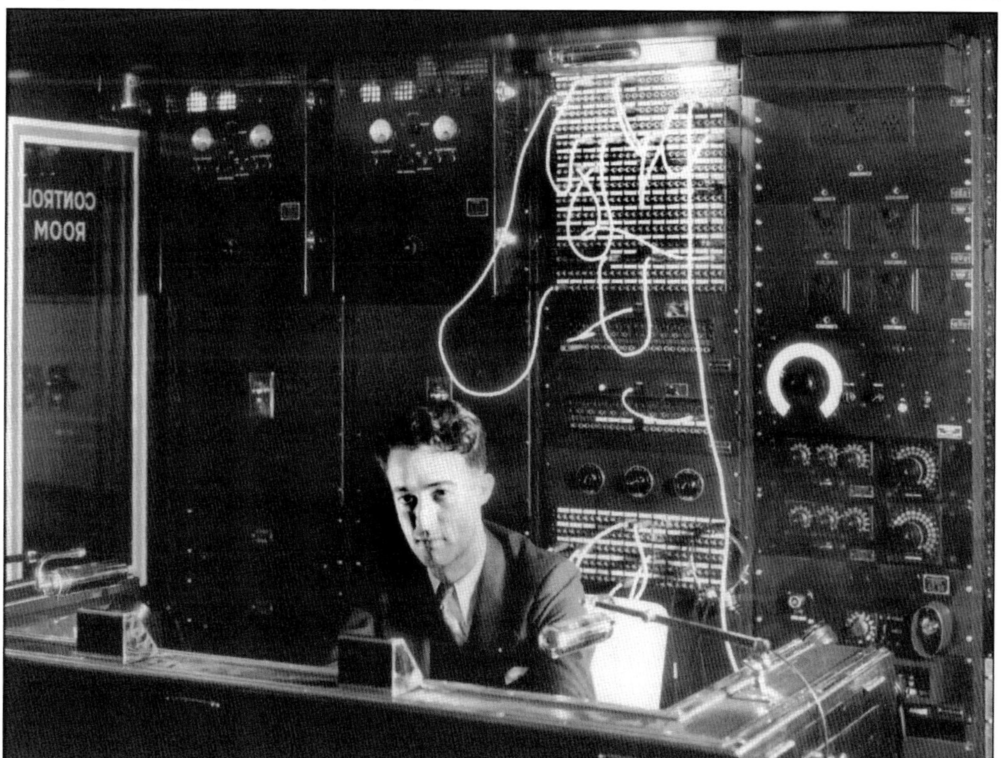

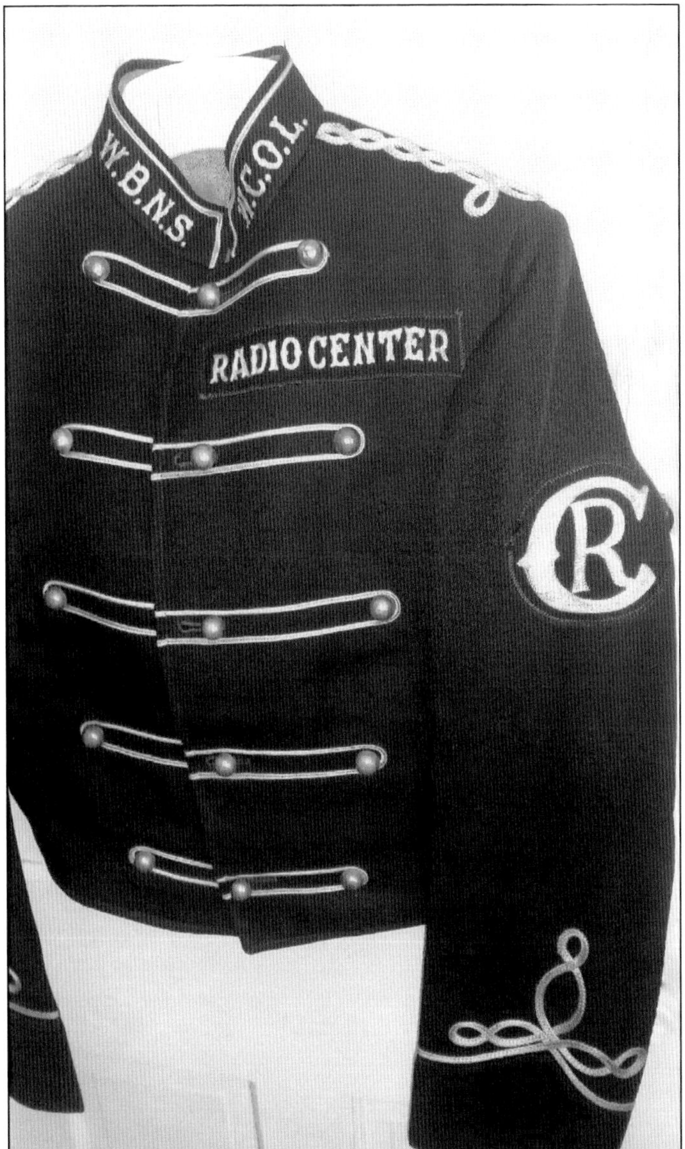

This is an usher uniform used when WBNS and WCOL shared common ownership at the North High Street facility. On its collar, the stations are listed as W.B.N.S. and W.C.O.L. While NBC in New York was called "Radio City," in Columbus it was "Radio Center." Uniformed ushers would meet those with studio audience tickets at the front door and escort them to their seats for the live program. A single telephone operator/receptionist for both stations answered incoming calls with the words "Radio Center." The Radio Center arrangement with WCOL and WBNS was never one of equal stature for the stations. In the Robert Dildine history of WBNS, the 250-watt WCOL was the farm team, and there was always the possibility that a WCOL person could be "promoted" to WBNS, the 5,000-watt CBS big brother. When the Wolfes had to divest themselves of one of two stations, the choice was obvious. In the late 1930s, the WCOL part of Radio Center was NBC Blue, and that became ABC in 1943. Columbus did not have any NBC Red affiliate, as the powerful 50,000-watt WLW in Cincinnati carried that network, apparently exclusively. NBC Red carried the most popular NBC offerings. (Brian Wolf.)

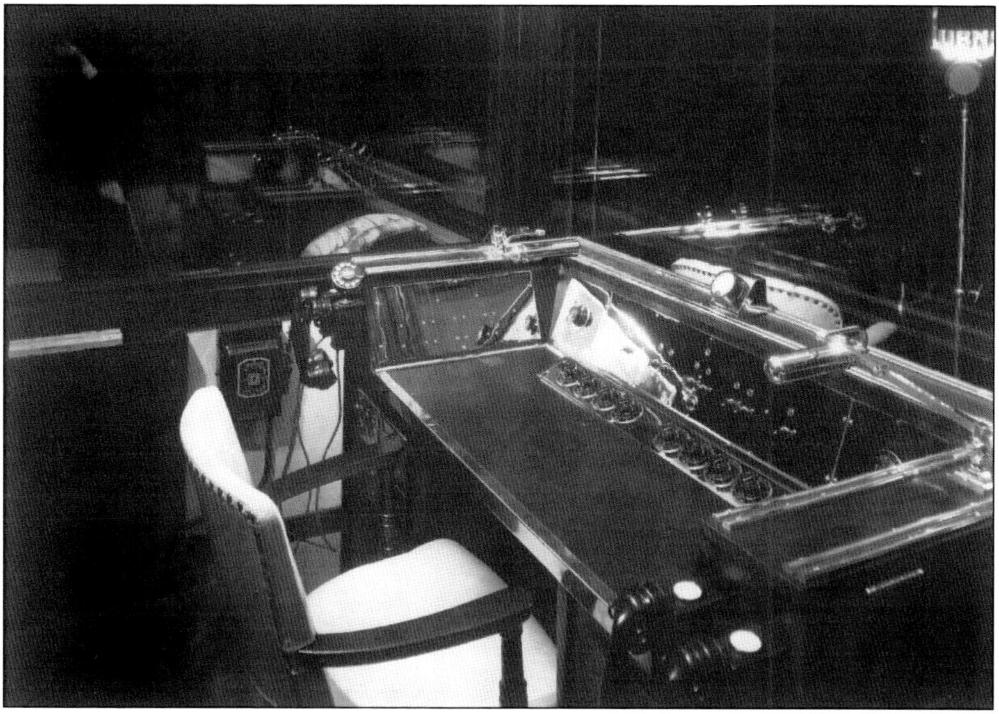

Compared to its established "parent," WCOL was a low-powered appendage that might have been an entry-level job for talent and technical personnel. The best radio job in town was always WBNS—it was a stable, well-appointed, high-class career. If the FCC had not declared at the end of the 1930s that an owner could only have one AM radio station per market, WBNS may have continued to own WCOL. (Greg Armstrong, Radio Ohio, WBNS.)

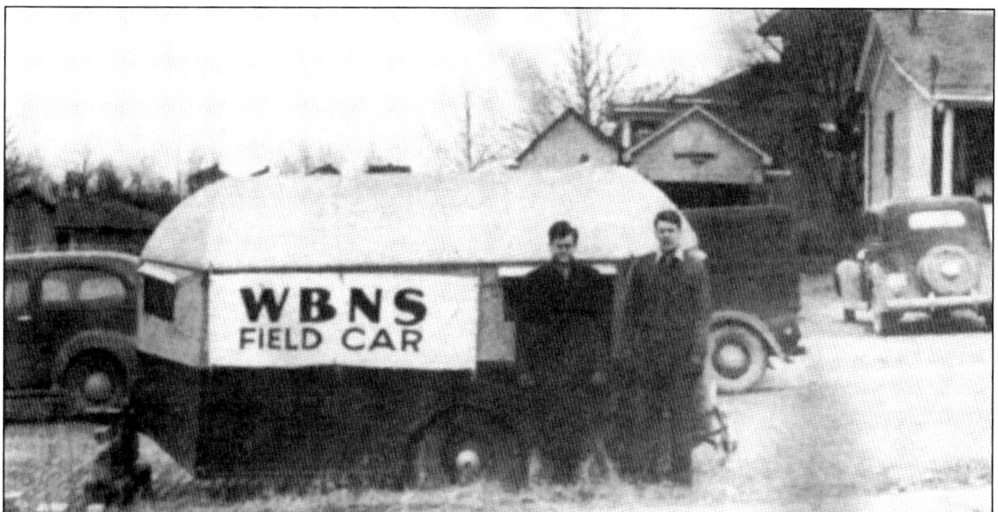

The WBNS Field Car was equipped with shortwave transmitters to broadcast on-the-spot news of a 1937 Ohio River flood. As a public service, the station also handled two-way communications between state officials and the Red Cross. Local radio was often the only way to get so-called "breaking news," and it replaced the newspaper extra when people needed news quickly. (WBNS 25th Anniversary booklet, author's collection.)

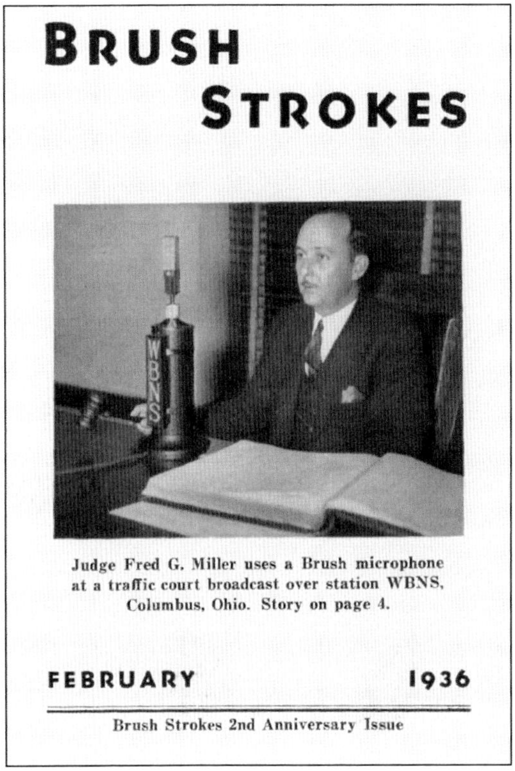
BRUSH STROKES

Judge Fred G. Miller uses a Brush microphone at a traffic court broadcast over station WBNS, Columbus, Ohio. Story on page 4.

FEBRUARY 1936

Brush Strokes 2nd Anniversary Issue

In this advertisement from the Brush Microphone Company in 1936, it is said that Judge Fred G. Miller uses a Brush microphone for his traffic court broadcasts on WBNS. In all of the WBNS photo collection of equipment, there is no such microphone, leading this researcher to believe that it was only product placement. (Author's collection.)

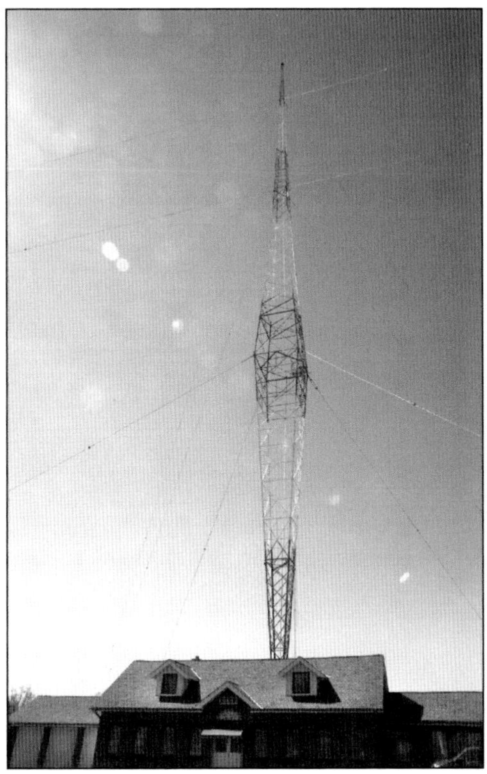

An exterior of the WBNS AM tower and transmitter building features the famous Blaw-Knox tower, a distinctive diamond shape designed in the 1930s. WBNS is one of only five that have survived into the present day. They are WSM Nashville; WLW Cincinnati; WBT Charlotte; WFEA Manchester, New Hampshire; and WBNS. To an engineer, this tower design is art. WBNS has recently refurbished and repainted its version of the Blaw-Knox. (Author photograph.)

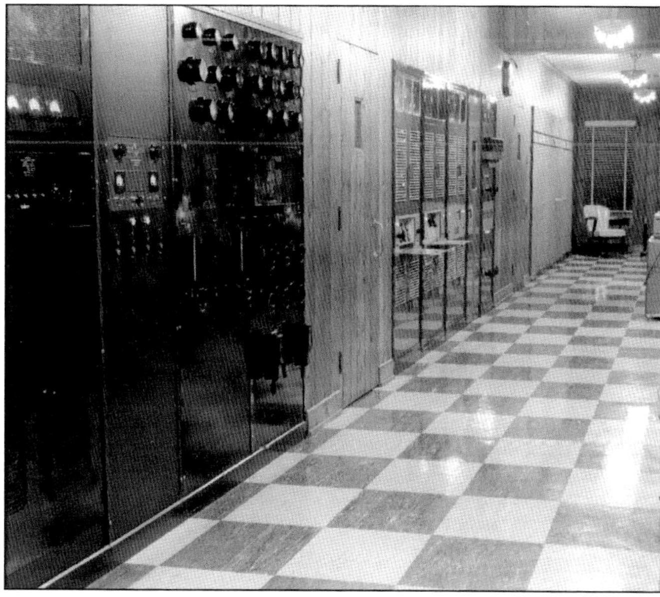

The interior of the WBNS AM transmitter building is pictured in the 1930s. This image shows a line of mostly AM transmitters and audio processing equipment connected by telephone line to the newly constructed studios in downtown Columbus. This facility at various times served as the location for the early FM transmission equipment. In March 1938, the FCC granted 5,000 watts for daytime power and 1,000 watts for nighttime using a directional pattern. (Greg Armstrong, Radio Ohio, WBNS.)

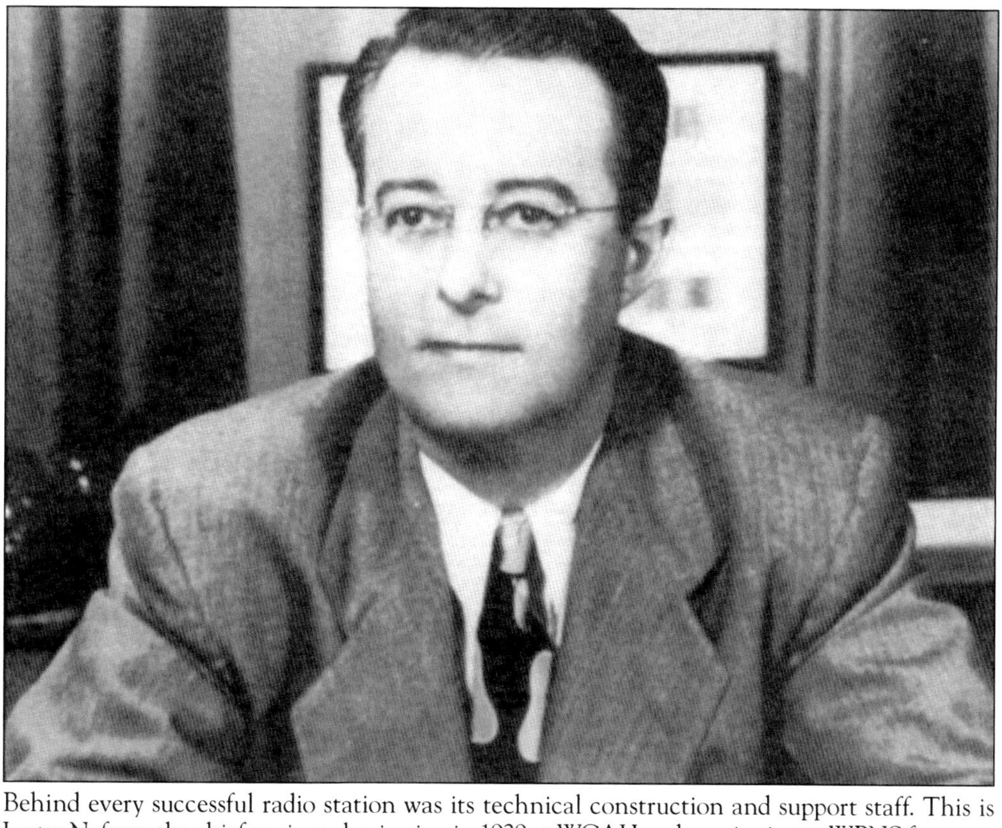

Behind every successful radio station was its technical construction and support staff. This is Lester Nafzger, the chief engineer beginning in 1929 at WCAH and continuing at WBNS for many years into the 1960s. For decades, he was in charge of the WBNS AM and FM stations and was involved in the early planning for WBNS-TV. Under Nafzger's leadership, WBNS received one of the very first FM licenses in 1940. (WBNS 25th Anniversary booklet, author's collection.)

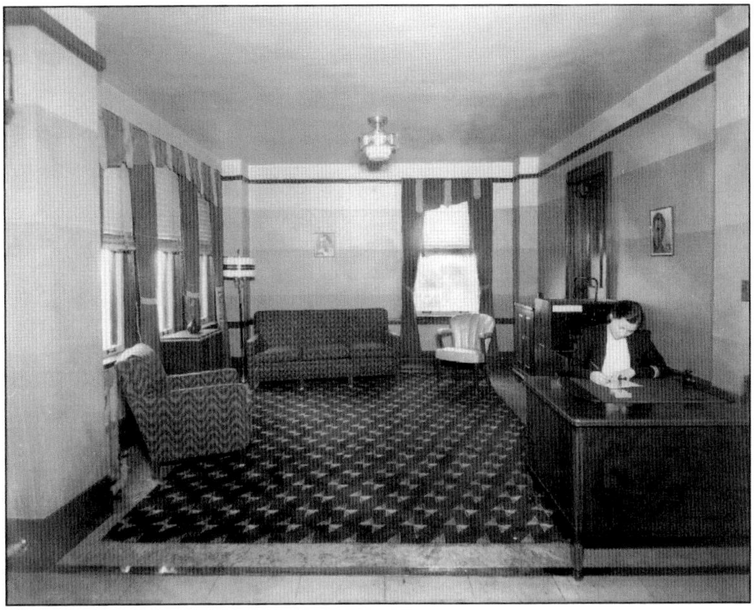

At the new WBNS facilities at 33 North High Street, the reception room is larger than some entire radio stations today. This room is where one would wait in comfort to go on the air as a guest or meet with the sales or program department. A uniformed usher escorted visitors to their destination. (Greg Armstrong, Radio Ohio, WBNS.)

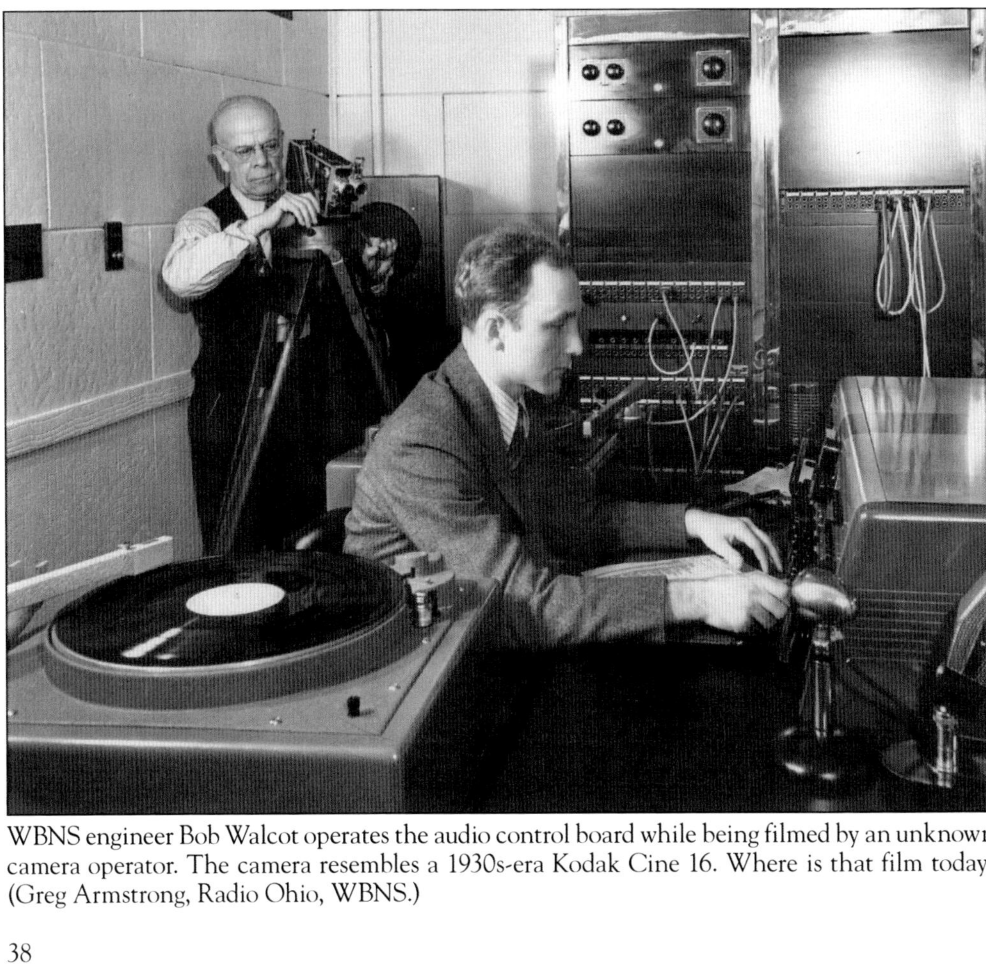

WBNS engineer Bob Walcot operates the audio control board while being filmed by an unknown camera operator. The camera resembles a 1930s-era Kodak Cine 16. Where is that film today? (Greg Armstrong, Radio Ohio, WBNS.)

By the early 1930s, WEAO had matured and demonstrated its great possibilities for the image and the mission of the university. It could entertain, it could educate, and it had to be rebranded as WOSU. Pictured is Dorothy Humphries, and since she is standing next to a piano and holding sheet music in her hands, it can be assumed that she is singing over WOSU. (The Ohio State University Archives.)

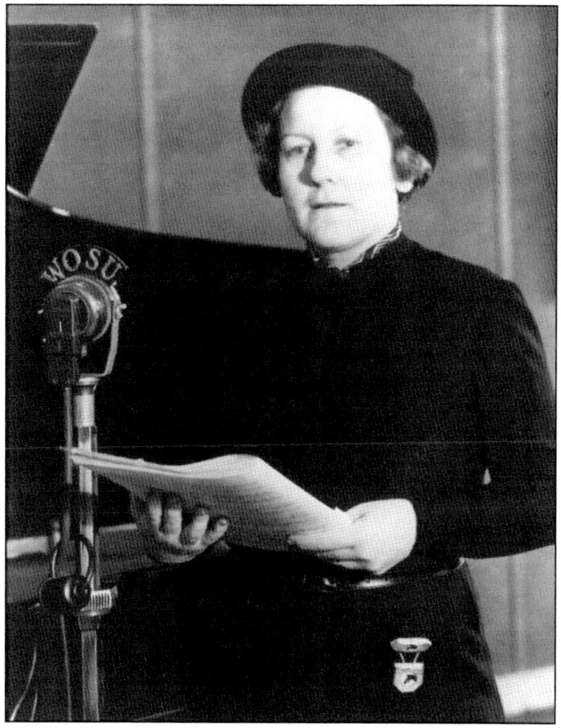

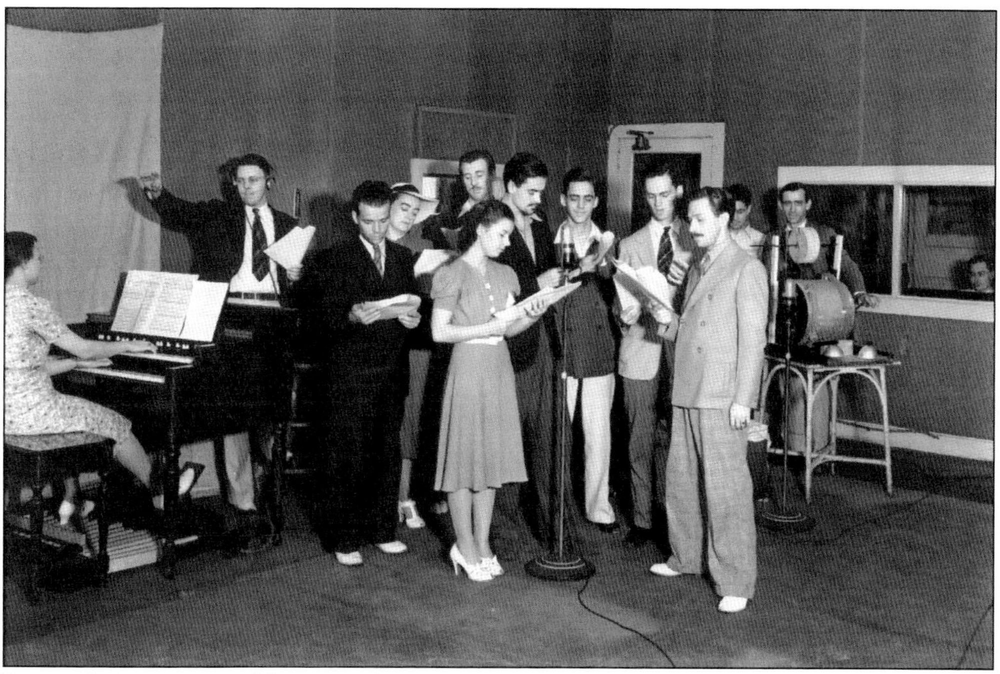

During the Depression of the 1930s, there were government programs to employ artists, and WOSU had this drama troupe funded by a New Deal program called the Works Progress Administration (WPA). The WPA was a jobs program employing over eight million people and saving the economy and many families. The organ pictured is a 1936 Hammond BC. (The Ohio State University Archives.)

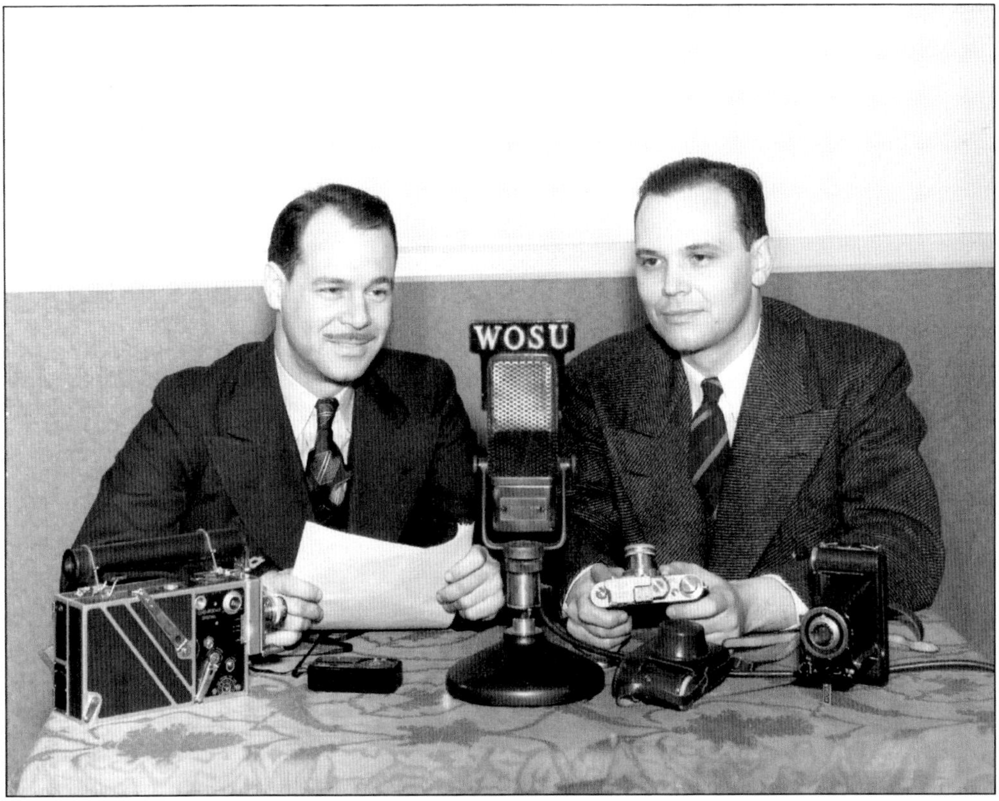

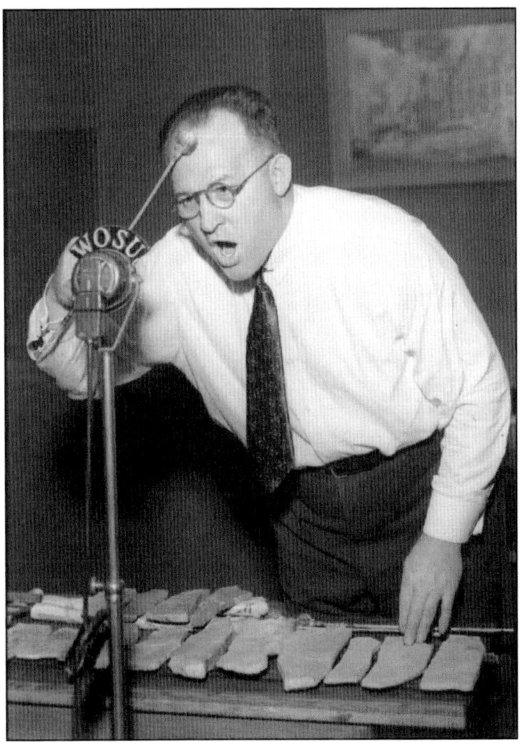

Here is an example of a 1930s WOSU educational program, the illustrated lecture using audio only. This show is obviously about cameras, but the folks at home will have to imagine that on the table there are, from left to right, a 16-millimeter film camera, a Leica rangefinder, and a Kodak bellows camera. (The Ohio State University Archives.)

This 1930s program, another demonstration, might be considered an audio novelty. The host is Charles Werderman, and the show in called *Unusual Instruments*, one of which is played by banging it on his head. (The Ohio State University Archives.)

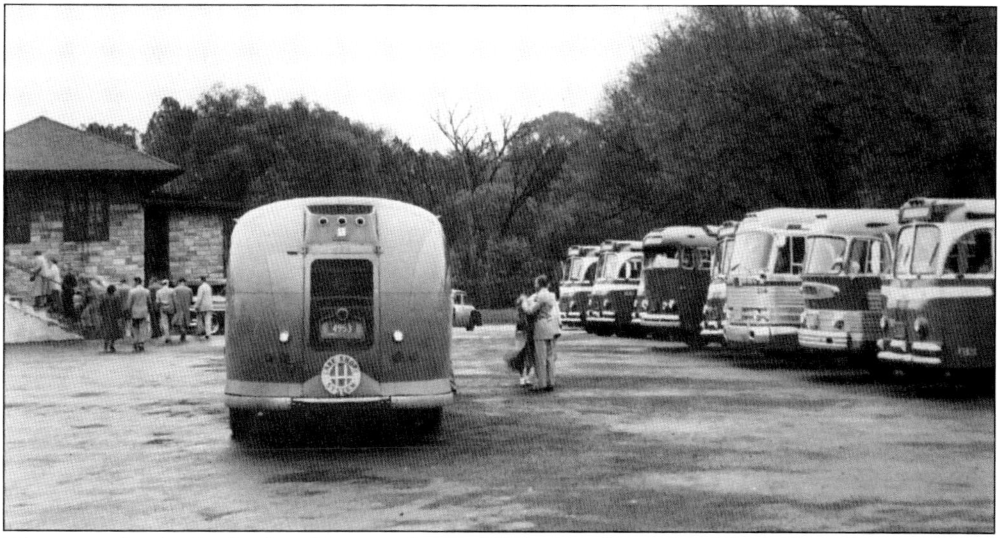

They came by the busload to dance to the big bands at Valley Dale Ballroom in rural Columbus. In the 1930s and 1940s, live broadcasts from there featured Kay Kyser, Paul Whiteman, Glen Gray and his Casa Loma Orchestra, Buddy Rich, Russ Morgan, Tommy Dorsey, and many more. It was all broadcast from Columbus to the world. This was the big band era, it was wartime, and Americans wanted to get away from it all, if only for a night. (Landa Brunetto.)

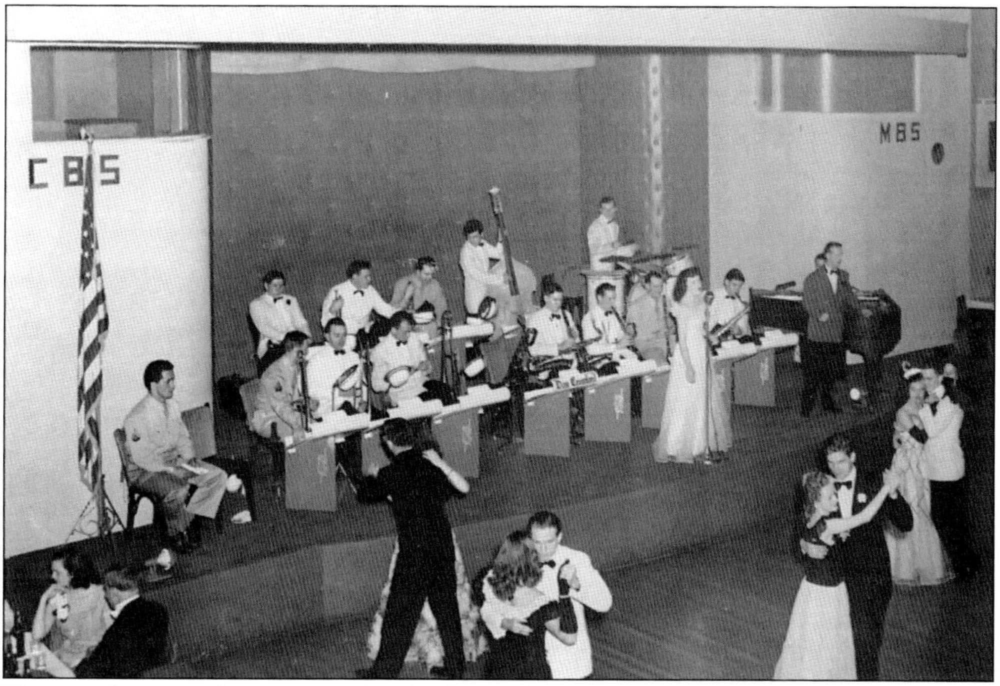

This was the event that connected Columbus to the rest of the country: the weekly broadcasts from Valley Dale. On the left side of the stage is the CBS broadcast booth. Microphones on stage would pick up the band and singers, connected to an audio mixer, where they would be sent by telephone line back to WBNS, then to New York for nationwide airing over CBS. The announcer would introduce the show: "Live, from beautiful Columbus, Ohio, and the giant Valley Dale Ballroom, it's Kay Kyser and his Kollege of Musical Knowledge!" (Landa Brunetto.)

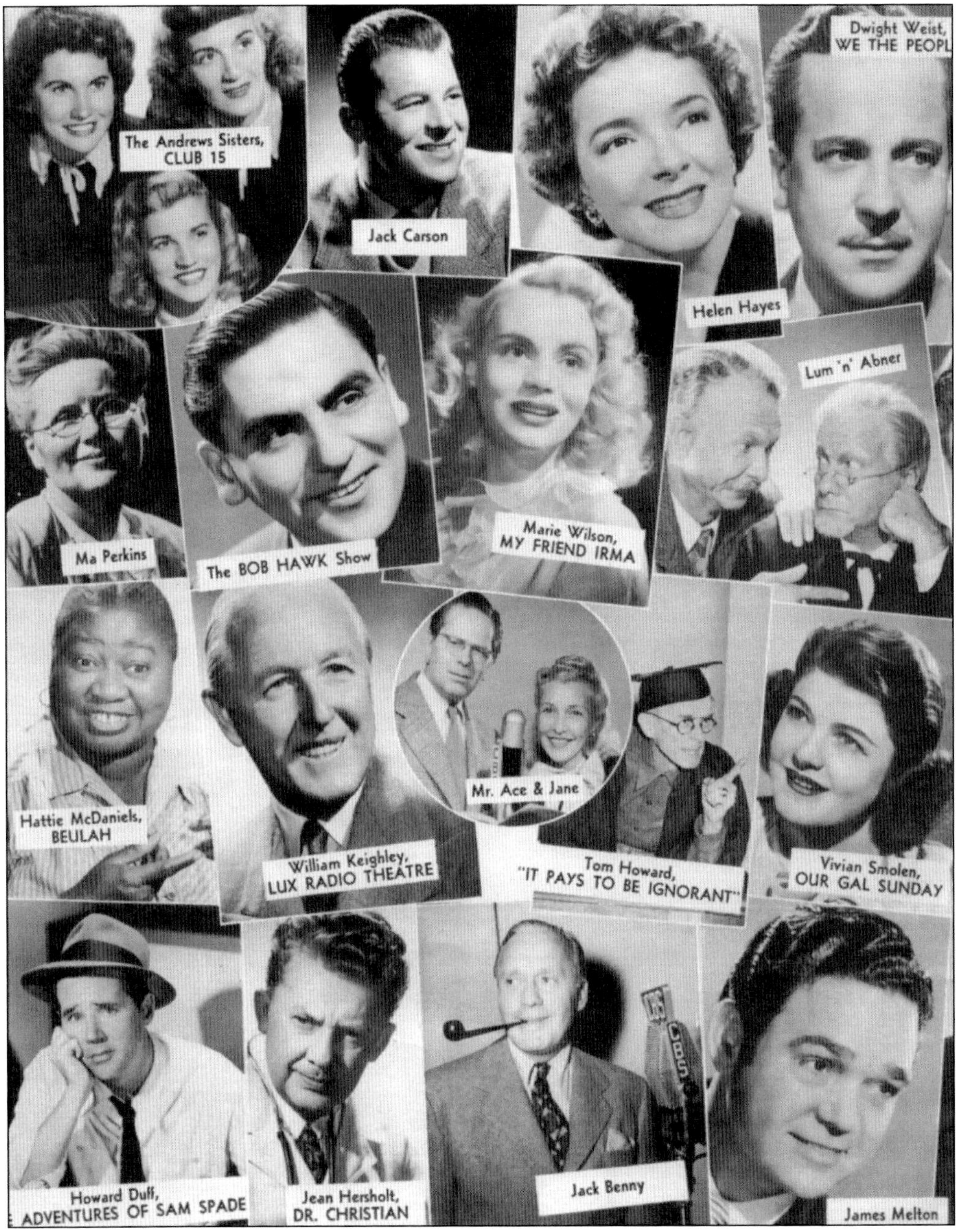

"The Stars Are Out Tonight on CBS" was a phrase used on the CBS radio network during the station break before and after a show. Seen in this CBS promotional picture are examples of the familiar names who were welcomed weekly into Columbus homes. WBNS was one of the earliest CBS affiliates, and CBS was the most popular radio network. Radio had moved from a local scientific curiosity during the 1920s into a nationwide entertainment medium by the end of the 1930s, and it stayed that way until dethroned by television in the 1950s. The so-called "Golden Age of Radio" started in the mid-1930s, as major talent in music, acting, and comedy were packaged by sponsors into 30-minute and one-hour programs. This ended in the mid-1950s; call it slow death by television. (WBNS 25th Anniversary booklet, author's collection.)

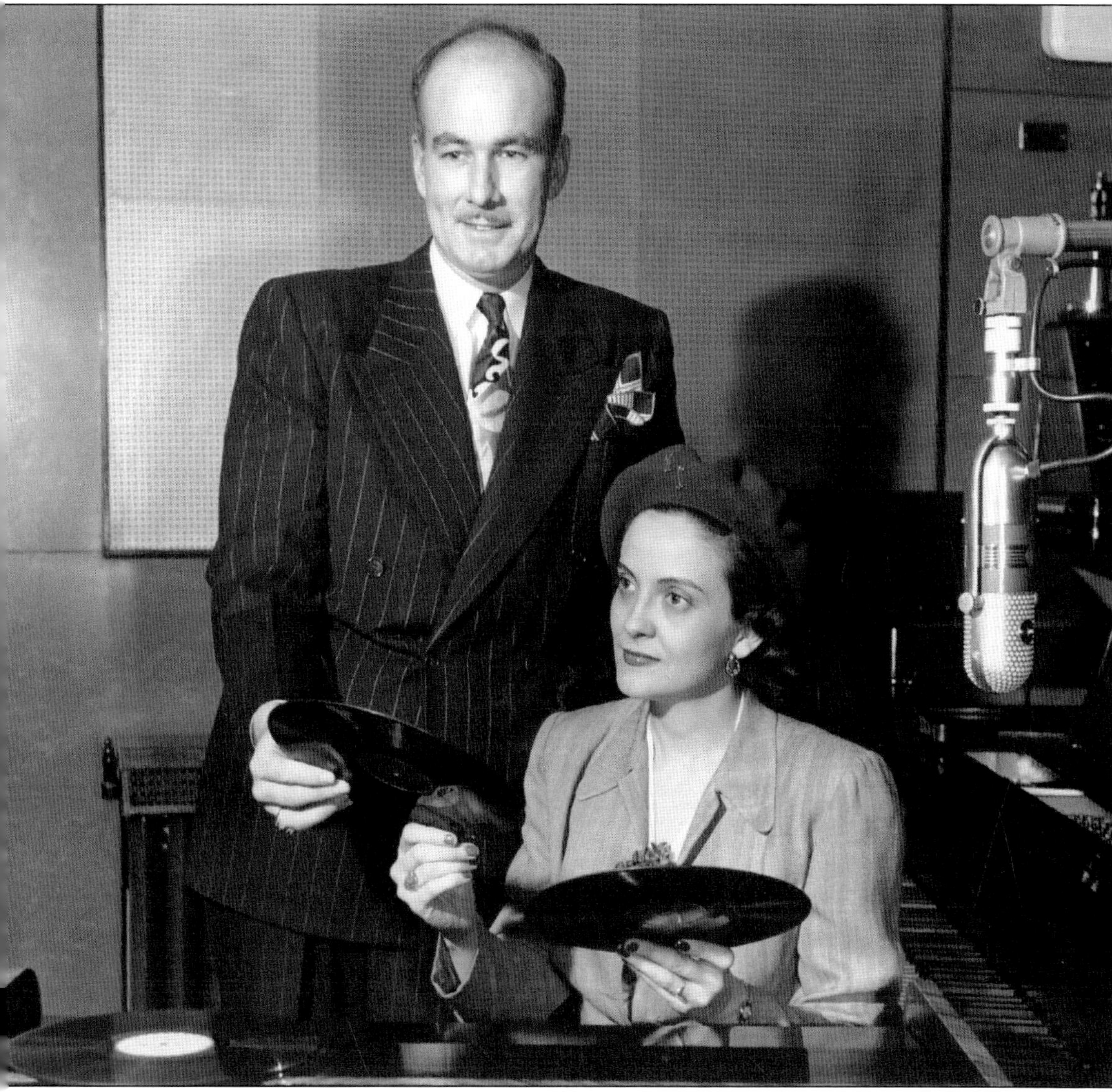

This is announcer Bill Corley with Muriel Lightfoot, comparing records in the WBNS studios. Corley was a long-time voice on WBNS, a studio announcer from the 1930s into 1970s. One of his long-standing announcer duties was the broadcast of Ohio State football. Lightfoot was the WBNS pianist and organist, one of the many musicians employed. This photograph illustrates the seriousness that embodied radio and especially WBNS in those early days, when it ruled the ratings. WBNS and its staff exuded high class locally and carried the best talent and national programming from CBS. (The Ohio History Connection, MSS1328AV.)

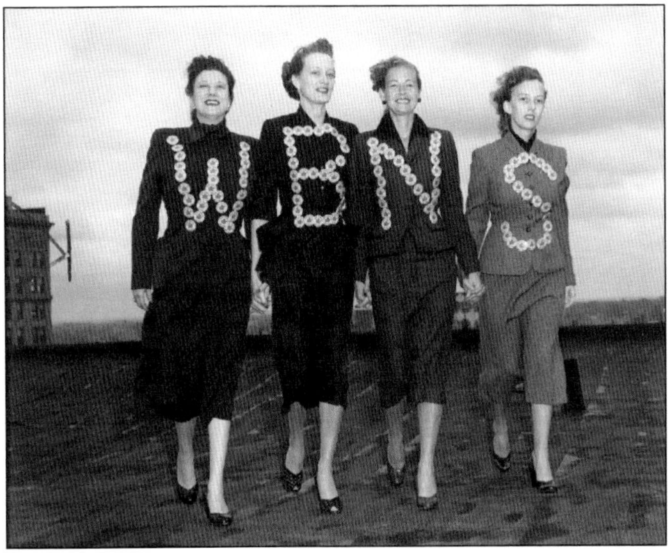

This WBNS promotion would only be effective if each of the four walked a certain way. They would have to know their letters so they always spelled WBNS. The participants are Naomi, Kitty, Audrey, and Mary, and it was their job to walk around downtown to show off the brand. The concept of promotions would become increasingly important as more stations led to more competition. (The Ohio History Connection, MSS1328AV.)

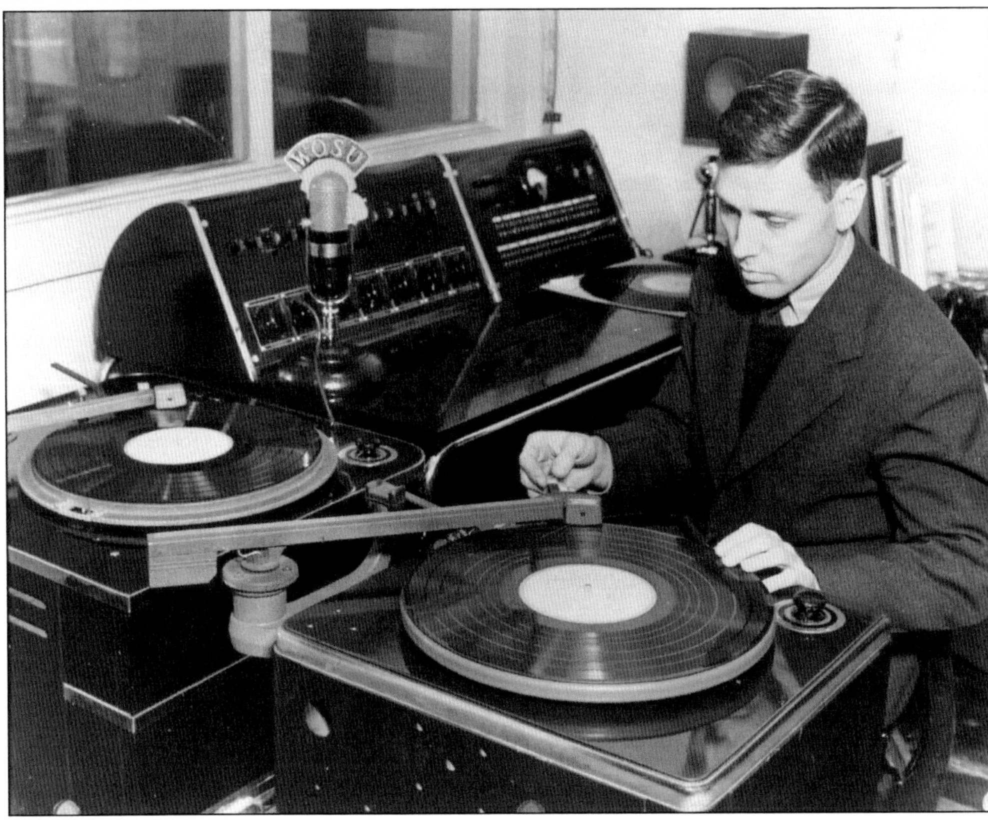

An unnamed WOSU announcer prepares his next recorded program or music selection while the turntable on the far left is on the air. A close look at the records indicate that these are 16-inch 33 1/3-rpm transcription discs, a format that allowed distribution of library music, complete programs, or groups of public service announcements. CBS invented the so-called LP or 12-inch long-play record album in 1949, also 33 1/3 rpm, so it could be played on existing equipment. (The Ohio State University Archives.)

Four

From War to Television

Radio soared during wartime in the 1940s, then crashed in the 1950s as television took the programming and the audiences of the network radio stations. First, the major network-affiliated stations served the war effort with news from Europe and entertainment programming meant to soothe the nervous citizens and reinforce the American military effort. By the 1950s, network radio was tired, with most stations supplementing that programming with big band records introduced by disc jockeys. Formerly successful stations struggled to find a purpose as their programming remained in the past. The famous radio dramas and comedies were reintroduced over the new device called the television. What was radio to do as its audience deserted it for their favorite programs that now featured pictures?

In Columbus, WBNS continued to lead throughout the 1940s and 1950s as other stations tried to catch up. There was WHKC and its fare of Mutual Broadcasting Network programming. By the mid-1950s, it would change ownership and adopt the call letters of its ABC TV station, WTVN. Now WCOL was affiliated with the ABC radio network, and it would build a new facility in 1947. Others, like WRFD, originally serving the farmer, and the educational WOSU, were still serving small niche audiences. Several new AM stations were broadcasting by the end of the 1940s, including WCLT in suburban Newark and WVKO, both low-power, daytime-only stations. WMNI-AM debuted in 1958.

With World War II over, radio had become predictable—some would say boring. It was time for something extraordinary to happen to radio to move it into the remainder of the century. Baby Boomers would grow up to be teen consumers by the end of the 1950s, and there were profits to be made from rock and roll for the station that understood it. But for the 1940s and 1950s, radio would remain the same. Its first major threat was television, and the major suppliers of television programming were NBC, ABC, and CBS. It was only a matter of time before the networks lost interest in radio and put all their resources into this new and compelling visual medium. This left radio with a mostly DJ format that appealed to adult listeners, and while, by the end of the 1950s, station programmers everywhere were looking at the buzz surrounding hit music radio, most still believed that the music was crude and that they could not convince their advertisers to take a chance with the new teen audience. They were so wrong. But that is for later.

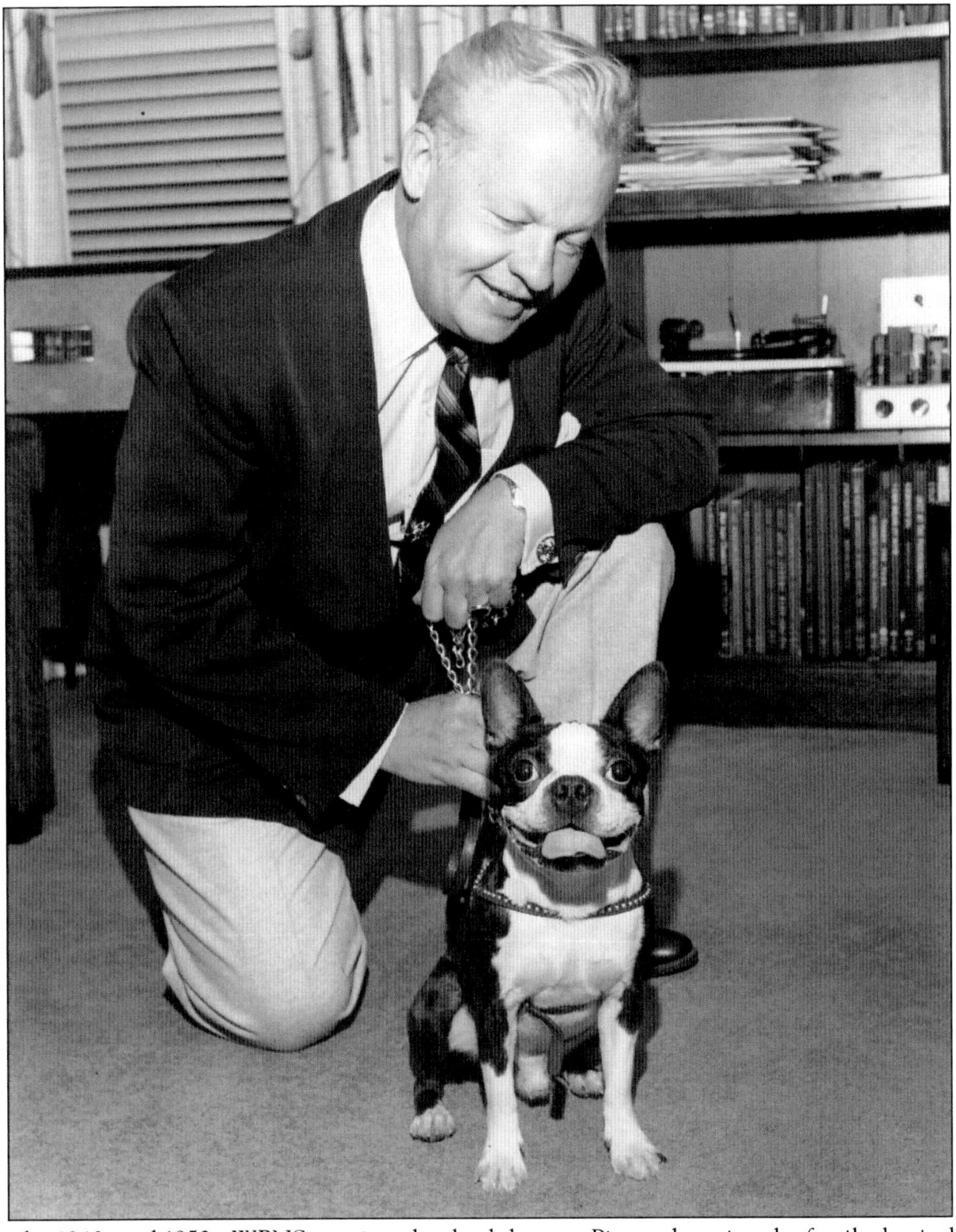

In the 1940s and 1950s, WBNS continued to lead the way. Pictured petting the family dog is the most famous of all Columbus radio personalities, WBNS morning show host Erwin Johnson. In 1940, Johnson began his career as the "Early Worm," and by the mid-1950s, he had given over 6,000 broadcasts. Johnson had two advanced degrees from Ohio State University and a Phi Beta Kappa key, and before getting into radio, he was a French professor at OSU. And although he was a French expert, in his words, "My knowledge of the language and the country keeps alive my desire to go there someday." He was a Columbus legend, likely the most recognized voice in the history of local radio. By the 1950s, Johnson was broadcasting from the studio three days a week and from home the other days. According to the WBNS publication *Radio-Photo News*, Johnson has made over "1,000 public appearances off the air," these for local nonprofits. (The Ohio History Connection, MSS1328AV.)

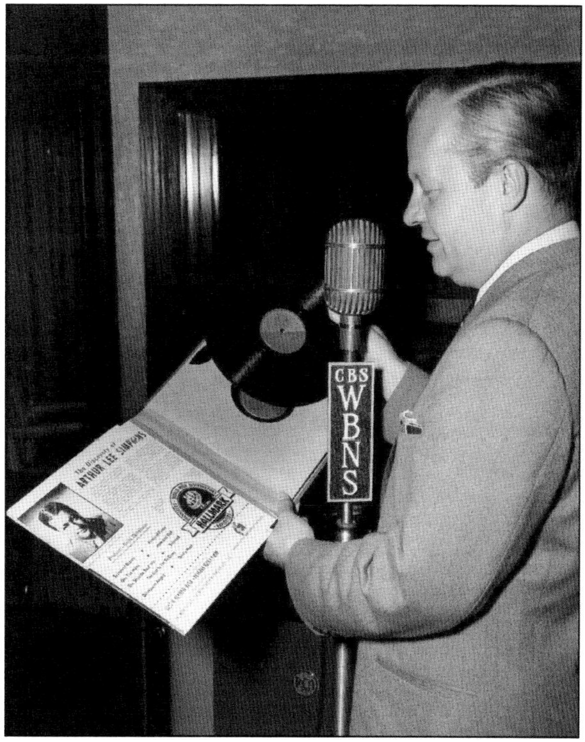

In the WBNS studios, the Early Worm is selecting music to be played on his morning show. While all radio stations would eventually be combo operations, meaning the DJ both announces and operates the audio board, Johnson just announced, and an engineer did the rest. Even from his home studio, he just talked, and an engineer at the station played the music. (The Ohio History Connection, MSS1328AV.)

The Early Worm relaxes at home in 1952. In the family room with his daughter, Nancy, and wife, June, Johnson is doing—what else—a DJ show for his family. Later in his career, Johnson tried television—WBNS, of course—following the path of many of his fellow radio announcers. (The Ohio History Connection, MSS1328AV.)

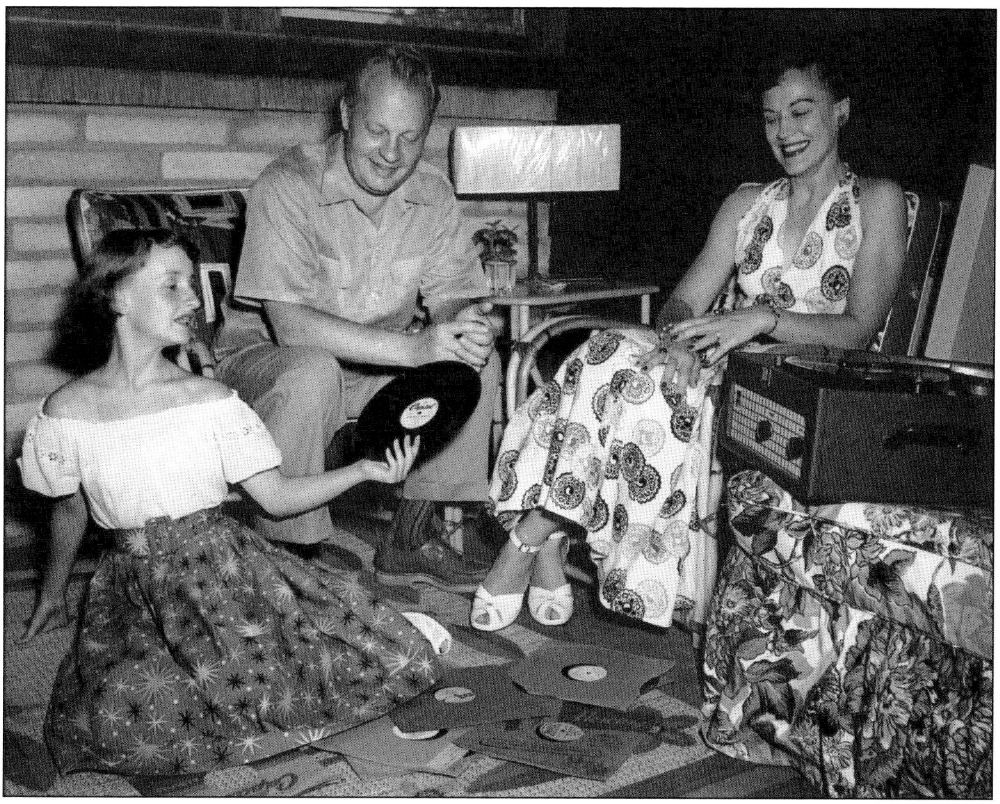

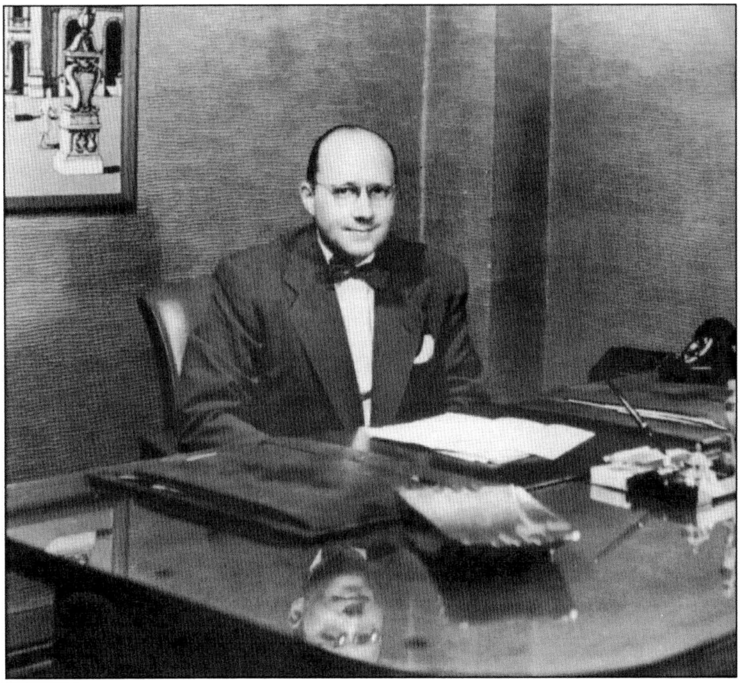

The boss of WBNS, Richard Borel, was station manager through most of the 1930s to the 1950s. During his management tenure, WBNS added FM and television Channel 10 as the CBS affiliate. He was apparently successful at hiring the best talent and technical people, as WBNS under his management was always on top of the ratings. (WBNS 25th Anniversary booklet, author's collection.)

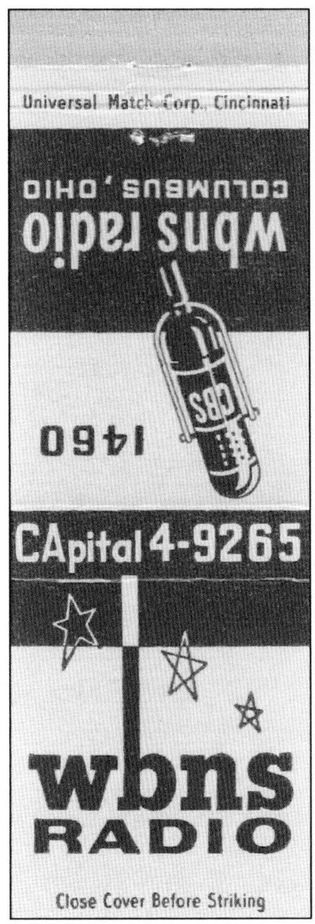

It seemed that everybody smoked in the early days of radio. Ashtrays were everywhere, and radio broadcast spaces, both control room and studio, were often smoke-filled rooms. An engineer at one Columbus station was assigned to scrape off the yellow cigarette smoke residue from the microphones and other equipment. And the warning on the matchbook, "close cover before striking," was always a good idea. (Author's collection.)

Every station was required by the FCC to air a few hours of religious programming on Sunday mornings. Pictured planning the WBNS version is a protestant minister, a rabbi, and a Catholic priest. In the early days of radio, so-called "full service" or "entertainment and information" stations needed to provide some diversity of religious programming and other non-advertising-supported public service, then called "sustaining programming." (WBNS 25th Anniversary booklet, author's collection.)

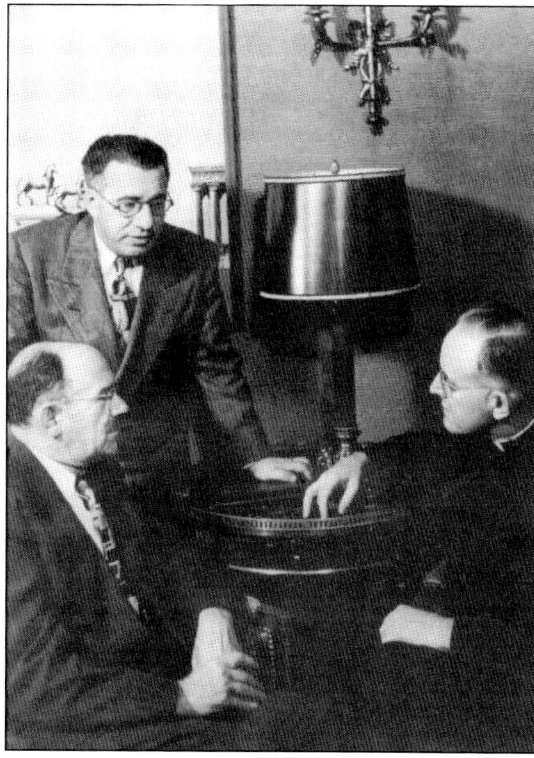

Duncan Hines is interviewed by Fern Sharp. He talks about—what else? Cakes. Fern Sharp began her radio career at WBNS in 1937 with a program called *Round Robin Review*, a show directed mostly at the homemaker stay-at-home mom. Every radio station had short programs that appealed to specific audiences, and all had a "woman's director." (WBNS 25th Anniversary booklet, author's collection.)

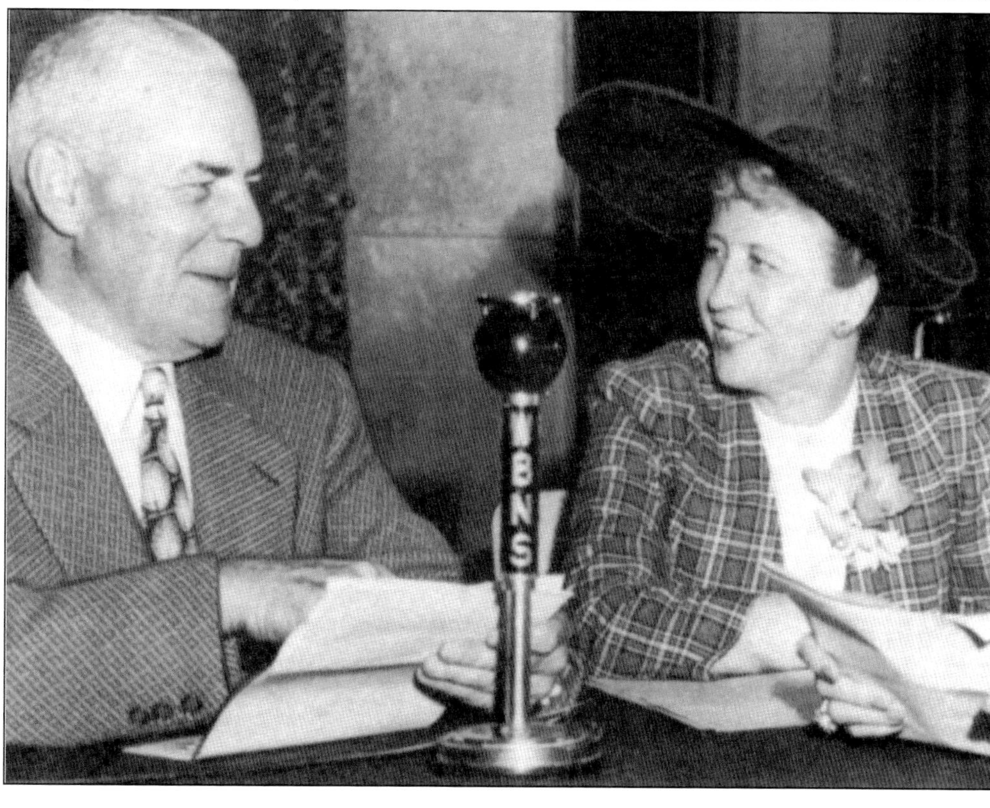

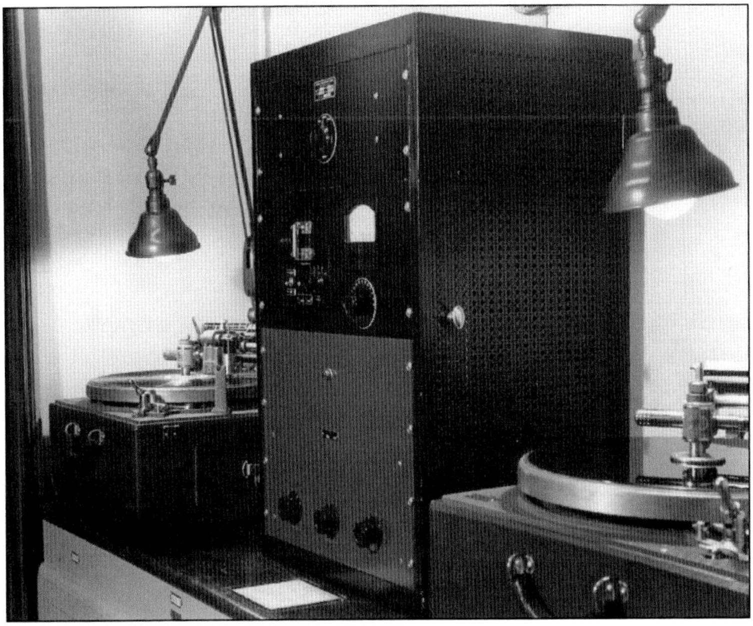

Before the tape recorder, saving a live program meant recording it on a 16-inch-diameter disc using what was called a cutting lathe. The adjustable lights above each cutter allow minute examination of the grooves, and often there was a microscope attached to enable the operator to see the grooves up close. (Greg Armstrong, Radio Ohio, WBNS.)

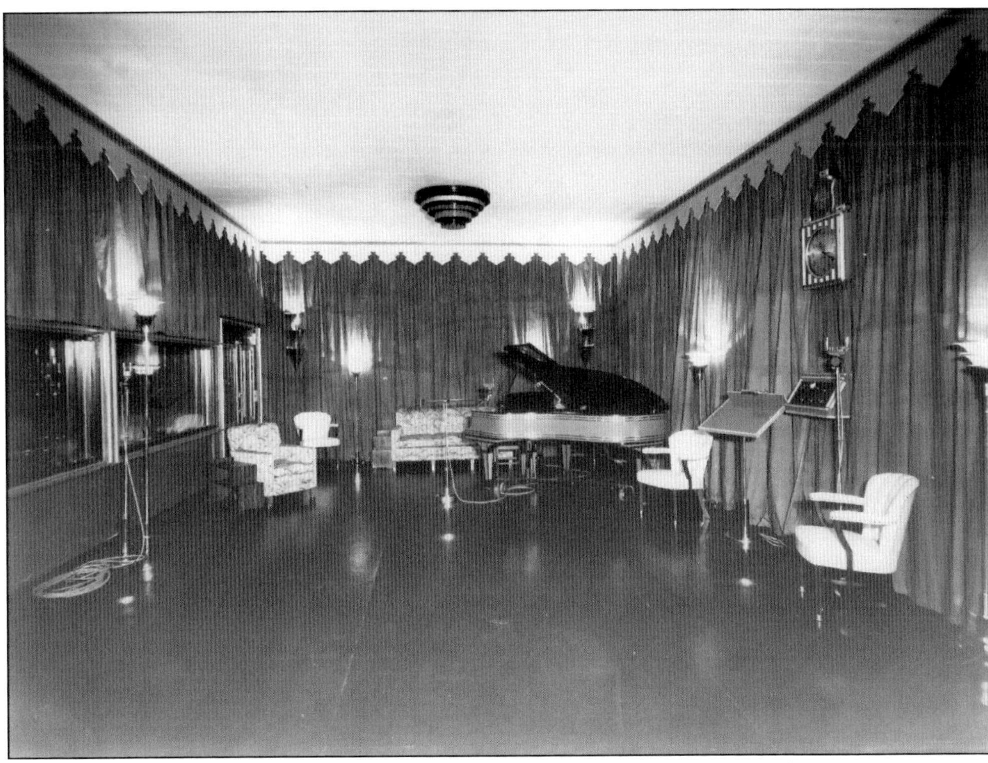

Studio A was promoted as the best of WBNS: "All programs that include large groups or casts originate here. The studio is tastefully decorated in soft pastels, has fluorescent lighting, air-conditioned and the latest acoustical effects. It includes an elaborate pipe organ with a special housing chamber on the roof of the building with pipes concealed in the ceiling." All of the studios had Steinway grand pianos as standard equipment. (Greg Armstrong, Radio Ohio, WBNS.)

Bill Corley of WBNS must be the morning announcer, as the clock indicates it is 4:00 a.m. and his clock radio has just gone off. A close look reveals that the radio dial is tuned to WBNS 1460 AM. Corley was the announcer for the Early Worm, meaning he read commercials and station breaks. (The Ohio History Connection, MSS1328AV.)

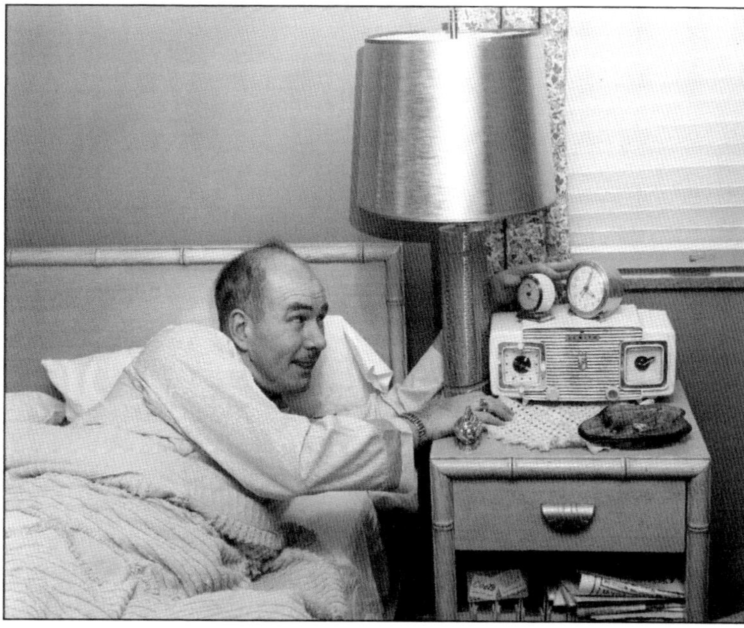

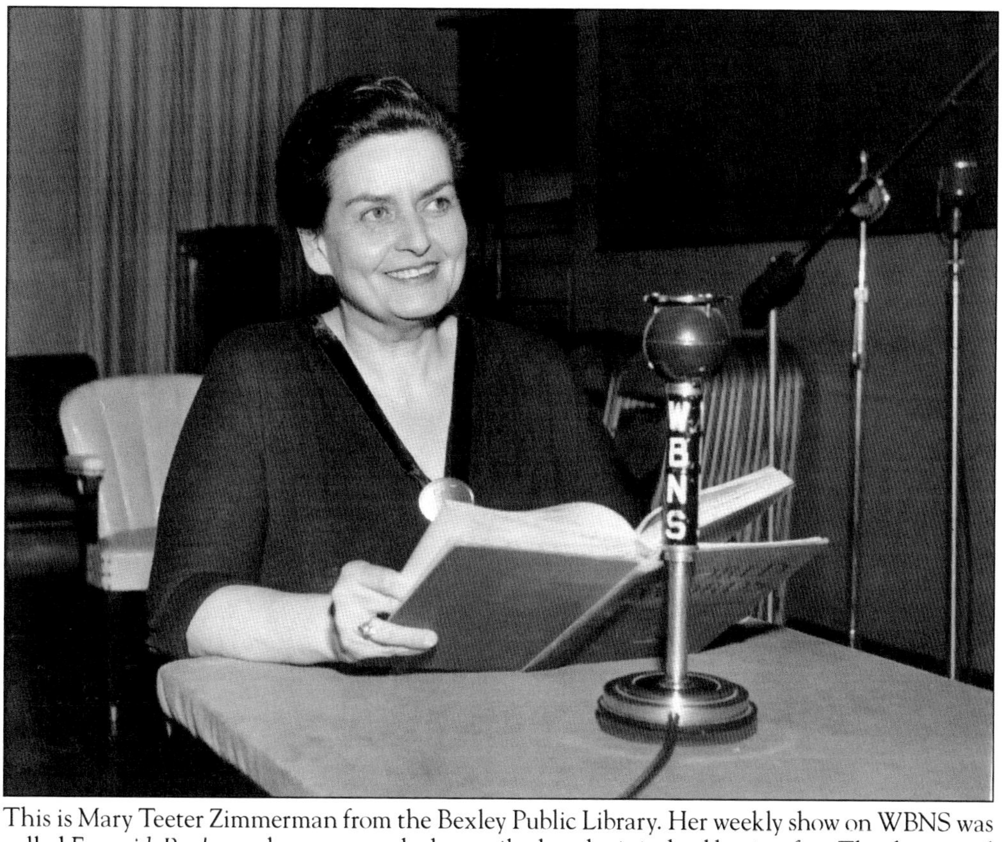

This is Mary Teeter Zimmerman from the Bexley Public Library. Her weekly show on WBNS was called *Fun with Books*, and one can see by her smile that she is indeed having fun. The show aired Saturdays at 4:15 p.m. It was probably logged as "public service, education." (The Ohio History Connection, MSS1328AV.)

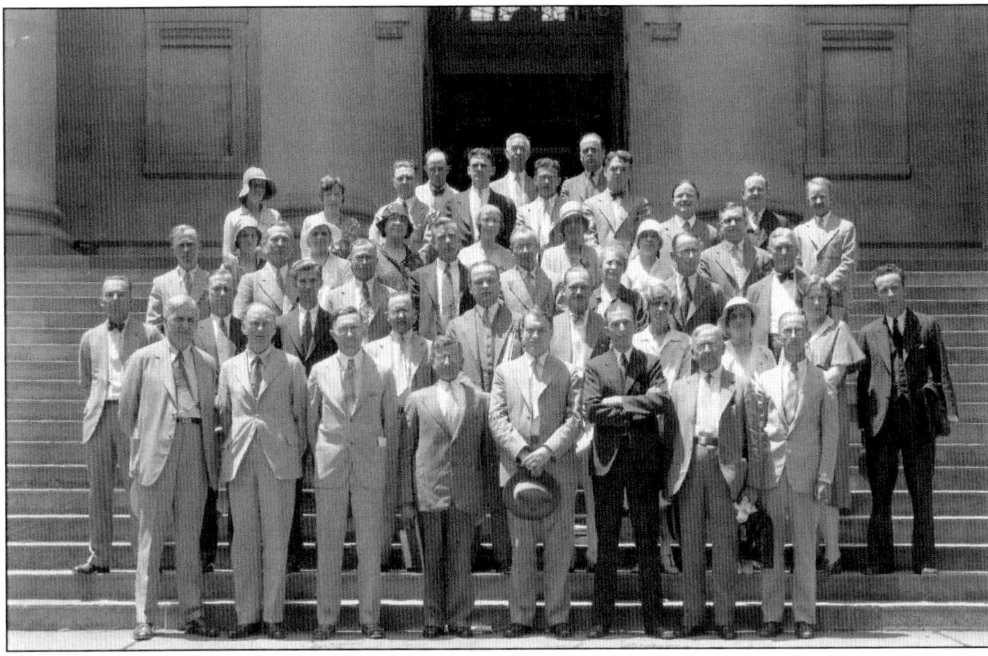

In the 1940s, several Ohio State professors demonstrated how radio could support education. The WOSU *Junior College of the Air* allowed working adults to take classes at home over the radio, and K-12 teachers could use radios in their classrooms to offer supplemental lectures. WOSU sponsored a national organization called the Institute for Education by Radio, pictured here at its annual conference in Columbus. (The Ohio State University Archives.)

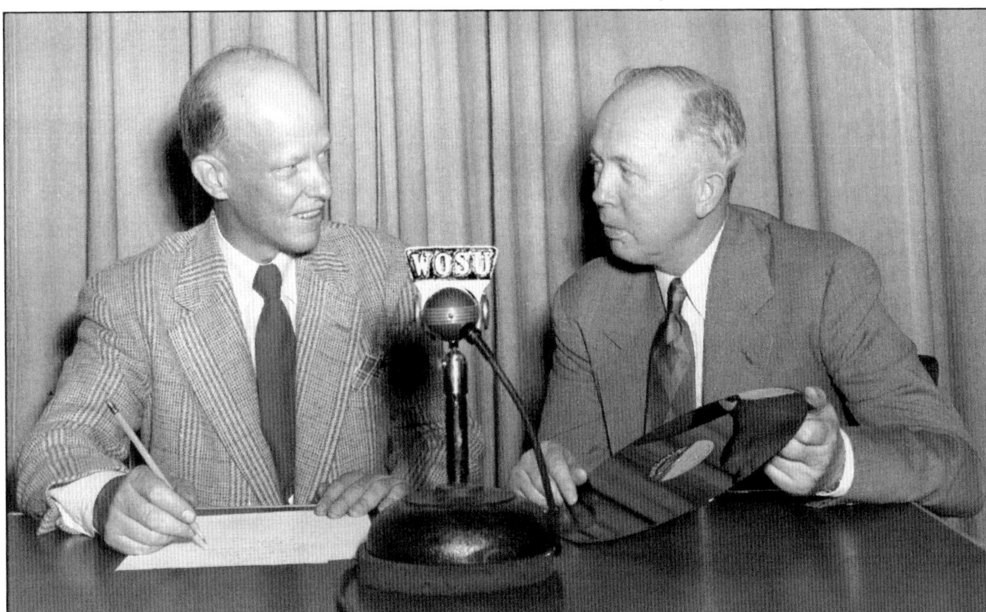

Dr. I. Keith Tyler and Dr. Edgar Dale are two professors who contributed much early to education using media. Professor Tyler created and ran the WOSU Institute for Education by Radio, and Professor Dale wrote the book *Audiovisual Methods in Education*, showing teachers how to use film, slides, and audio to enhance instruction. (The Ohio State University Archives.)

Of course it wouldn't be the same Ohio State without the football Buckeyes. In a survey done by WOSU, listeners were asked to name their favorite radio programs. The winner will not surprise. It is Ohio State football—the pregame, the play-by-play, the postgame, and all the OSU sporting news. (The Ohio State University Archives.)

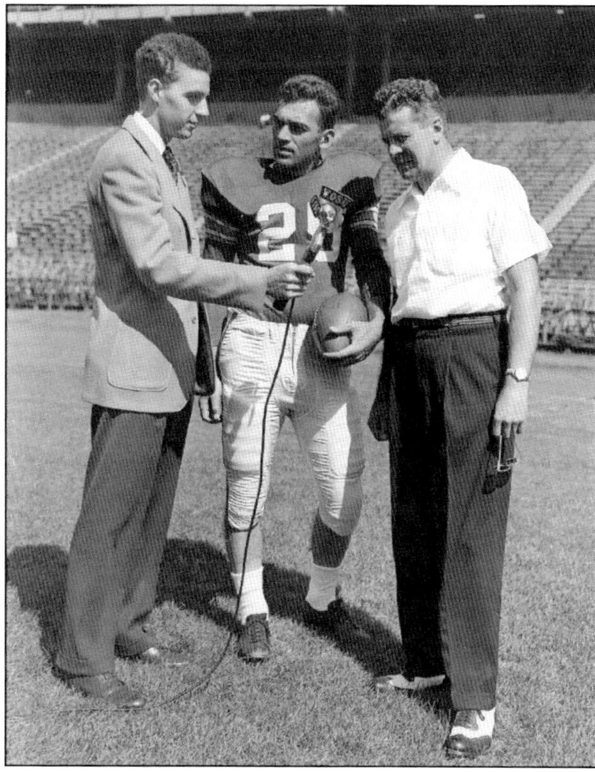

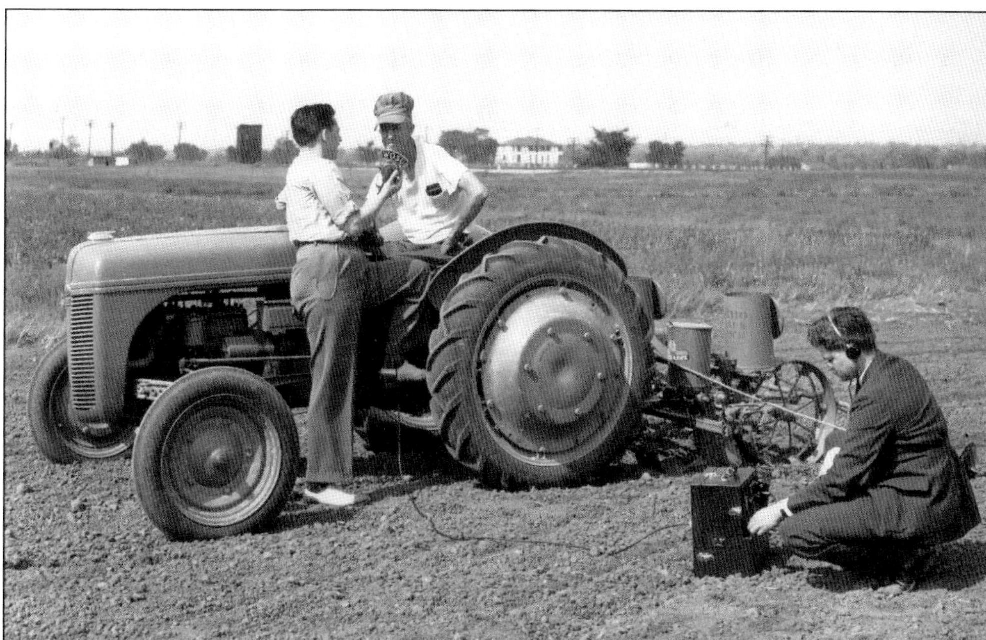

In second place with listeners responding to these early ratings were the programs for the farmers, who found early radio an up-to-date way to hear the farm news and the prices they could expect for their milk and corn. This is a live show called *The Farm and Home Hour*, sent back to the station by shortwave from a mobile unit. (The Ohio State University Archives.)

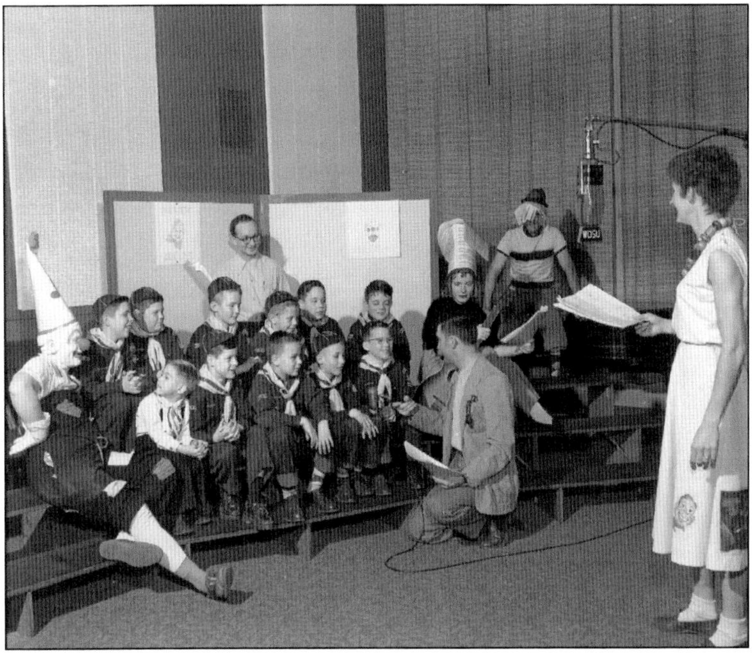

Remember when children's shows were on the radio? There were many on the radio networks, and some local stations had them as well. The goal was to get kids to listen and learn positive values by making them laugh and giving them prizes. Here is the 1950 version of WOSU's *Time for Fun*, a non-sponsored educational program. (The Ohio State University Archives.)

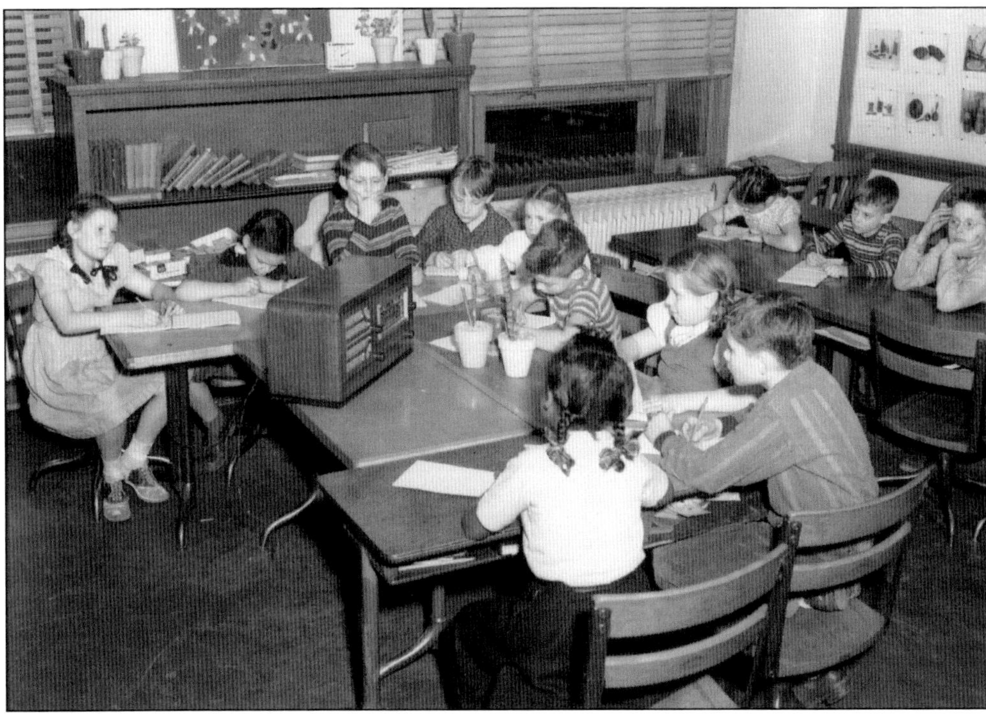

There was another genre of shows for kids, these provided by the more serious Institute for Education by Radio. The goal of this gambit was to place radios in the classrooms and have a master teacher in a studio giving a lecture. The results were always measured to see if radio-supported education worked. Did students actually learn more by listening to broadcast course content? This exact idea was replicated by educational television in the 1950s and on the Internet today. (The Ohio State University Archives.)

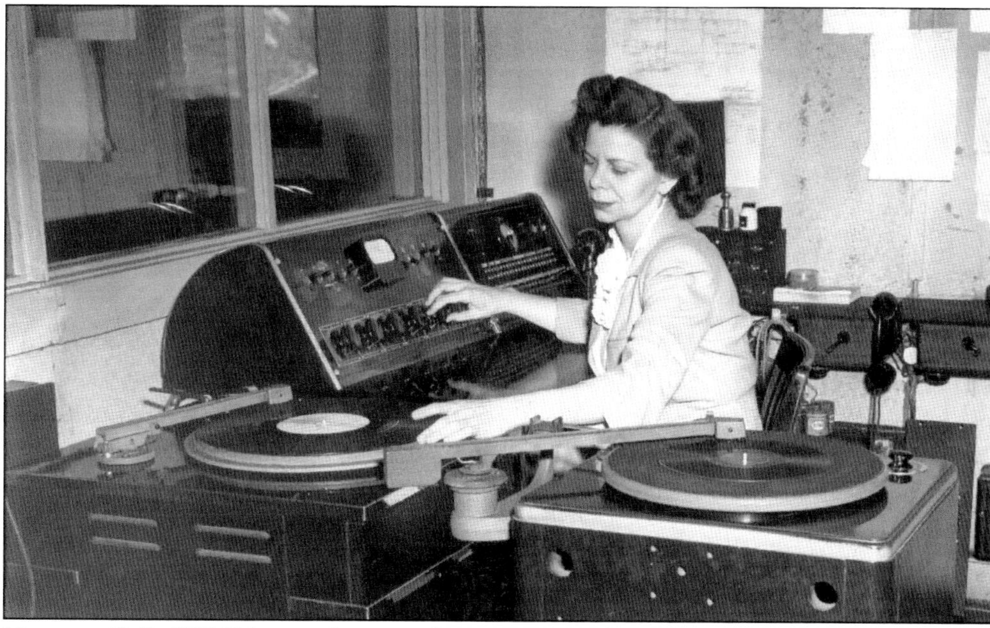

Here is a 1940s WOSU control room, where operator Alice McCuskey has cued up a record. The way this works is that the operator stops the record from spinning when the first sound is heard, then reverses the record to just before the sound begins. The turntable continues spinning under the record, which is stopped. Now she can release it, and it plays instantly. (The Ohio State University Archives.)

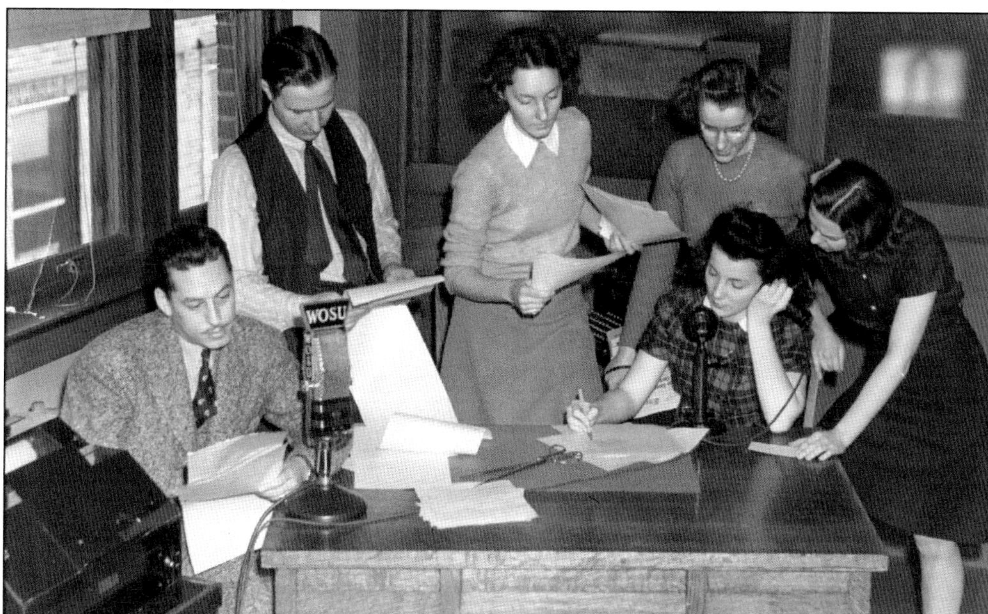

Gradually, in the 1940s, many major universities with large print journalism programs expanded their mission to include radio news. Here, a group from a news class is preparing the news, which will likely be read by a WOSU staff announcer—perhaps the one seated next to the microphone. WOSU was never a student-operated station, unlike many university FM stations today. (The Ohio State University Archives.)

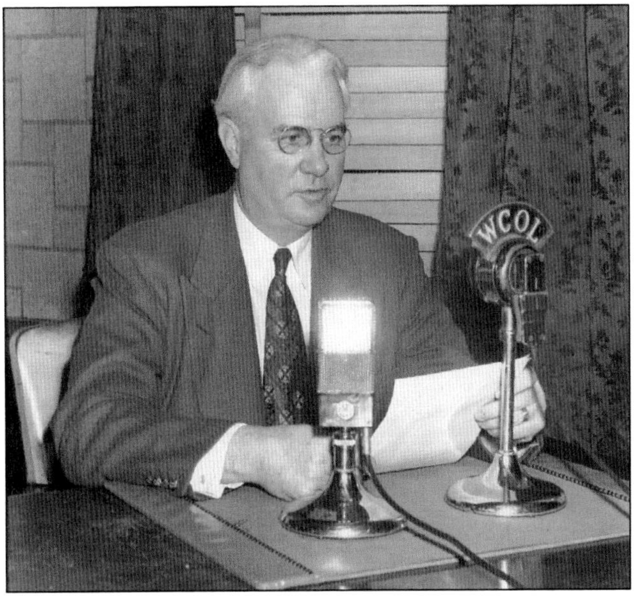

Here is a Republican giving an address on a soon-to-be Democrat-owned radio station. John Bricker was the 54th governor of Ohio and the Republican nominee for vice president in 1944. Politicians seemed to own Columbus radio: Charles Sawyer, secretary of commerce under Truman, would in 1951 own WCOL as Air Trails Broadcasting, and William Howard Taft, 27th president of the United States, would soon have family ownership of WTVN under Taft Broadcasting. (*Columbus Citizen-Journal*/Photohio.org.)

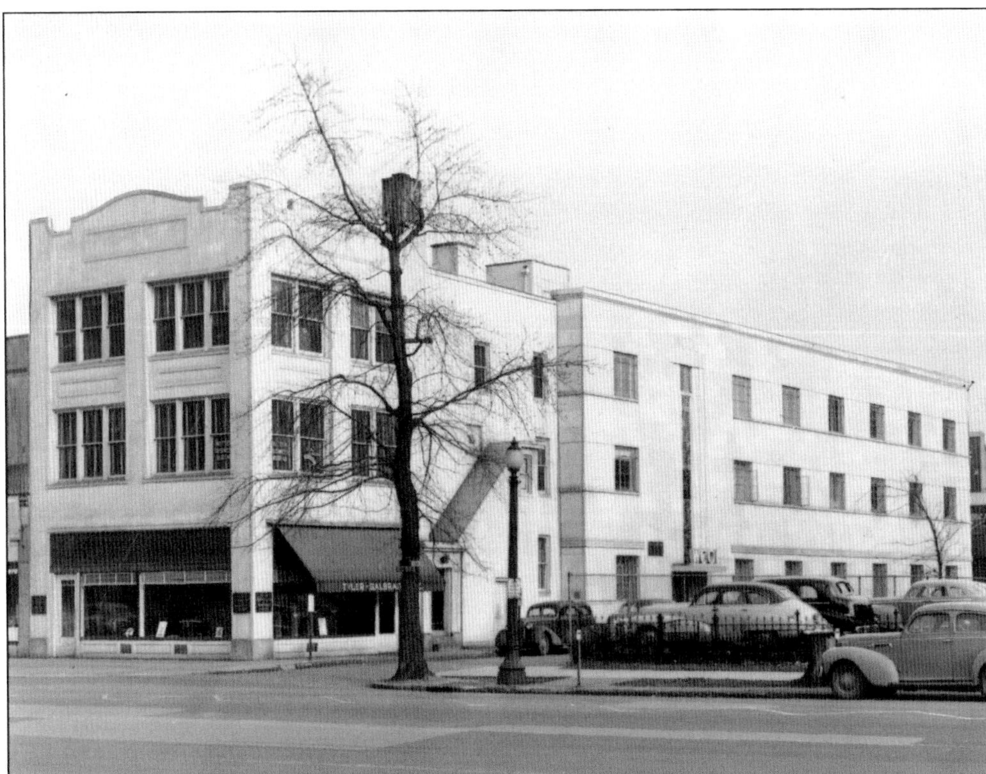

In 1947, the new WCOL building was constructed at the corner of Broad Street and Young Alley. Starting life as a religious broadcaster, then co-owned by WBNS, WCOL was an ABC radio affiliate in the 1940s and 1950s. The new broadcast facility in downtown Columbus was just a few blocks from the state capitol. For that reason, WCOL called itself "The Capitol Station." (*Columbus Citizen-Journal*/Photohio.org.)

This ribbon-cutting ceremony was held for the new headquarters of WCOL. With its ABC radio network affiliation, it still carried their newscasts and popular programs, like *Candid Microphone* and *You Bet Your Life* with Groucho Marx, two of hundreds of shows that would gradually migrate to television, leaving radio behind. (*Columbus Citizen-Journal*/Photohio.org.)

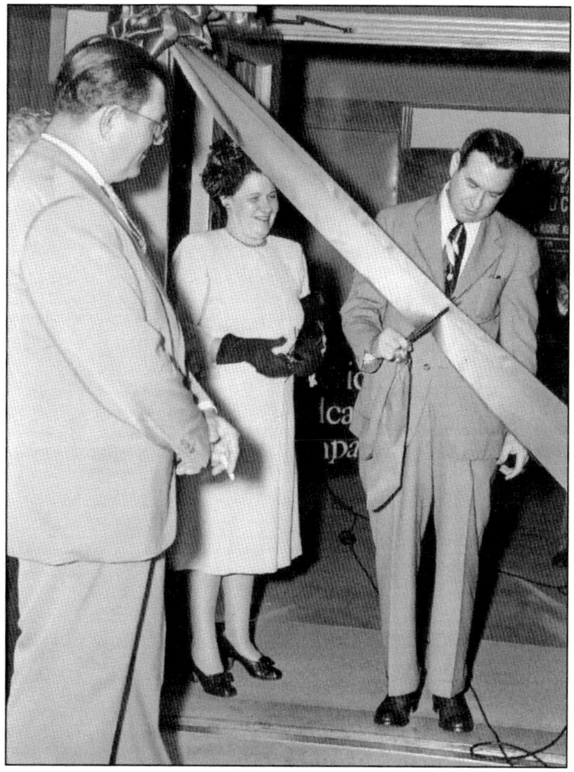

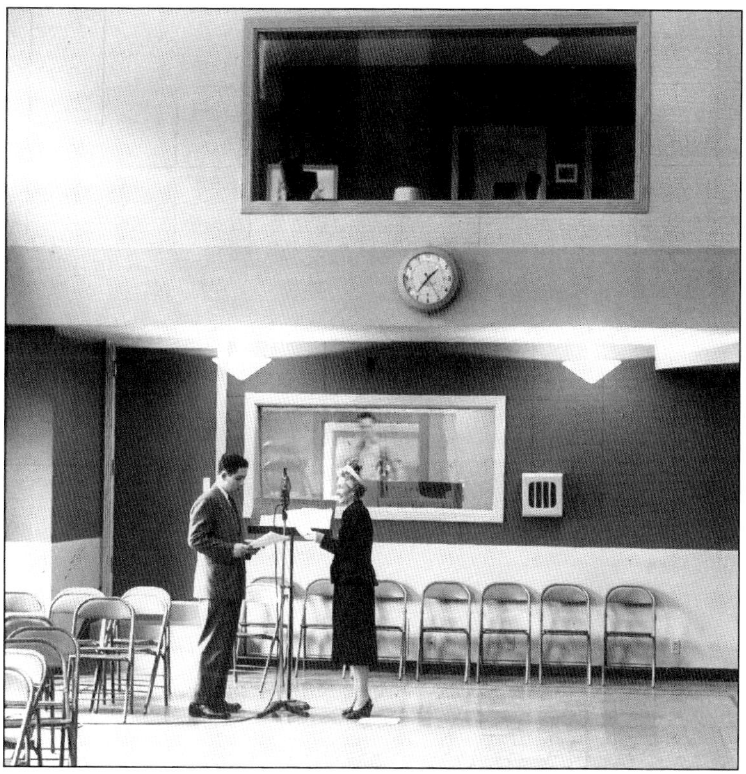

The studio interior is pictured in 1947, constructed just in time for the winding down of the traditional radio station facility design. Even though WCOL was a network station, it still had the occasional live broadcast of music or a local show that had an invited studio audience. Television would take that all away within a decade. Stations would repurpose their unused studios for offices and storage. (*Columbus Citizen-Journal*/Photohio.org.)

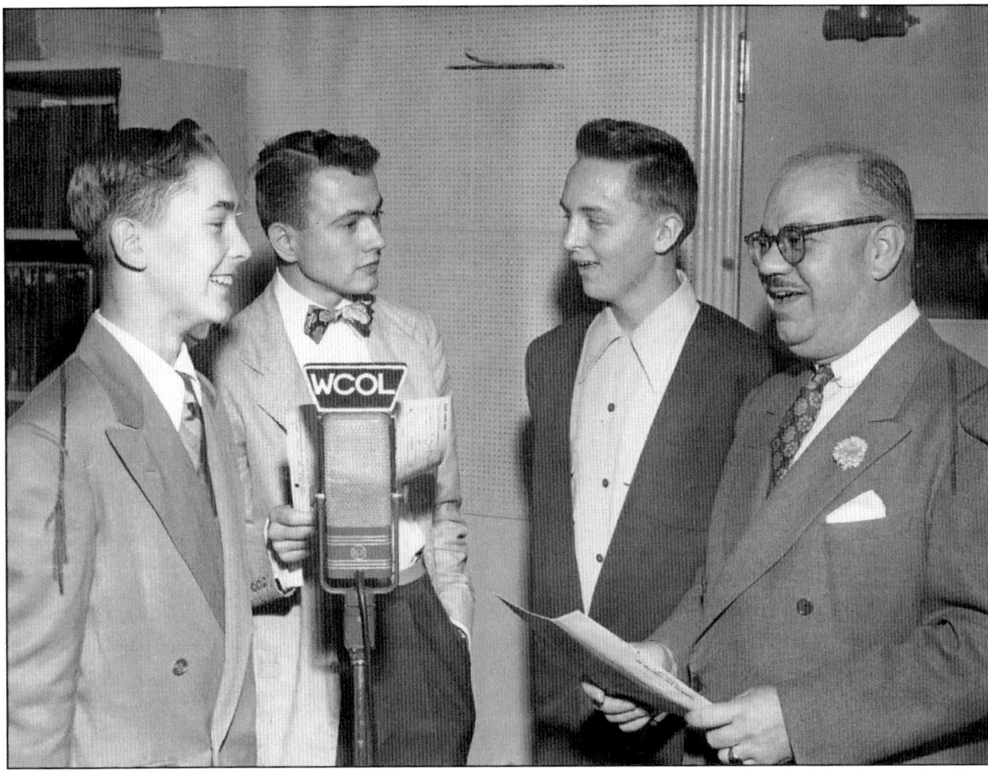

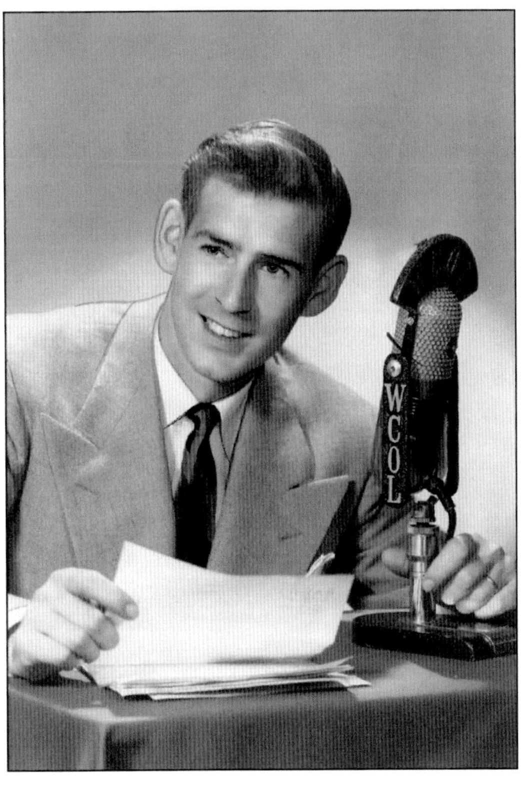

In 1950, a photographer from the *Columbus Citizen* captured this image of a live radio presentation recognizing outstanding paper carriers, so-called "paperboys." Newspaper home delivery was an entry-level job for a teenager during the first half of the 20th century. The former *Columbus Citizen-Journal* did not own any radio or television stations. The major Columbus paper, the *Columbus Dispatch*, owned WBNS. (*Columbus Citizen-Journal*/Photohio.org.)

WCOL announcer Jack Buck is pictured here in 1950. The role of announcer changed considerably between radio's beginning in the 1920s and the end of long-form programs 30 years later, a change exacerbated by television. The announcer moved from a voice giving the station break between network shows to a music host, called the disc jockey. (*Columbus Citizen-Journal*/Photohio.org.)

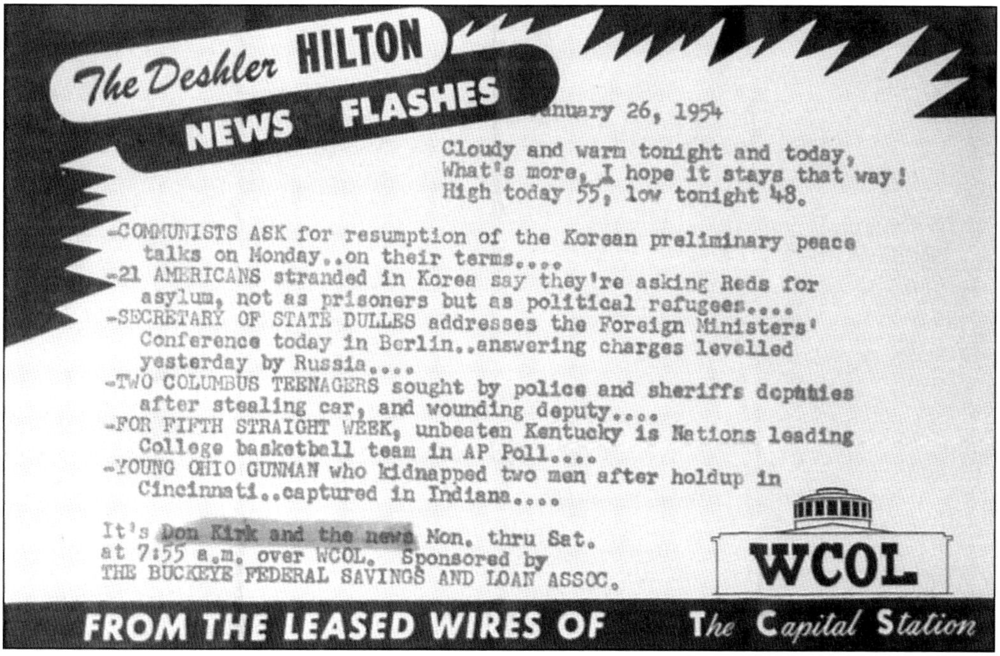

With its immediacy, radio had already caused competition for the newspapers. Print media formerly had to print many editions or "extras" when breaking news occurred. Radio filled the need for immediate news, and newspapers gradually went to a single daily edition. Here, in 1954, WCOL has created customized news and weather summaries to place in local hotels, this for the Deshler Hilton. (Author's collection.)

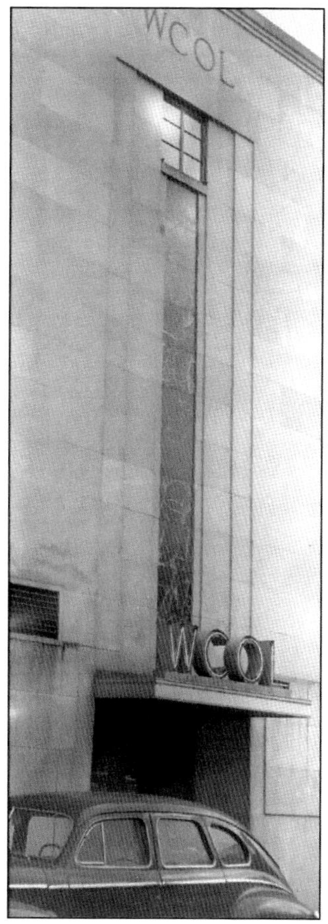

The front door was always the side door. While WCOL was at the corner of Broad Street and Young Alley, employees and guests always used this entrance at 22 South Young. This photograph was taken in 1947 and shows the call letters inlaid into the concrete far above the door. Today, the WCOL building remains vacant and in disrepair. (*Columbus Citizen-Journal*/Photohio.org.)

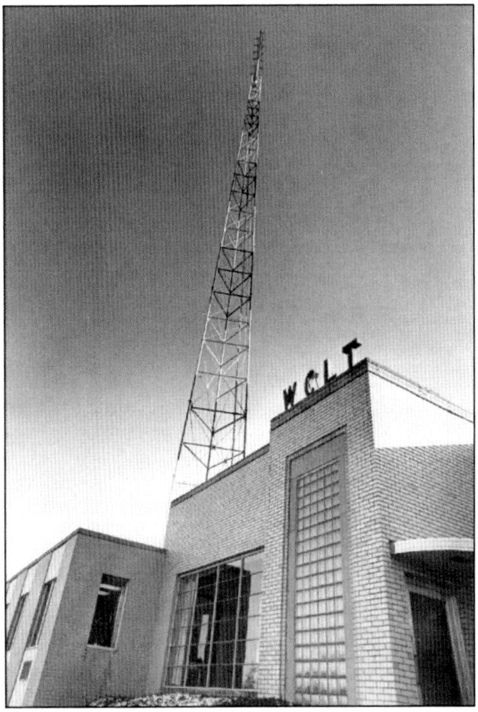

Concurrent with WCOL's new facility, a brand-new radio station went on the air in nearby Newark in 1947. WCLT, first FM only then AM, was a classic art deco–style building in a parking lot with the tower attached. Standing at its entrance, one is suddenly in awe of the mighty tower. It spoke to what radio was all about. (Douglas Pricer, WCLT.)

The WCLT studio for live programming was designed to be non-reflective of sound—not completely dead but conducive to broadcasting by using then-modern acoustic treatments. The studio always had a window into the control room for communication between talent and engineer. Here is a studio wall showing the sound-deadening panels. (Douglas Pricer, WCLT.)

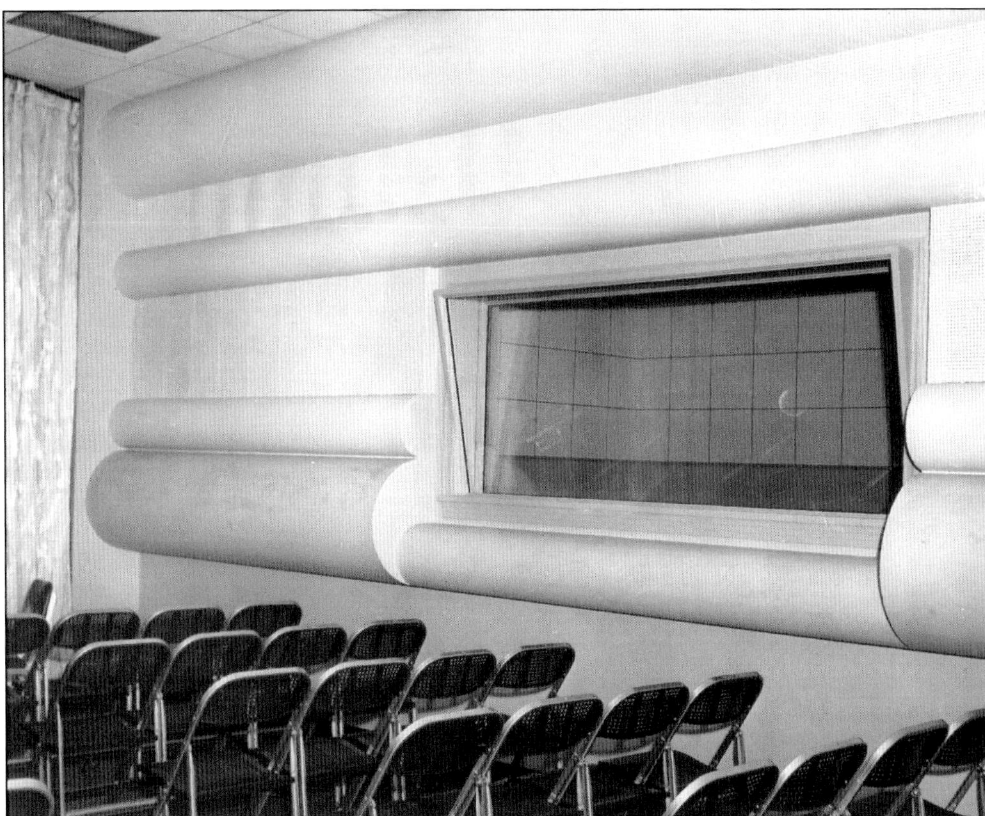

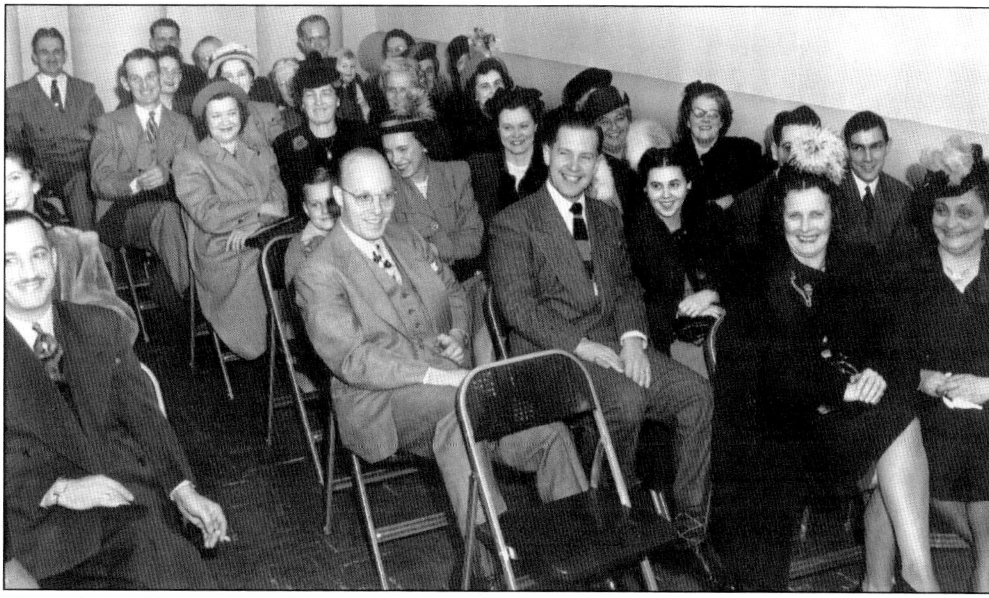

The audience likes it! One of the tenets of broadcasting in the early days was the concept of serving the community, in this case the city of Newark and Licking County, both part of the Columbus metro media market. A small station, usually without network affiliation, has to create its own programs and audiences. This one is happy. Now applaud, please. (Douglas Pricer, WCLT.)

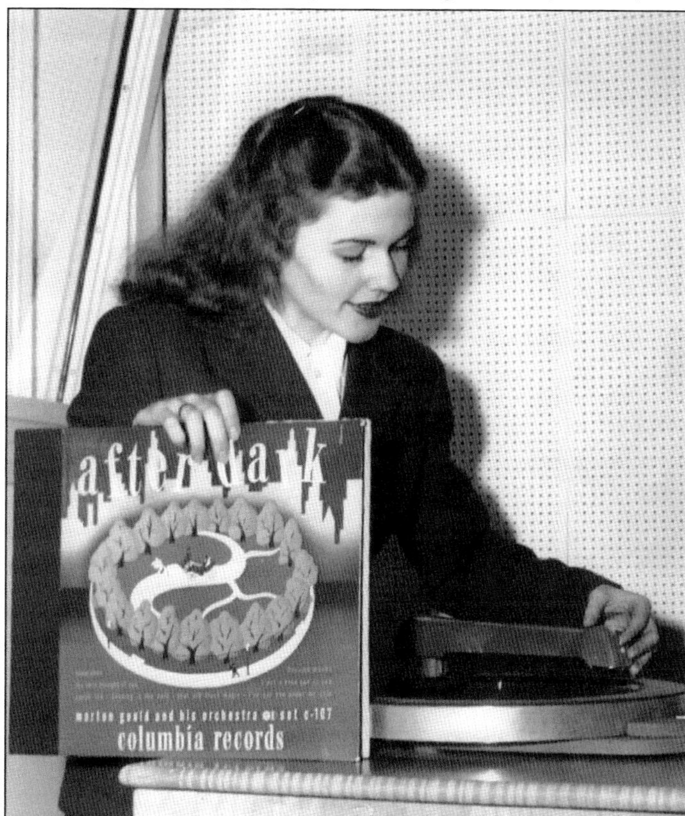

Freddie Terry selects music for a show in the 1950s. At a small station like WCLT, everyone would have to do more than one job. They might write commercials, sell time, and answer the phones in addition to their shows. Every radio station maintained an extensive record library of the music they aired, plus large discs with entire programs and music to use as background on commercials. (Douglas Pricer, WCLT.)

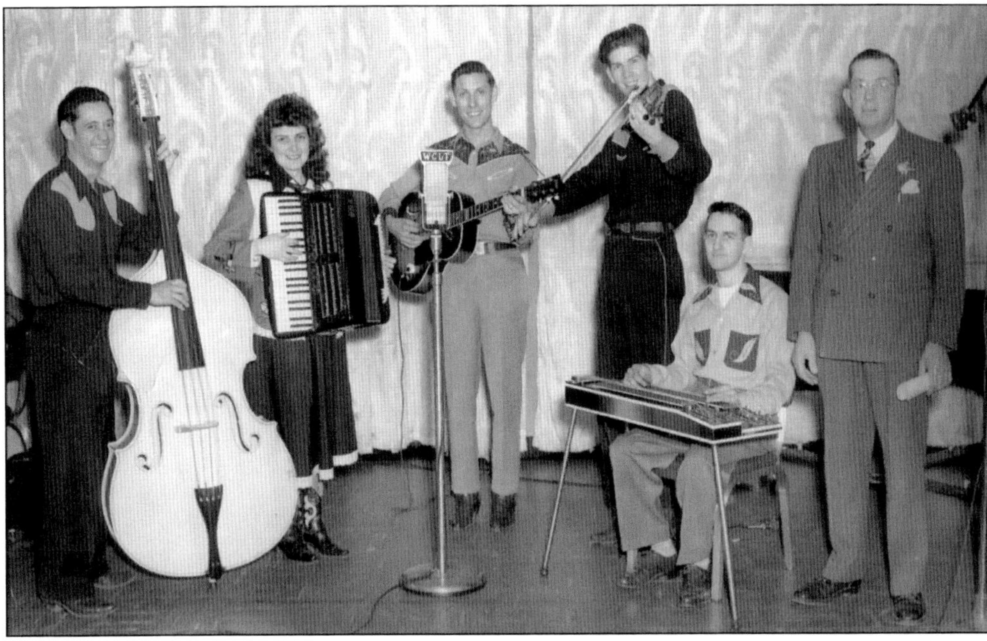

This is a live program by a Western swing band, perhaps a Newark version of Bob Wills and the Texas Playboys, the well-known group from the 1940s. There is a steel guitar, and one can almost hear Bob Wills in the background saying, "aaaaaaa Leon." Live music was popular on small stations, some indigenous to a region and therefore important programming content. (Douglas Pricer, WCLT.)

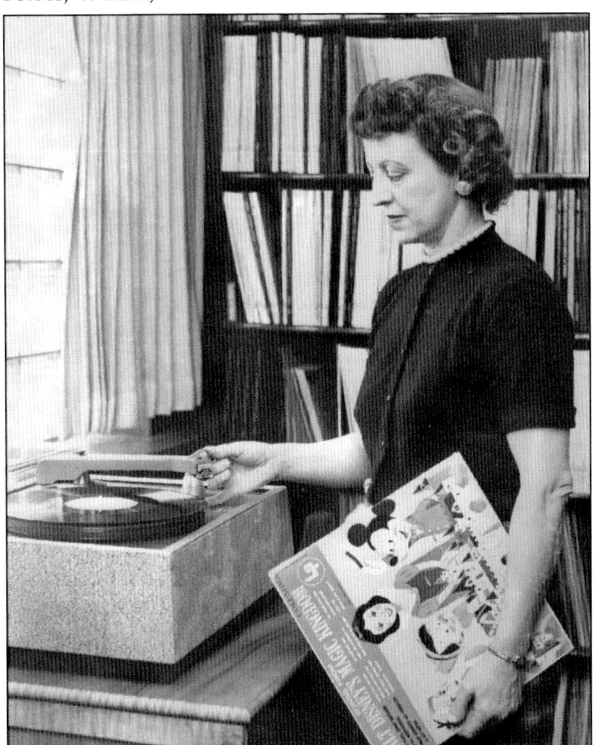

Mae Jackson, the WCLT record librarian, listens to tracks on an album and will select and recommend it to the announcers. In early music radio, at stations large and small, records were preselected from a large library, and a script was often written for the announcer. (Douglas Pricer, WCLT.)

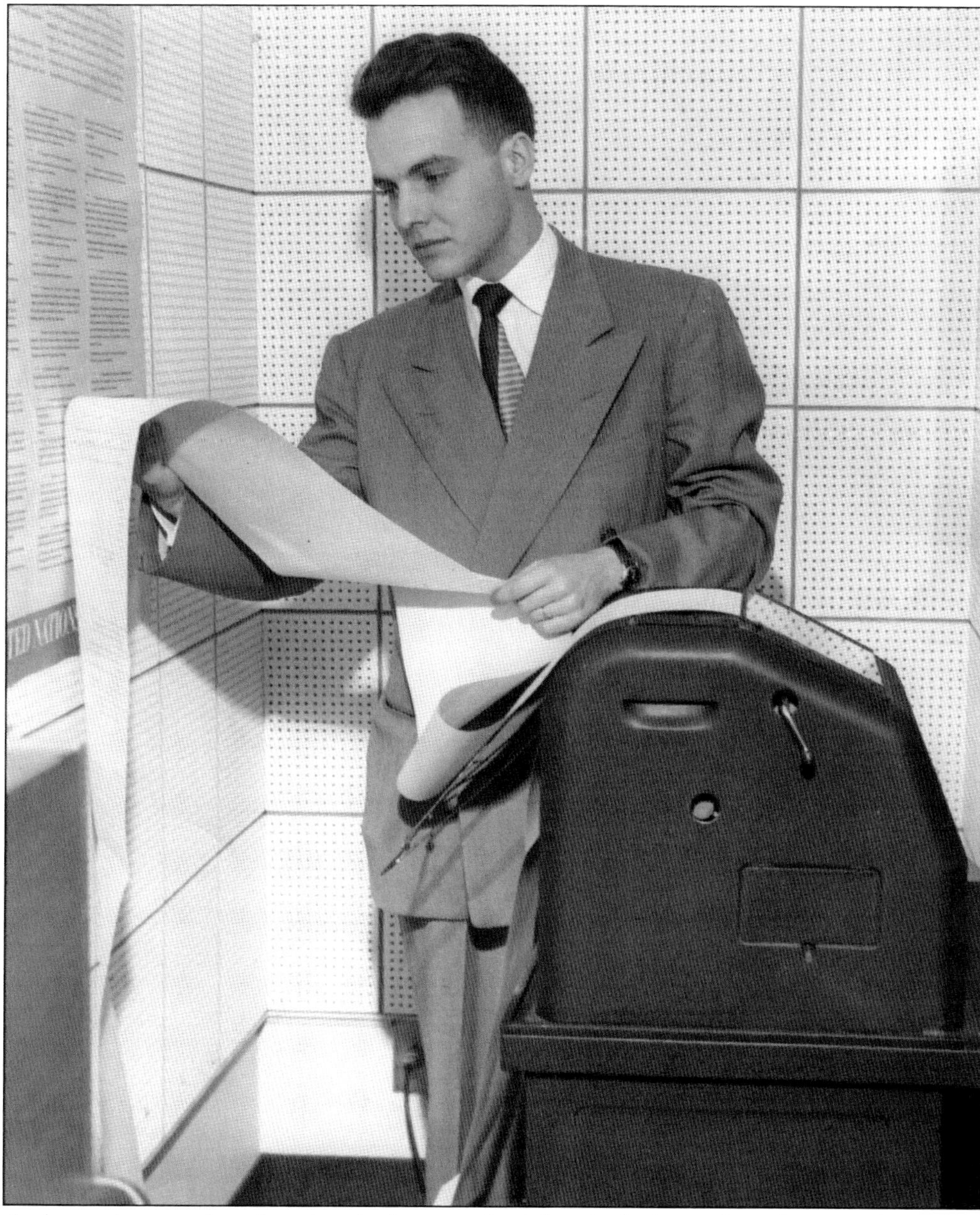

And now the news. Local stations had two methods by which they collected news to be read on the air for their listeners. The news reader would call the local police and fire and city hall sources each day and write stories of local interest. For the larger perspective, there were two major national news sources called wire services that aggregated stories contributed from reporters around the world. There was the Associated Press and United Press International, both produced by the same companies that served newspapers. The radio version of the wire news was written to be read aloud for radio, and they were organized into "headlines," "world in brief," and longer news summaries. They were packaged, timed, and ready to read. This gave rise to the term "rip and read," as there was a cutting edge on the device, a large typewriter in a soundproof box, and the announcer could tear off the news and be on in seconds. There were bells at various times that would alert to features being printed, 10 bells being a major news bulletin. (Douglas Pricer, WCLT.)

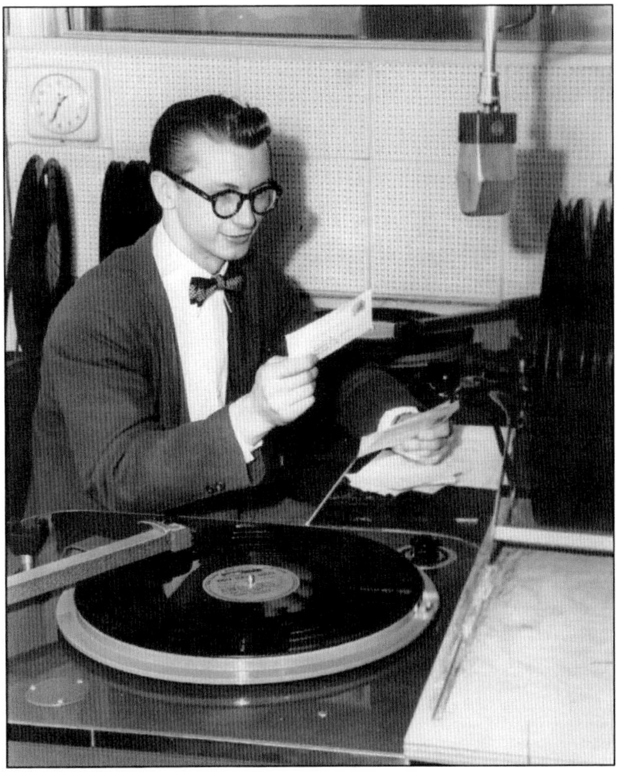

Jack Davis reads requests from listeners in the 1950s. Before the Internet and e-mail, listeners used the penny postcard to contact the local station. Sometimes, they wrote to hear a particular song at a certain time; at other times, they wanted to say happy birthday to a loved one. By being responsive to the audience, not ignoring them, stations would continue to have a loyal audience and sponsors would be happy. (Douglas Pricer, WCLT.)

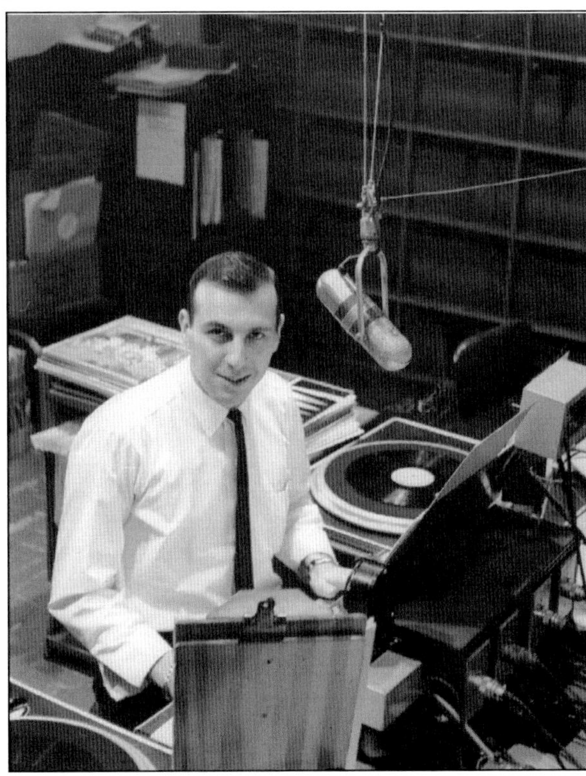

Carey Justice of WCLT is on the air. Radio at the small-station level was never specialized. In large radio markets, there was a union that announcers belonged to saying they could only announce. In a small station, one might finish the DJ shift and then go out and meet advertisers and sell airtime. (Douglas Pricer, WCLT.)

Boy announcer Milton Shoup speaks into a very big microphone. No, the microphone pictured is not really two times larger than the announcer's head, it only seems that way. The microphone in the foreground is the famous RCA 44BX, one of the best-sounding and most desired microphones in radio. Every announcer wants to speak into this one. (Douglas Pricer, WCLT.)

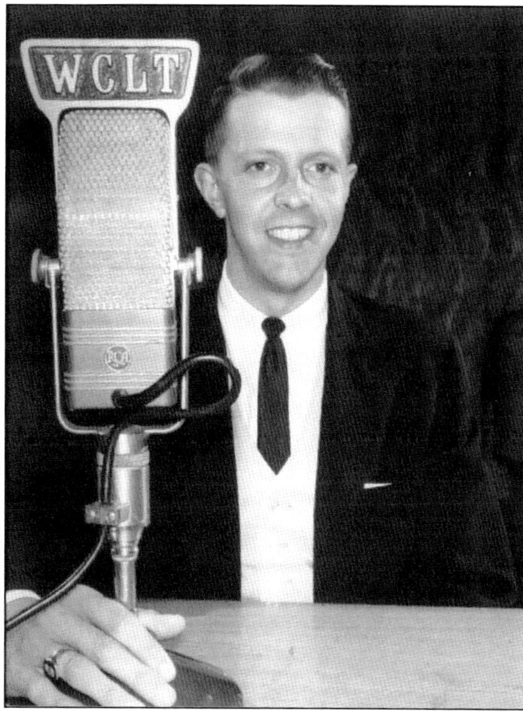

Here is a promotional photograph of a morning DJ, a stereotypical wake-up show. The morning block of time was often the most-listened-to part of any station, as people planned their days around the information they expected about traffic, weather, school closings, and other news. This was taken in the late 1940s or early 1950s. (Douglas Pricer, WCLT.)

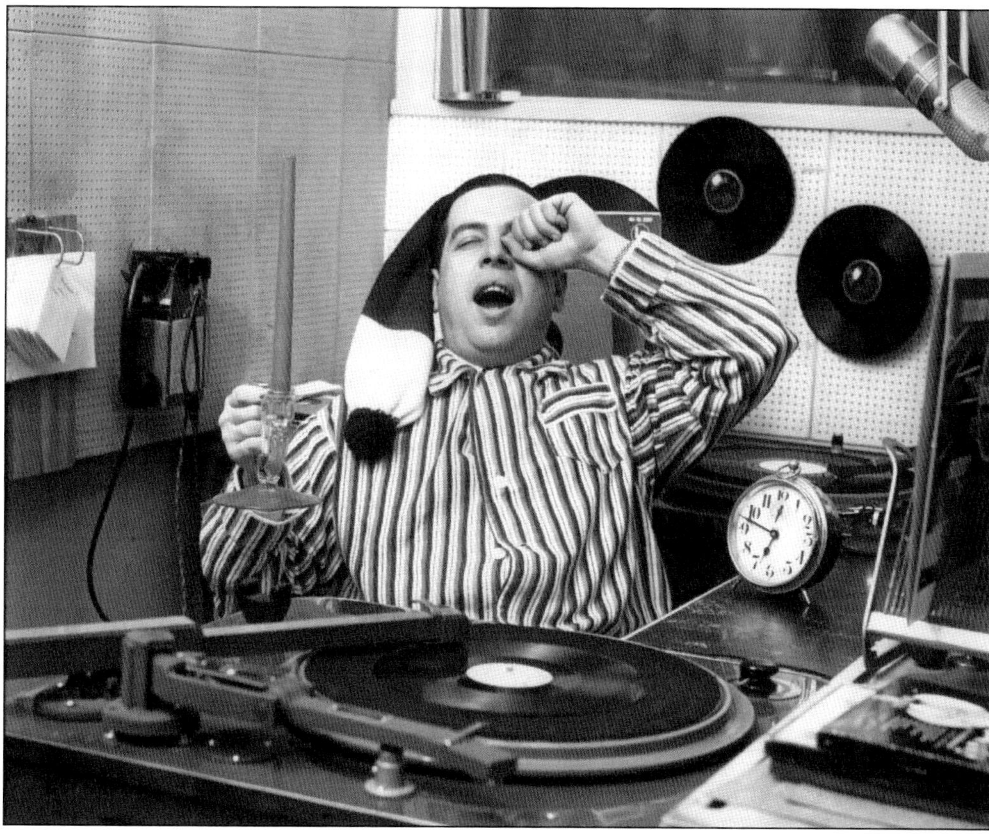

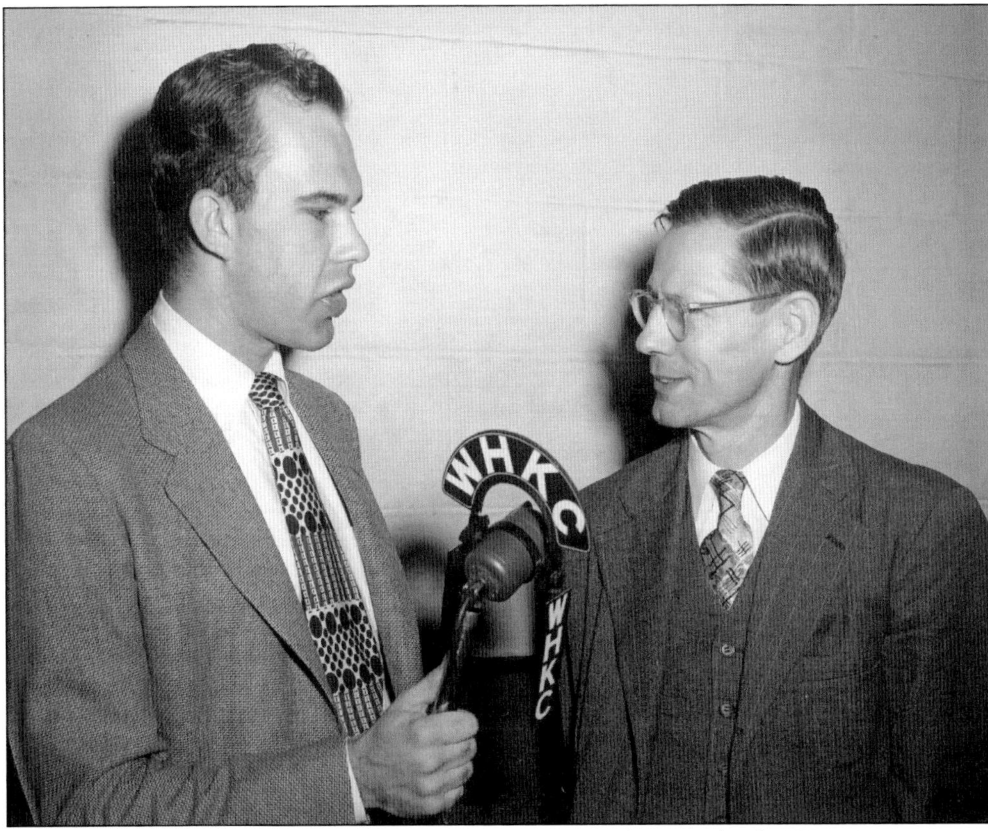

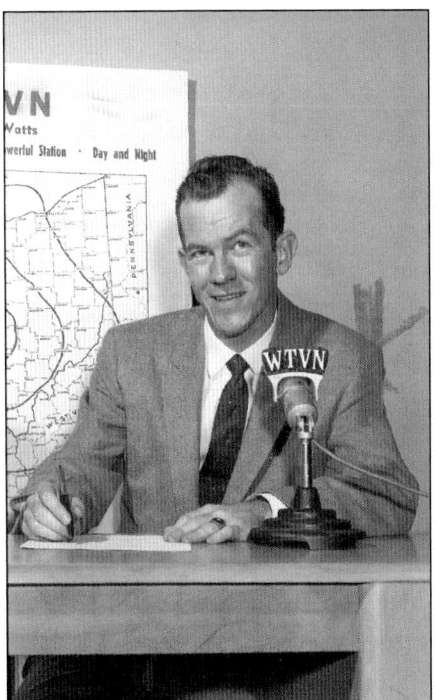

This is a 1949 photograph of a WHKC announcer interviewing an unidentified man. A tireless search for the history of WHKC in the 1940s did not yield much information other than they were not a popular station and they were affiliated with the fourth-place Mutual Broadcast Network, MBS. This image is all that remains. (*Columbus Citizen-Journal*/Photohio.org.)

By 1957, Taft Broadcasting had owned the former WHKC for several years and renamed the call letters to match its television channel identification, WTVN. Here, announcer Bob Adkins, host of the *Partyline* show, poses in front of a WTVN coverage map. Being on 610 kilocycles at 5,000 watts made WTVN the Columbus station with the greatest coverage area. Listeners could receive it over most of Ohio. (*Columbus Citizen-Journal*/Photohio.org.)

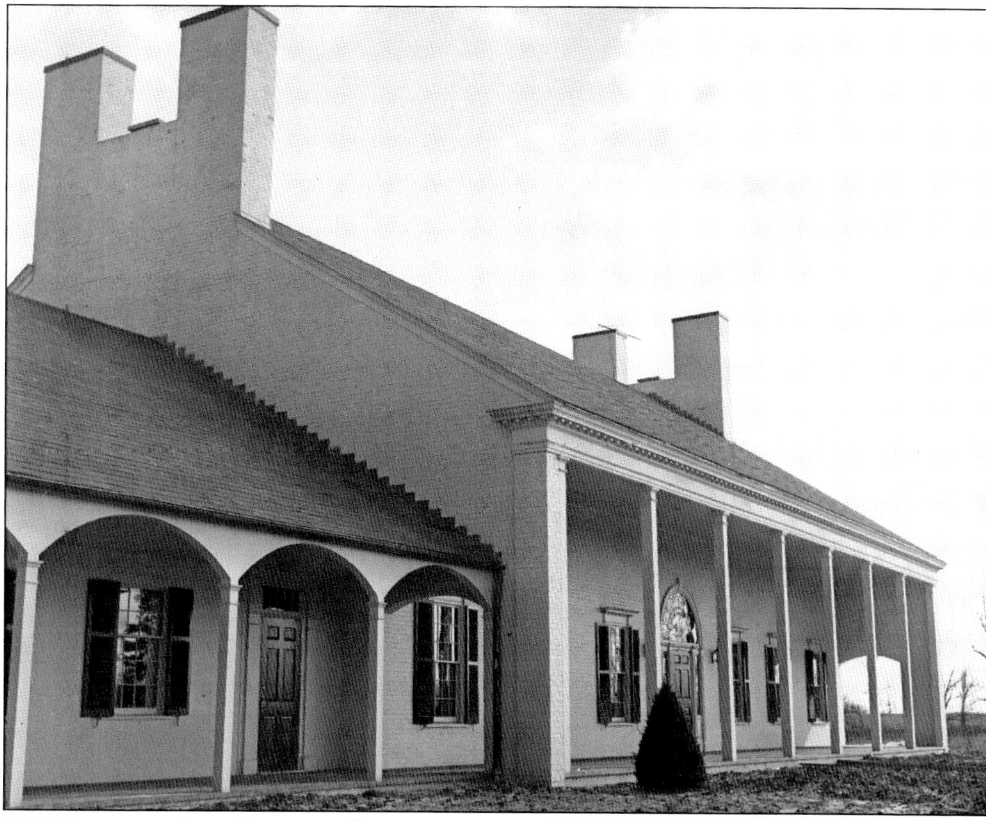

WCOL was not the only station that built a new facility in 1947. WRFD in suburban Worthington constructed this church-like structure north of Columbus. The Farm Bureau Mutual Insurance Company, now Nationwide Insurance, originally owned WRFD. The station was known in its first three decades for its farm news. In the 1970s, its FM station, WNCI, would rule the ratings. (*Columbus Citizen-Journal*/Photohio.org.)

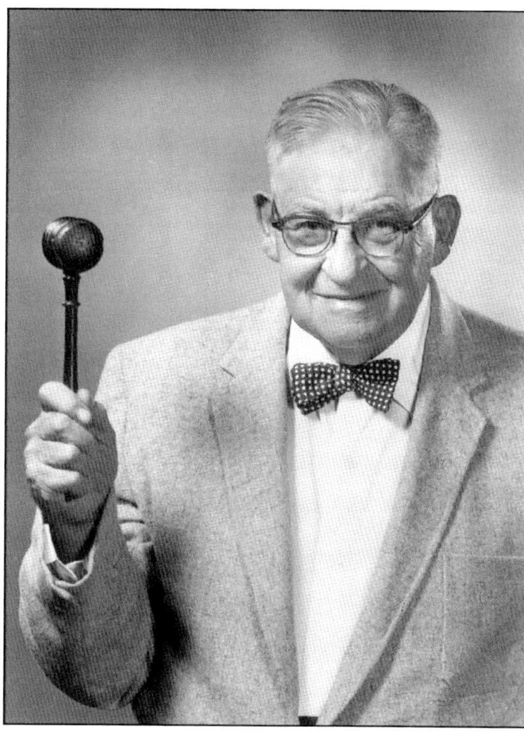

It is not known what Mr. Hess was auctioning off, but it is advised that he be taken seriously. Most likely, his auction has something to do with cows and pigs, as WRFD was the farm station. (*Columbus Citizen-Journal*/Photohio.org.)

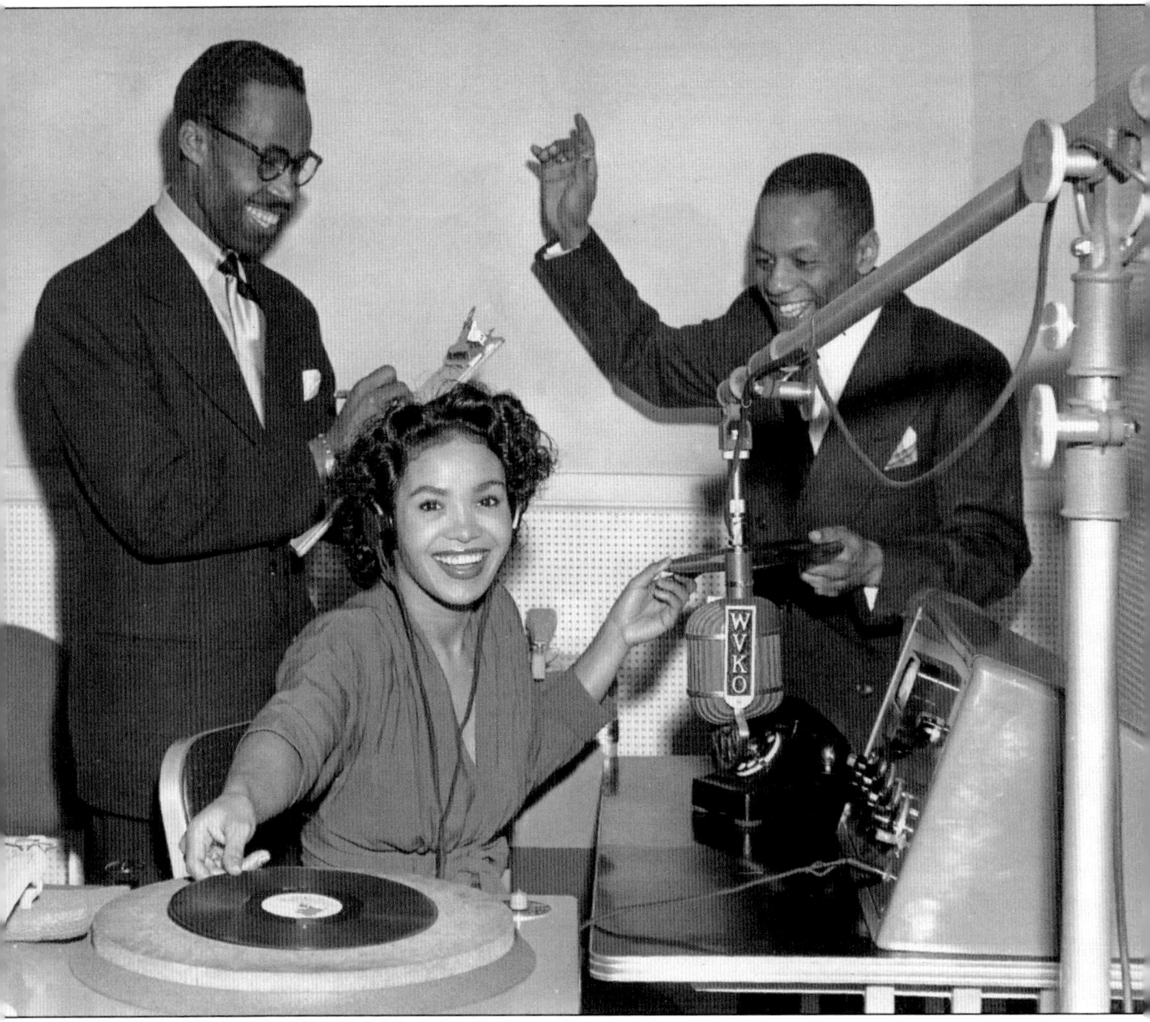

In this image from the mid-1950s, Eddie Saunders and some friends are having their usual good time broadcasting on WVKO. Saunders was an icon in the Columbus African American community through his on-air work and his many appearances for charity. Pictured here on the right, he was on WVKO from the early 1950s through 1979. According to the Saunders papers, "He joined WHKC (later WTVN) in 1944 and inaugurated programs titled 'Helping Hand,' and 'Swanee Hour.' Saunders became Central Ohio's first African American disc jockey when he hosted 'Platter Chatter' on WRFD in 1947. He joined WVKO, the first African American radio station in Columbus in 1951. Saunders continued to play gospel music, but also programmed rhythm and blues, the first disc jockey to do so in the area." (The Ohio History Connection, MSS422AV.)

Thanks to Eddie Saunders for his contributions to this book. The fact that he saved, organized, and placed his photographs and papers from his WVKO days with the Ohio History Collection means that his story can be told again and again. (The Ohio History Connection, MSS422AV.)

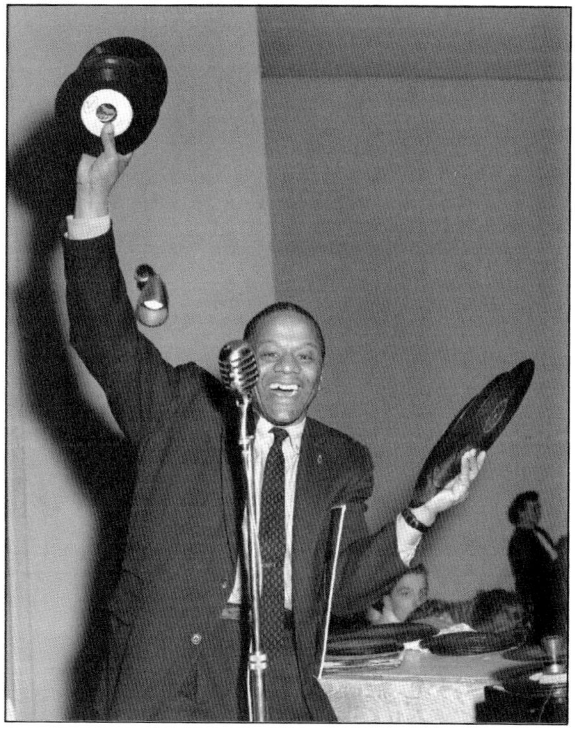

In 1952, DJ Eddie Saunders and Norma Brown of WVKO look at some of the contest entries sponsored by the East Side Chest X-Ray Program. Through Saunders, WVKO was doing what radio stations were licensed to do: serve the community. (The Ohio History Connection, MSS422AV.)

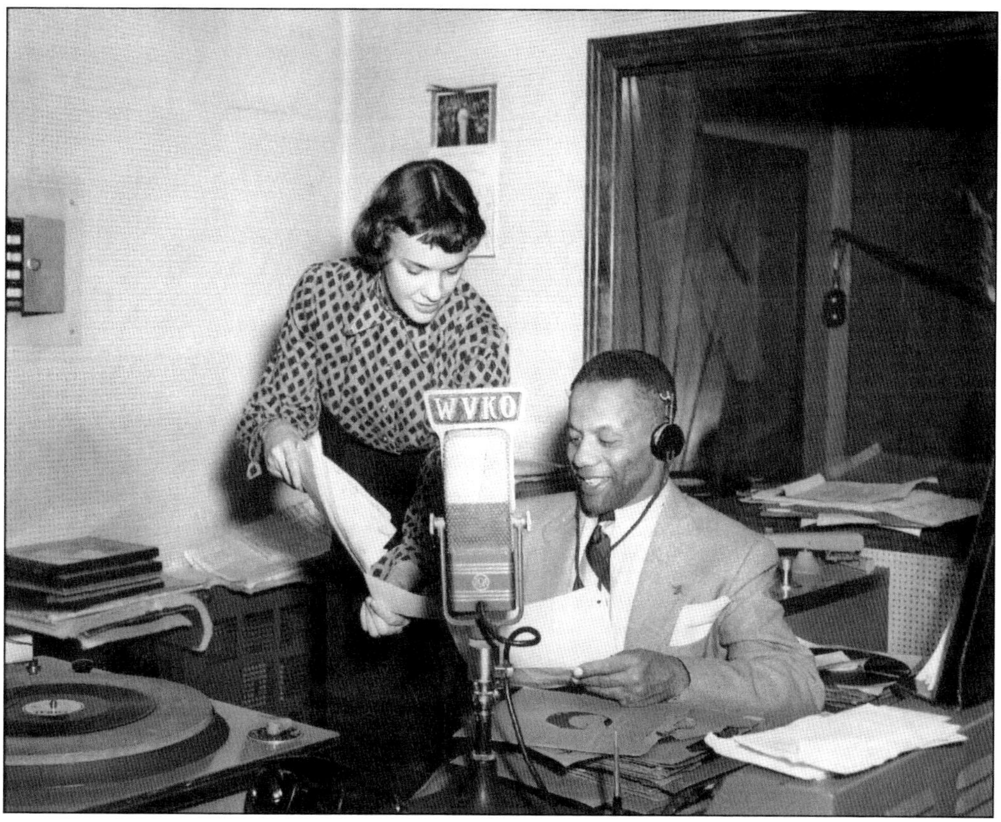

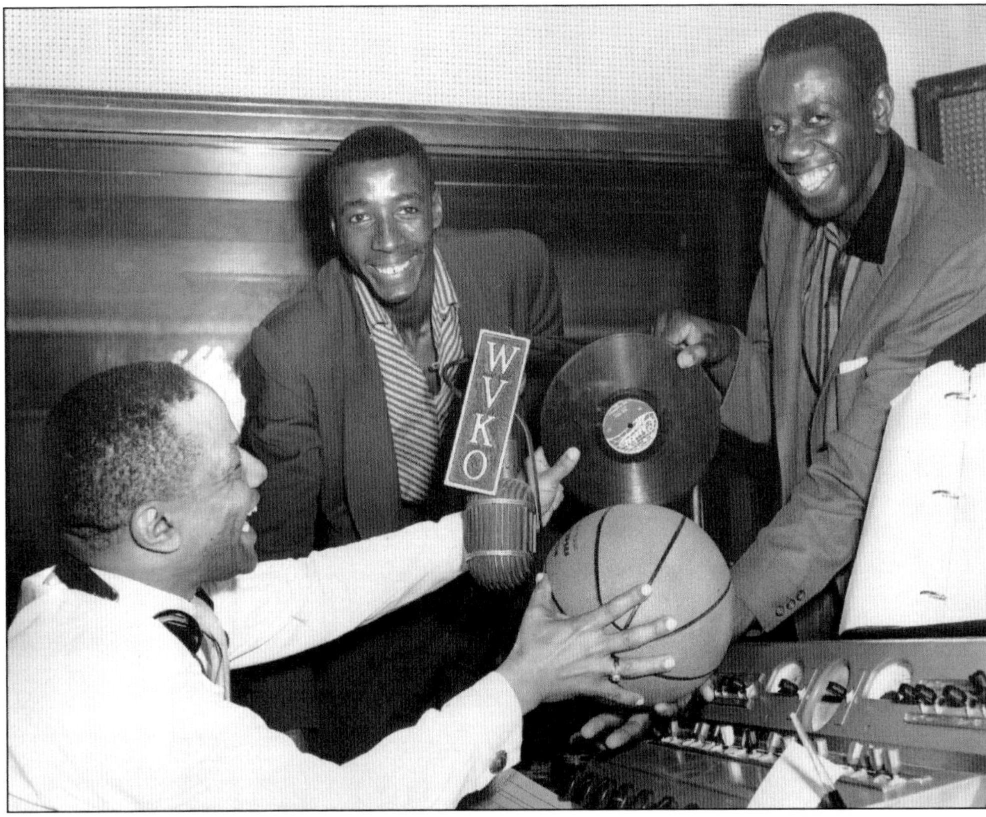

Here is a very special guest on WVKO. Saunders wrote on the back of this photograph: "the all time great crown prince of basketball, the late 'Goose' Tatum, pictured right." Eddie seems to want to trade Goose a record for his basketball. (The Ohio History Connection, MSS422AV.)

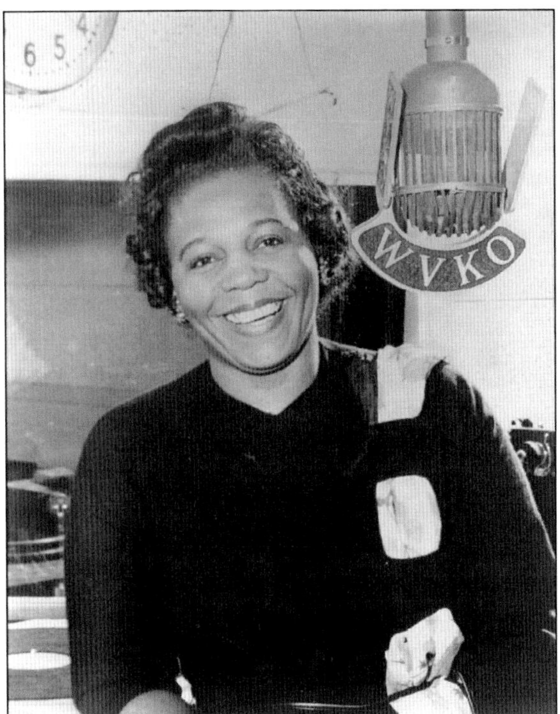

Every radio station had a women's issues director, and this is Ann Walker of WVKO in the 1950s. Usually, there was a 30-minute or one-hour show on the weekends featuring interviews with local women active in the community. (The Ohio History Connection, MSS422AV.)

Dean Lewis of WBNS conducts a radio interview with a well-known star of radio and later television. On the left is Art Linkletter. His CBS show was called *People Are Funny*. Like most popular radio shows, by the 1950s it had moved to television, leaving radio as a recorded music service introduced by a DJ. (The Ohio History Connection, SC4593.)

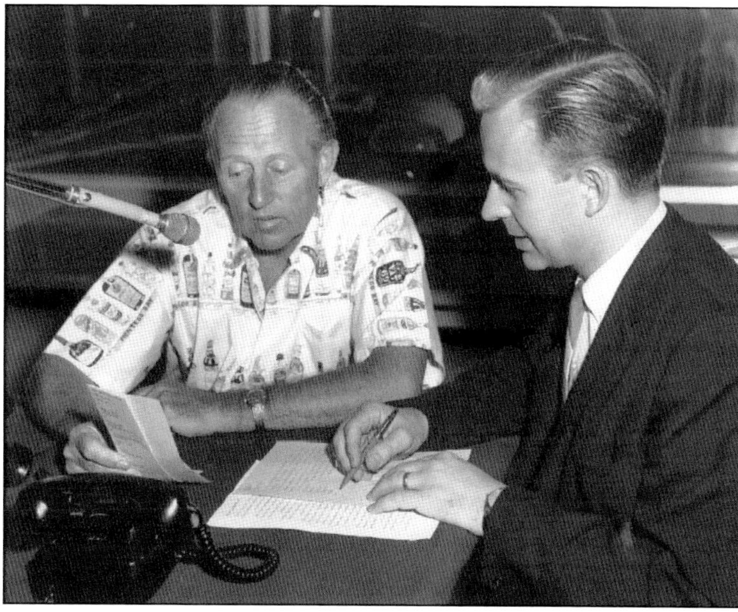

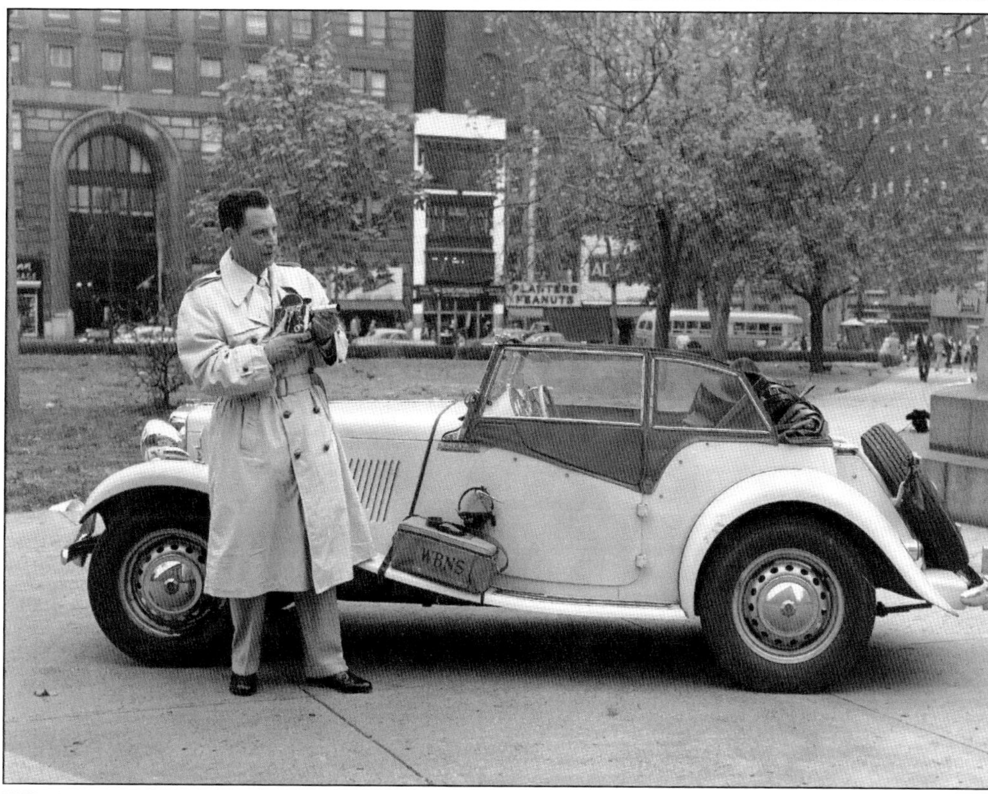

WBNS news reporter Chet Long, disguised as a British spy, has parked illegally on the statehouse sidewalk. Nattily dressed as always, Long poses by his British roadster holding a Bolex 16-millimeter film camera. In addition to his radio news duties and that of the co-host of the *Gas Company* radio broadcast, Long was also a news anchor on WBNS TV. (The Ohio History Connection, MSS1328AV.)

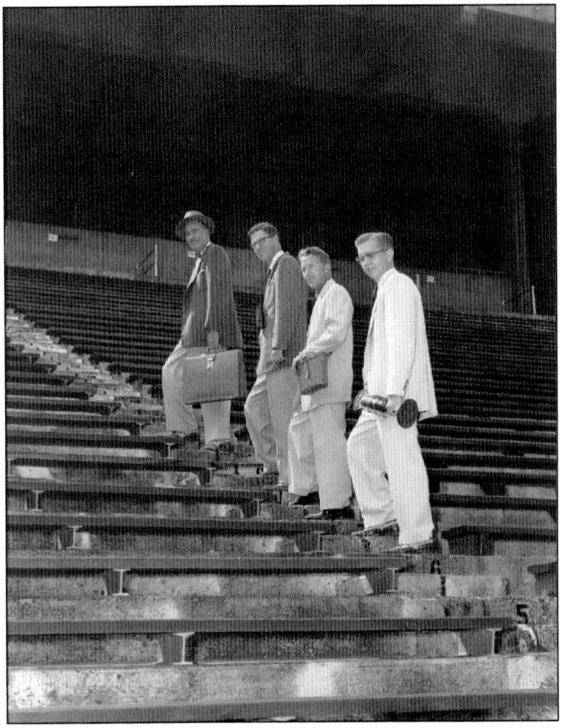

Marching in tight formation to the press box, here is the WBNS Ohio State University football broadcast team climbing the bleachers. Play-by-play announcer Bill Corley leads the broadcast team. (The Ohio History Connection, MSS1328AV.)

Here is one of several WBNS news vehicles. Said to be not very good as a car and even worse as a boat, the Amphicar is photographed on the Scioto River. It would make news in its own right, especially as it sinks lower and lower into the water. This car is obviously on its way to a breaking underwater news story. (The Ohio History Connection, MSS1328AV.)

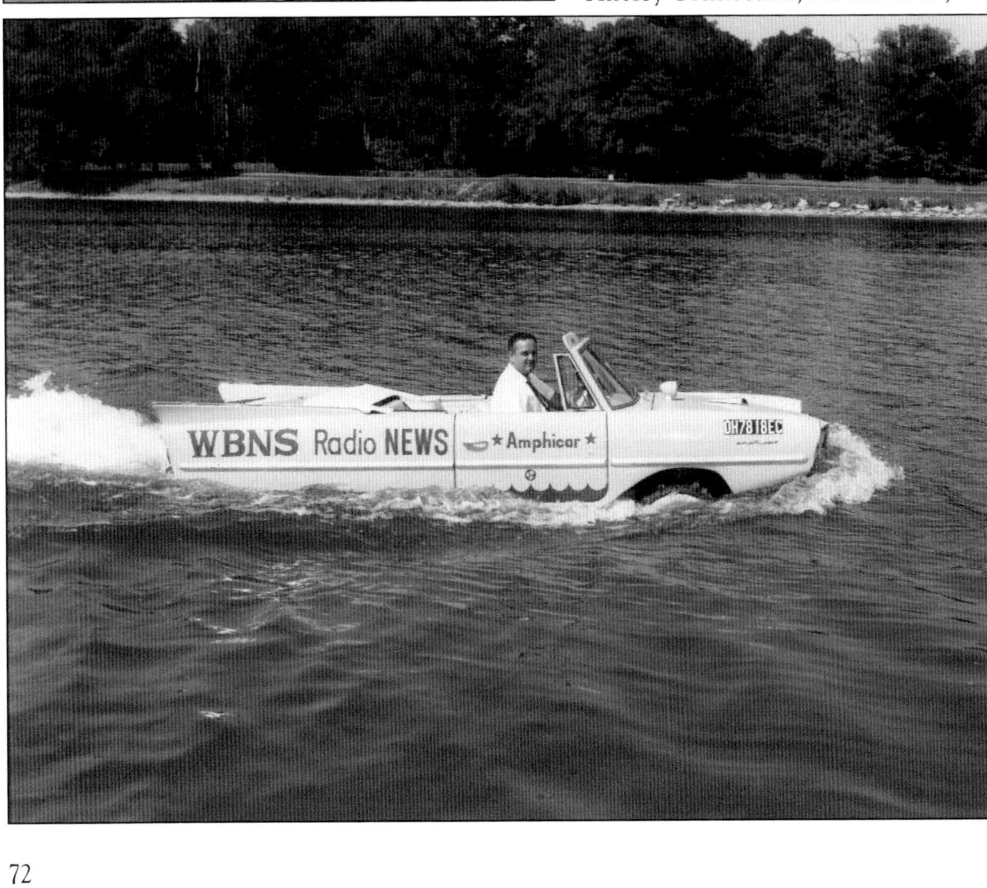

This is Mary Jane Berner of WBNS walking through the downtown to promote the portable radio as a way of life. Her sign reads "Miss Portable Radio, June 1958." (The Ohio History Connection, MSS1328AV.)

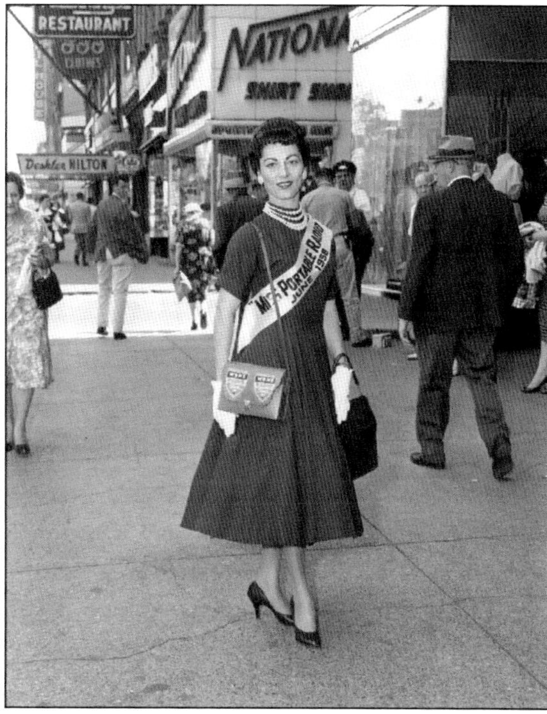

Pictured is 1950s WBNS DJ Gene Fullen entertaining two high school girls with the latest top tunes. Although they are holding what looks to be 78-rpm 12-inch singles, the 45-rpm version was becoming the lingua franca of that era. Fullen later moved to WTVN-TV as the host of *Gene's Canteen*, a dance party in the same vein as the *Dick Clark Show*. (The Ohio History Connection, MSS1328AV.)

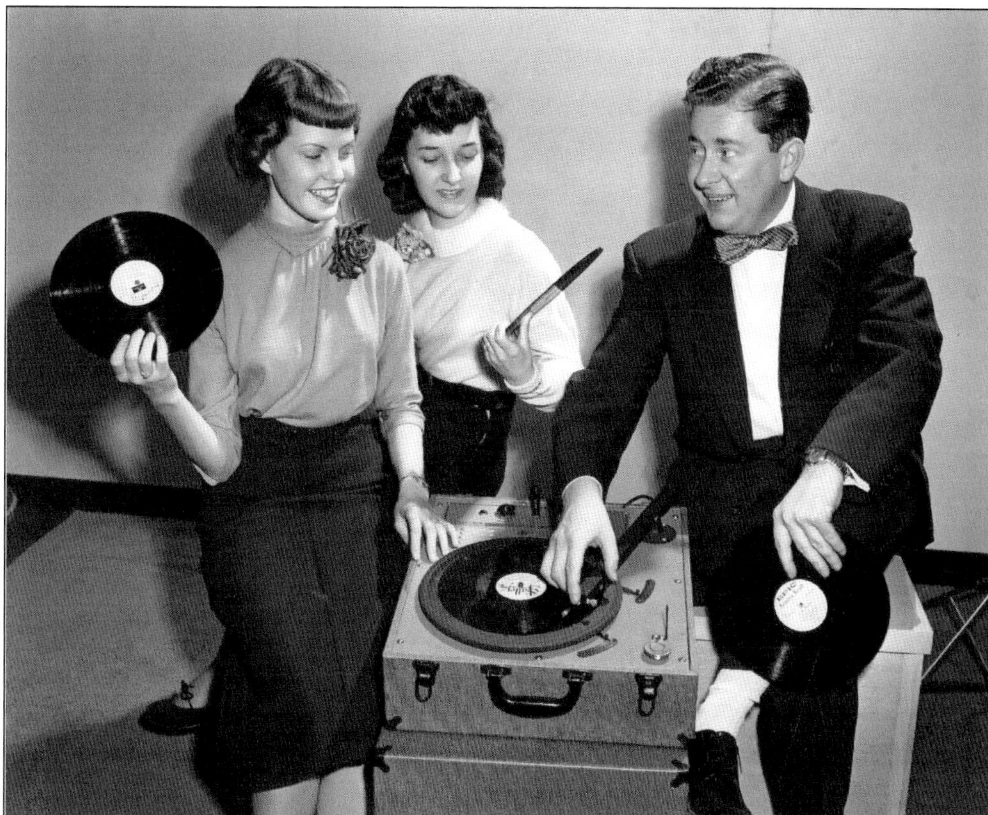

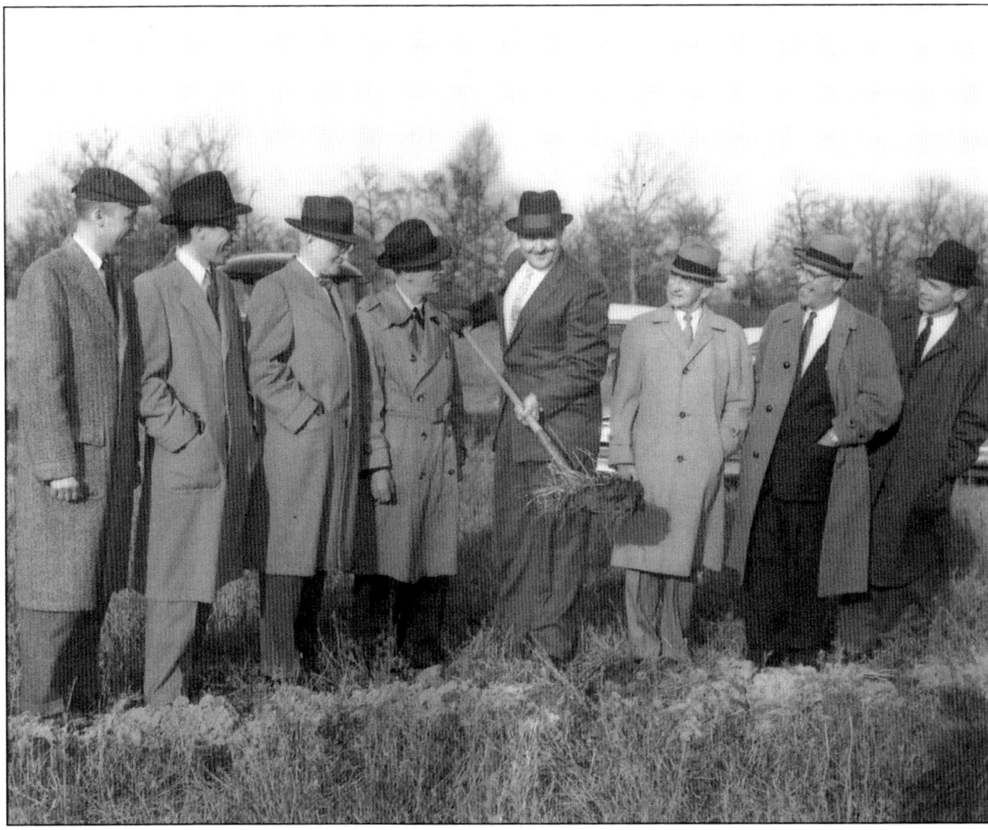

It is 1958, and this is the birth of the first new Columbus radio station in 10 years, WMNI 920 AM. Surrounded by local dignitaries and politicians, WMNI owner William Mnich digs a very large hole in which to plant his AM 920 tower. (Matt Mnich, WMNI.)

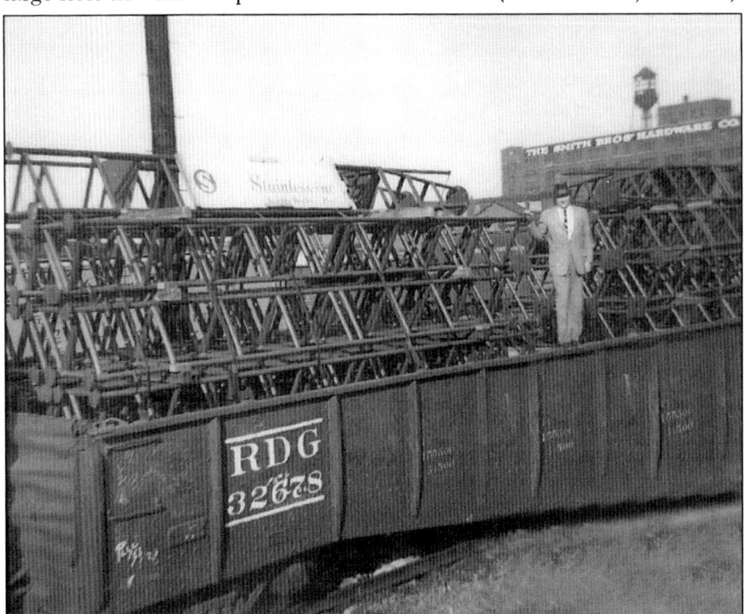

The late 1950s were an exciting time for the Mnich family, as this freight train announces the arrival of the actual WMNI tower. William Mnich is standing on the car next to his first antenna—some assembly required. (Matt Mnich, WMNI.)

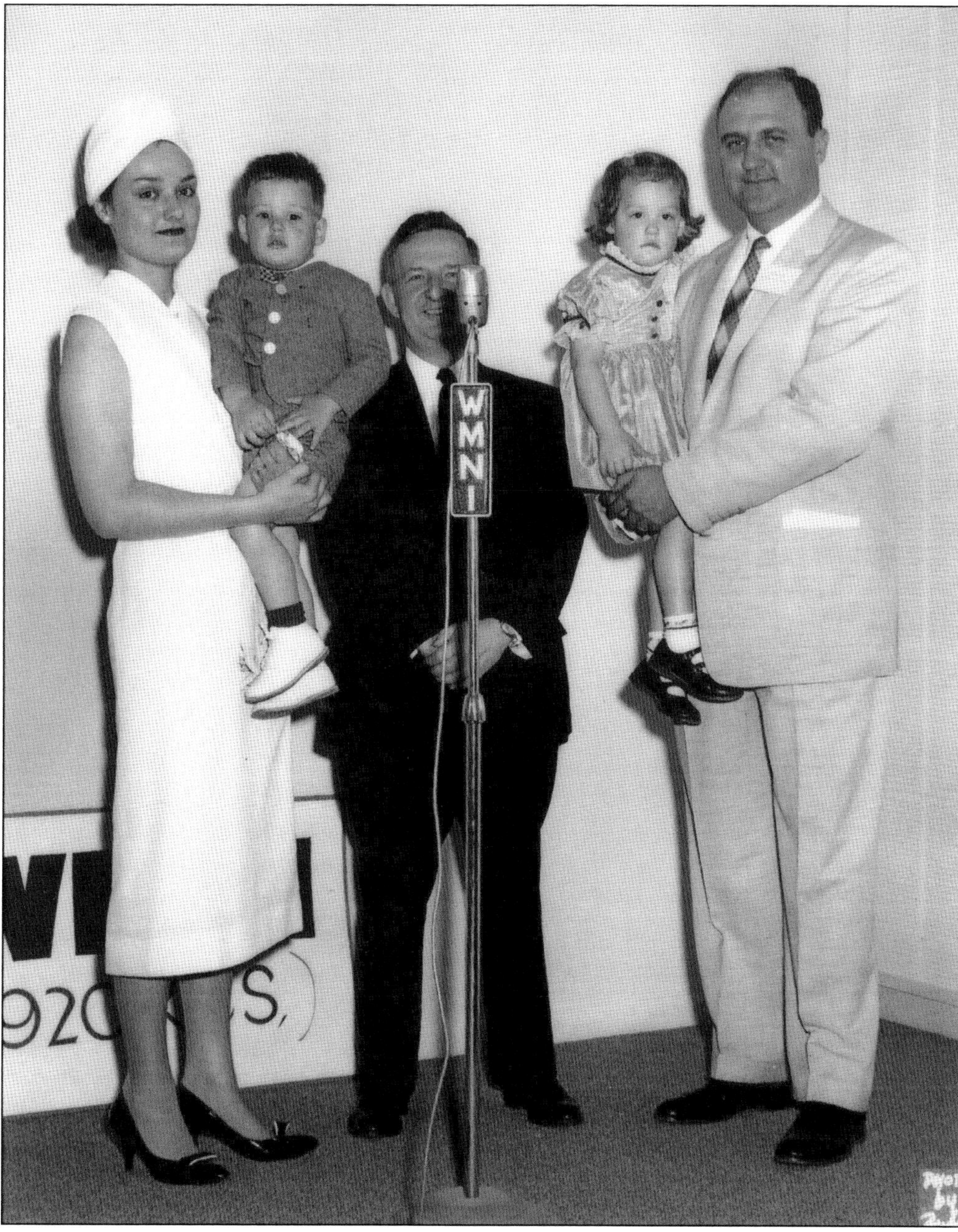

WMNI was truly a family station, and in this early image of the Mnich family, there is dad Bill, mother Norma, and children Louise and Bill. Baby Matt Mnich, not pictured, assumed leadership of WMNI upon the passing of his father. This is the occasion of their sign-on in April 1958. (Matt Mnich, WMNI.)

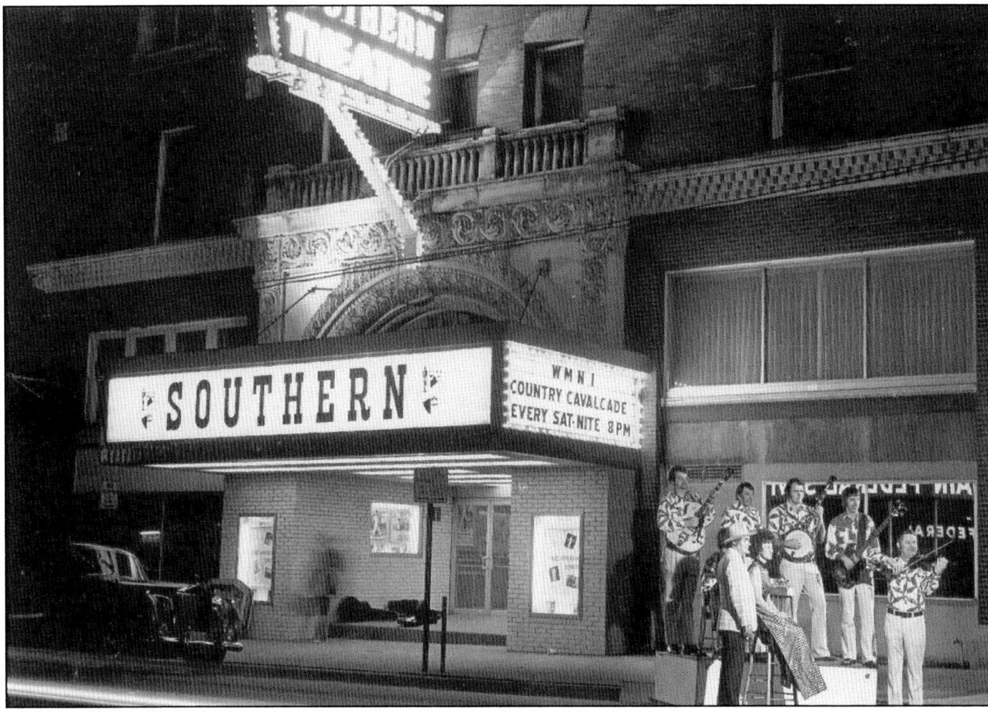

Built in 1897, the old Southern Hotel was the original home of the WMNI studios, and just like the famous WSM Nashville Saturday-night *Grand Old Opry* broadcasts, WMNI announced its "*Country Cavalcade* Every Sat Nite 8 PM." Outside the entrance, one of the bands about to entertain the home audience plays to attract passersby. The Saturday night show was aired live. (Matt Mnich, WMNI.)

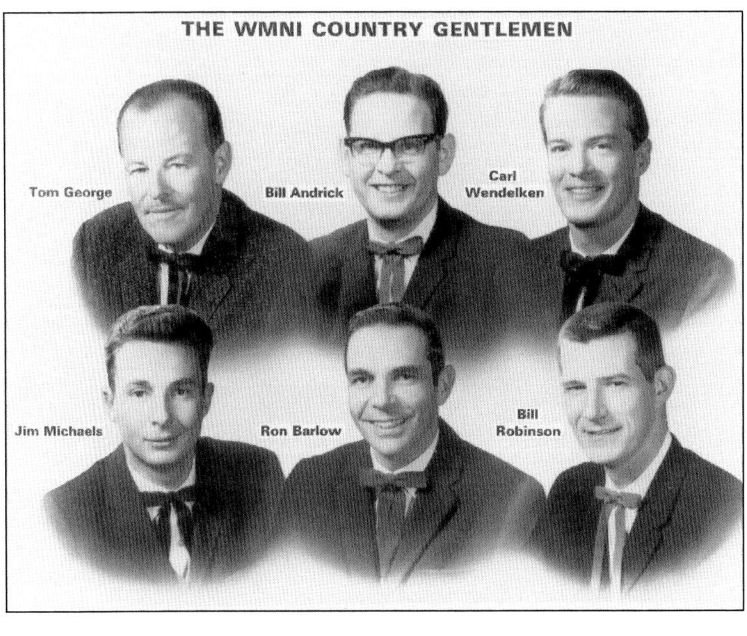

The WMNI Country Gentlemen DJ lineup is pictured in the early 1960s. Notice the matching string ties worn by this group, the country format version of the boring old neckties worn by all the other local DJs. (Matt Mnich, WMNI.)

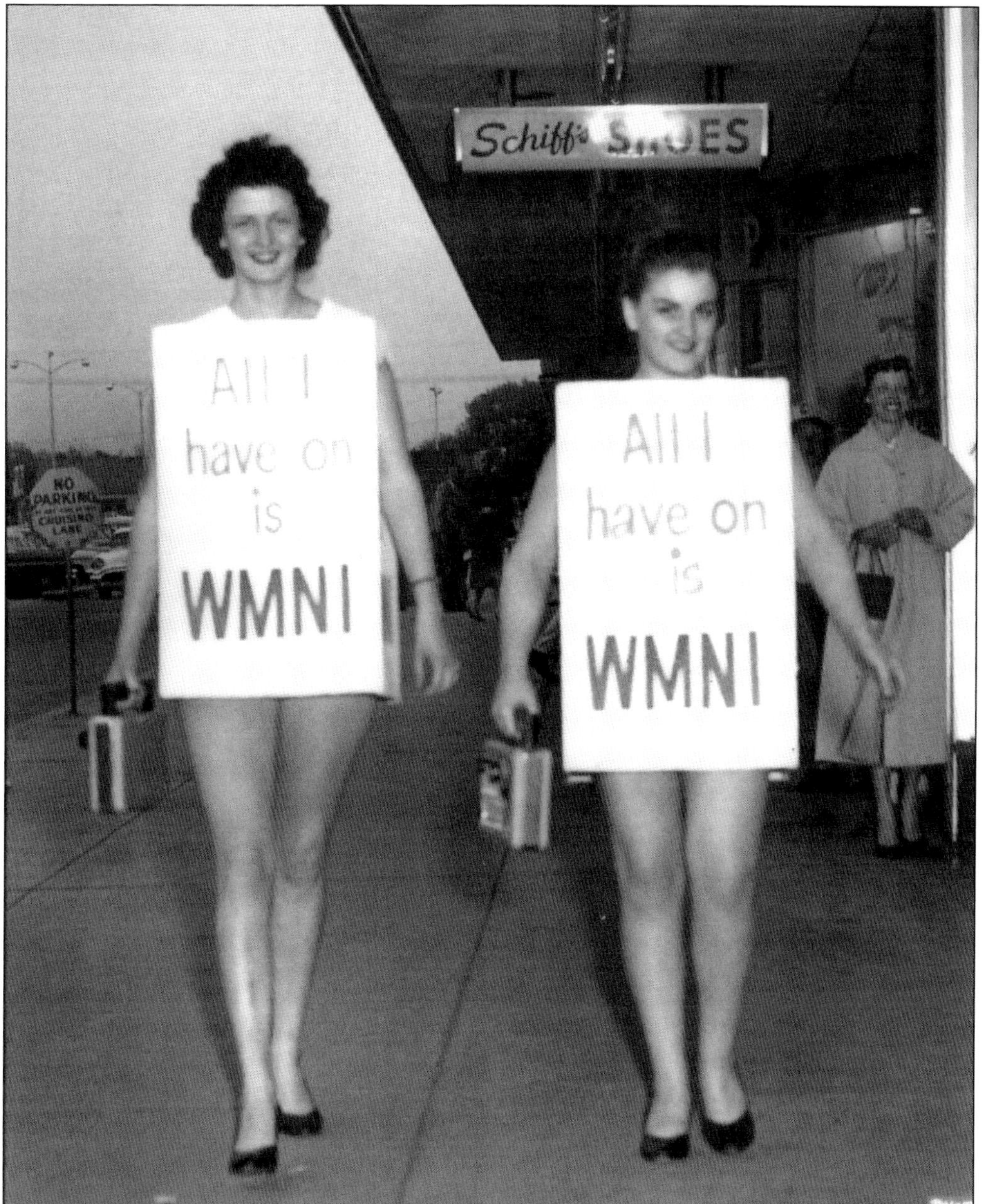

This provocative promotion might win someone a night in jail in conservative Columbus. But of course, being a family station, it's not all what it appears to be. These two each carry the latest in 1950s transistor radios, tuned of course to WMNI 920. This is what radio stations did to draw attention to themselves and their programming. (Matt Mnich, WMNI.)

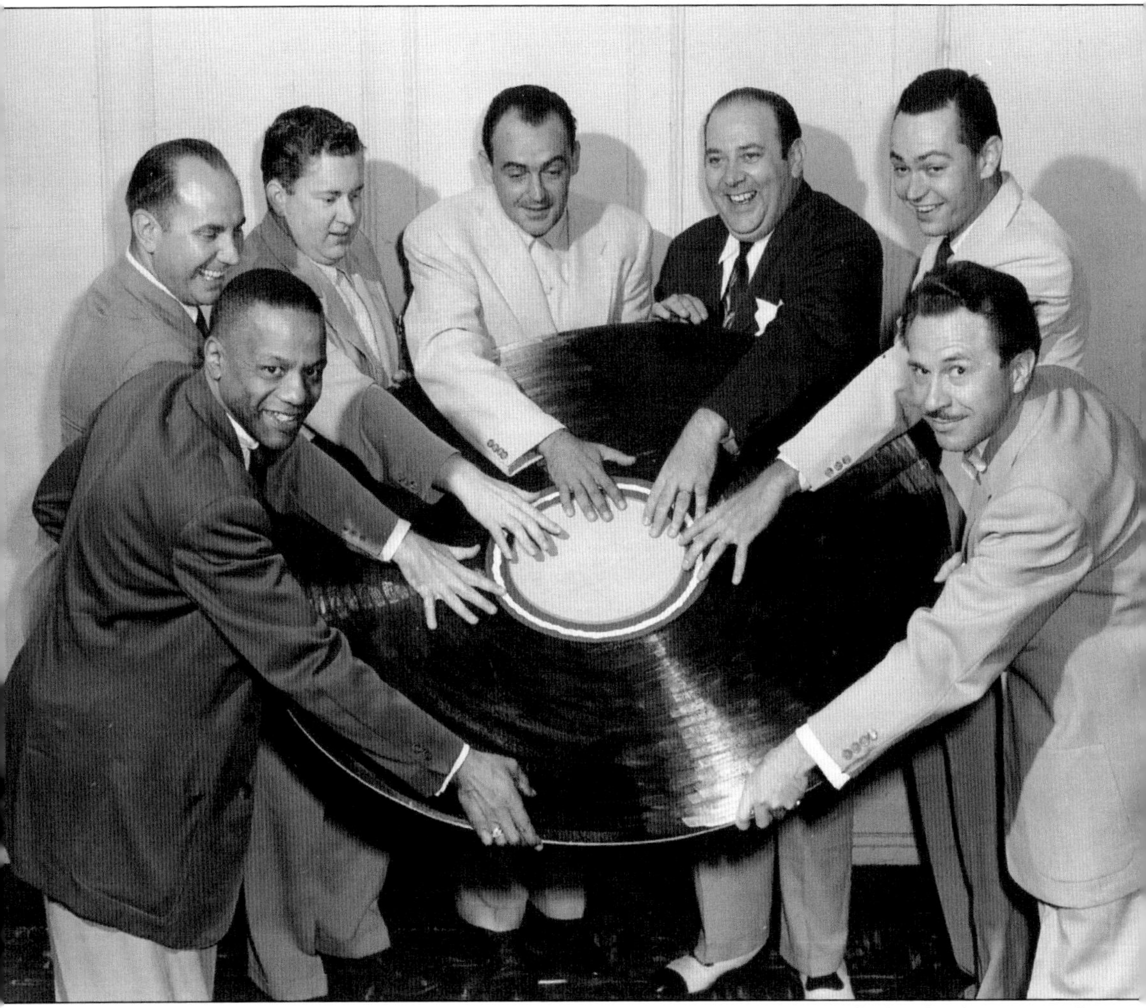

This is a classic image from the Eddie Saunders collection that he titled *All of Columbus DJs, 1957.* These men, except for the host of the event, Eddie Saunders, are unidentified, but as some readers will say, "Gee that face looks familiar." The voice would be. These were the DJs that played adult and big band music on so-called "full service" radio stations, notably WBNS, WTVN, WCOL. In 1957, there was no rock and roll on Columbus radio, and with the exception of Saunders (bottom left), who played R&B and gospel, the only music heard on Columbus radio was album music and so-called "standards," maybe with a bit of the softer popular music. Within a few years, all of these radiomen would take a back seat to the youthful DJs of the "New WCOL." (The Ohio History Connection, MSS422AV.)

Five

The Hits Just Keep on Coming

Where did the Columbus radio listener first hear rock and roll? There were some far away but powerful stations—in Cleveland, Chicago, New York—which could only be heard at night when the AM radio signal traveled farther. But in Columbus, the station that truly spoke to the teenage audience was WCOL, beginning its innovative Top 40 format in 1960. Other Columbus stations were earlier with popular music, but they did not connect with advertisers and audiences. WCOL was the one. It was smart, and because it already had a dwindling listenership, it had nothing to lose. Suddenly it had all the important advertisers and the highest ratings. The "New WCOL" was the king of Columbus.

Part of this was driven by demographics. The Baby Boomers were growing up and had discovered their own music: rock and roll. More importantly, these teen listeners had more discretionary income than their parents had growing up in an era of war and sacrifice. For advertisers that wanted to sell goods and services to that large and expanding group of young consumers, Top 40 worked. Concert tickets, clothing, soft drinks, records, acne cream—the kids bought it all. The theory was that if one could grab the ears and wallets of the Baby Boomer cadre, they would remain as loyal listeners into their 20s and 30s and beyond. It worked. They listened to any radio station that played their music, and WCOL was the most successful. After WTVN and WVKO tried briefly and then gave up, WCOL was the only hit music station until the 1970s, promising all the hits all the time, time and temperature, and more rock, less talk.

By the end of the 1960s, there were other niche music formats being tried, like soul and country, some successful, others not, but WCOL remained number one. Meanwhile, Columbus was growing rapidly, expanding into the suburbs and turning farmland into housing developments and shopping malls. WCOL could not follow. Its low power signal, especially at night with 250 watts, was difficult to receive beyond the original city limits. There needed to be a way to hear this music in cars and homes, without interference. In the 1970s, Columbus would discover FM, and WCOL AM would not survive.

Other stations in 1960s Columbus were WVKO with its soul/R&B format and WMNI with country. There were also two stations with large audiences that played so-called "adult music." WTVN and WBNS, both 5,000 watts, were still successful although not number-one rated. The 1960s belonged to the "New WCOL."

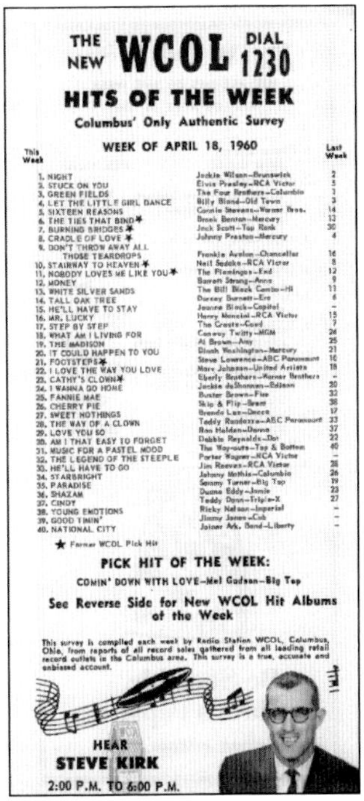

THE NEW **WCOL** DIAL 1230

HITS OF THE WEEK

Columbus' Only Authentic Survey

WEEK OF APRIL 18, 1960

This Week			Last Week
1.	NIGHT	Jackie Wilson—Brunswick	2
2.	STUCK ON YOU	Elvis Presley—RCA Victor	5
3.	GREEN FIELDS	The Four Brothers—Columbia	1
4.	LET THE LITTLE GIRL DANCE	Billy Bland—Old Town	3
5.	SIXTEEN REASONS	Connie Stevens—Warner Bros.	14
6.	THE TIES THAT BIND★	Brook Benton—Mercury	13
7.	BURNING BRIDGES★	Jack Scott—Top Rank	30
8.	CRADLE OF LOVE★	Johnny Preston—Mercury	4
9.	DON'T THROW AWAY ALL THOSE TEARDROPS	Frankie Avalon—Chancellor	16
10.	STAIRWAY TO HEAVEN★	Neil Sedaka—RCA Victor	8
11.	NOBODY LOVES ME LIKE YOU★	The Flamingos—End	12
12.	MONEY	Barrett Strong—Anna	9
13.	WHITE SILVER SANDS	The Bill Black Combo—Hi	11
14.	TALL OAK TREE	Dorsey Burnett—Era	6
15.	HE'LL HAVE TO STAY	Jeanne Black—Capitol	-
16.	MR. LUCKY	Henry Mancini—RCA Victor	15
17.	STEP BY STEP	The Crests—Coed	7
18.	WHAT AM I LIVING FOR	Conway Twitty—MGM	24
19.	THE MADISON	Al Brown—Amy	25
20.	IT COULD HAPPEN TO YOU	Dinah Washington—Mercury	21
21.	FOOTSTEPS★	Steve Lawrence—ABC Paramount	10
22.	I LOVE THE WAY YOU LOVE	Marv Johnson—United Artists	18
23.	CATHY'S CLOWN★	Everly Brothers—Warner Brothers	-
24.	I WANNA GO HOME	Jackie deShannon—Edison	20
25.	FANNIE MAE	Buster Brown—Fire	32
26.	CHERRY PIE	Skip & Flip—Brent	38
27.	SWEET NOTHINGS	Brenda Lee—Decca	17
28.	THE WAY OF A CLOWN	Teddy Randazzo—ABC Paramount	33
29.	LOVE YOU SO	Ron Holden—Donna	37
30.	AM I THAT EASY TO FORGET	Debbie Reynolds—Dot	22
31.	MUSIC FOR A PASTEL MOOD	The Way-outs—Top & Bottom	40
32.	THE LEGEND OF THE STEEPLE	Porter Wagoner—RCA Victor	-
33.	HE'LL HAVE TO GO	Jim Reeves—RCA Victor	28
34.	STARBRIGHT	Johnny Mathis—Columbia	26
35.	PARADISE	Sammy Turner—Big Top	19
36.	SHAZAM	Duane Eddy—Jamie	23
37.	CINDY	Teddy Vann—Triple-X	27
38.	YOUNG EMOTIONS	Ricky Nelson—Imperial	-
39.	GOOD TIMIN'	Jimmy Jones—Cub	-
40.	NATIONAL CITY	Joiner Ark. Band—Liberty	-

★ Former WCOL Pick Hit

PICK HIT OF THE WEEK:

COMIN' DOWN WITH LOVE—Mel Gadson—Big Top

See Reverse Side for New WCOL Hit Albums of the Week

This survey is compiled each week by Radio Station WCOL, Columbus, Ohio, from reports of all record sales gathered from all leading retail record outlets in the Columbus area. This survey is a true, accurate and unbiased account.

HEAR **STEVE KIRK** 2:00 P.M. TO 6:00 P.M.

This image is from the beginning of the 1960 WCOL format change, a "New WCOL" classic "Hits of the Week Survey" from April 1960, indicating the station was just a month into its decade-long run as the number-one station in Columbus. WCOL dropped its ABC affiliation, received a power increase to 1,000 watts in the daytime, and became a 24-hour Top 40 station in 1960. (Mike Eiland, iHeart Media.)

Seated is Collis A. Young, general manager of WCOL from 1957 to the early 1970s. Collis Young ("call me Collie") ruled WCOL with an iron fist, keeping wages down and hours long. It is fair to say that all feared him. On the other hand, he kept the format pure, time and temperature, no deviation allowed, and so the station did remain number one under his parentage. On his wall is a photograph of station owner Charles Sawyer, secretary of commerce under Harry Truman. (Author's collection.)

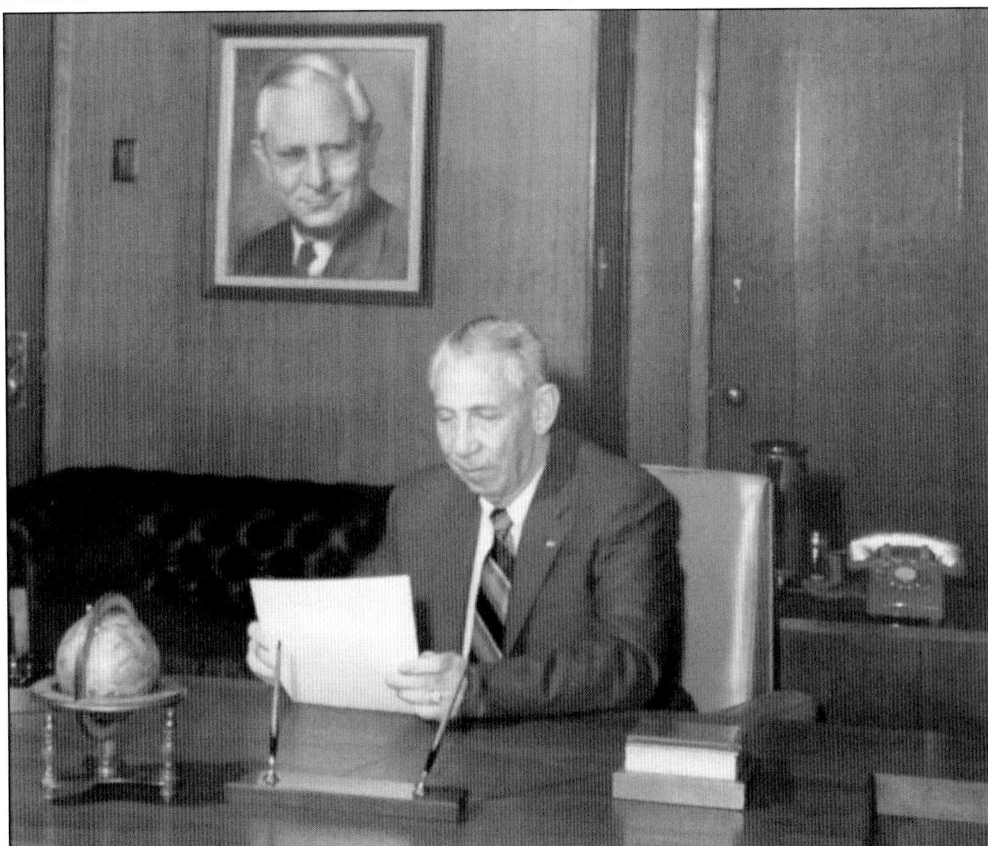

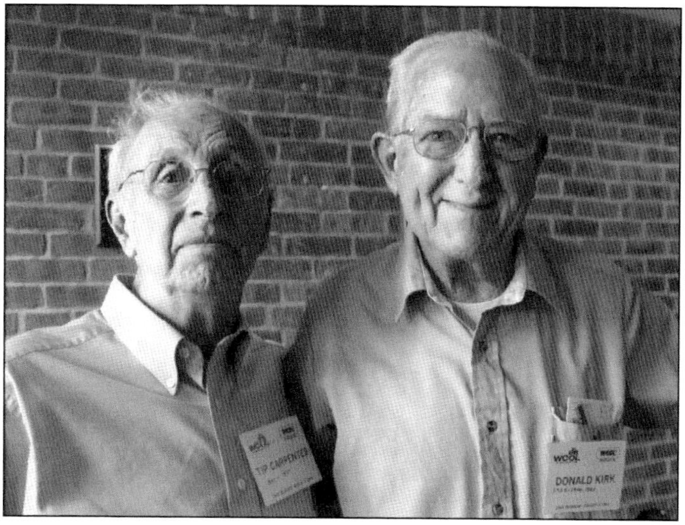

At left is Tip Carpenter, who began at WCOL in 1948 and became chief engineer in the 1960s. In many ways, Tip was responsible for WCOL's on-air sound. Because he understood modern audio processing techniques, he had the loudest AM station in Columbus. Next to Tip is Donald Kirk, a WCOL announcer in 1953. This photograph is from the 2003 WCOL reunion. (Author's collection.)

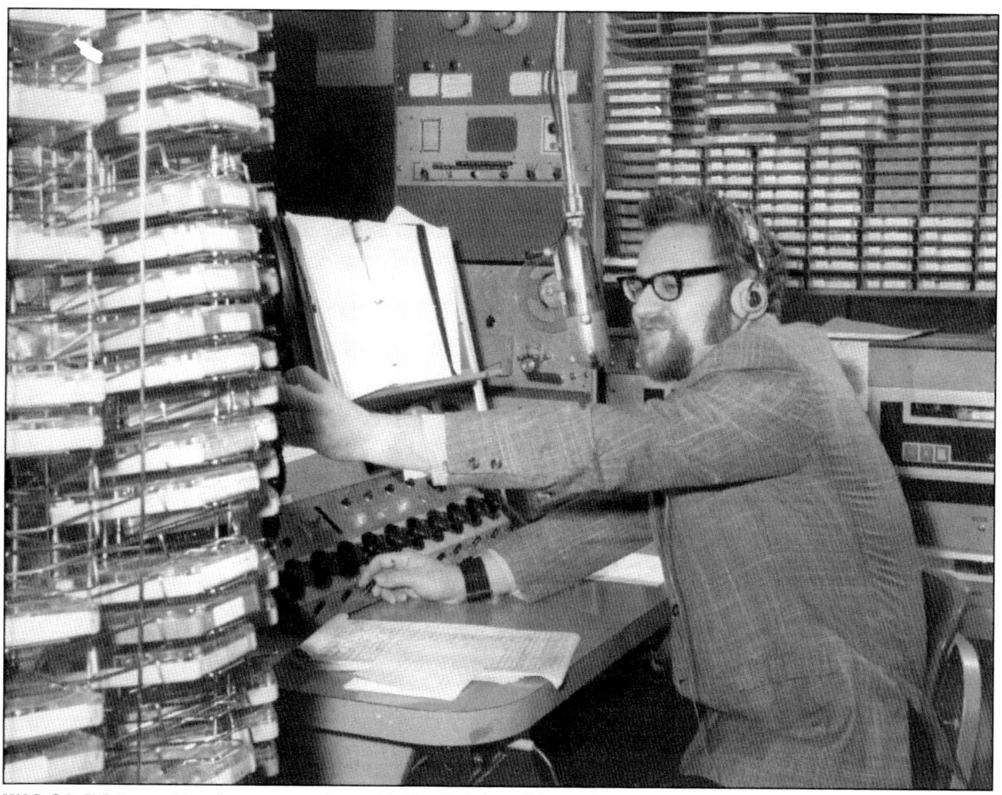

WCOL DJ Jerry Gordon remembers 1968: "I did middays there, one of two new hires brought in to inject more personality into the station. Management there was very clever, and even though they had ratings dominance they were concerned about the future. They were very sales oriented—in the front lobby instead of posting pictures of the station's DJs they had pictures of the sponsors locations." (Jerry Gordon.)

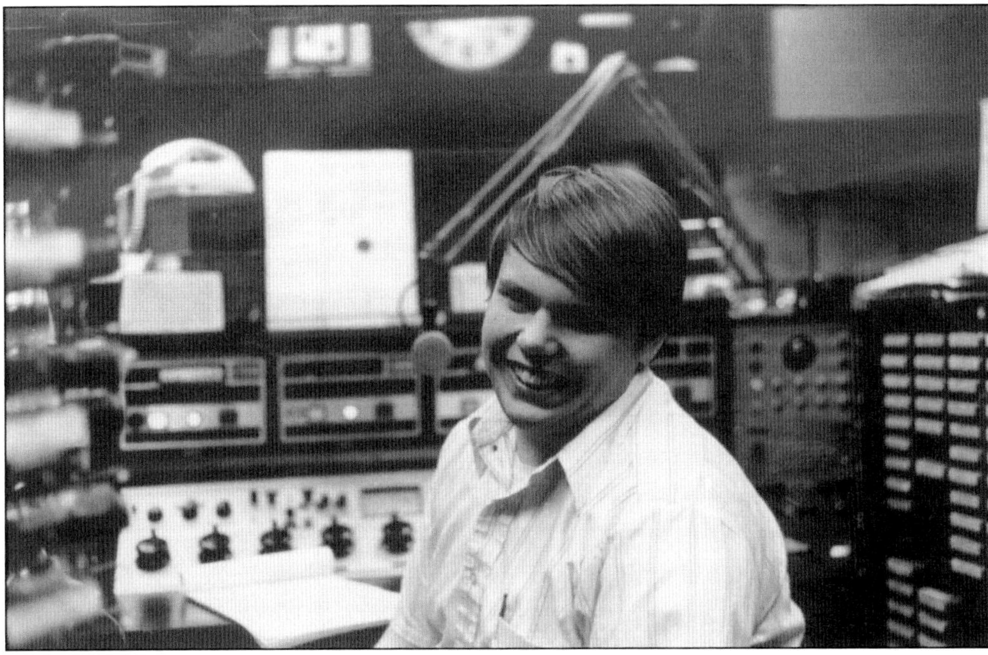

But these are just babies! This is WCOL DJ Phil Golovin posing for a promotional photograph, probably to be used on the official music survey. Readers of the local newspapers saw photographs of those announcing on the so-called adult stations in Columbus, and they would seem severe, serious, and very gray. Conversely, the WCOL DJs were really young, many of them just out of high school. (Author's collection.)

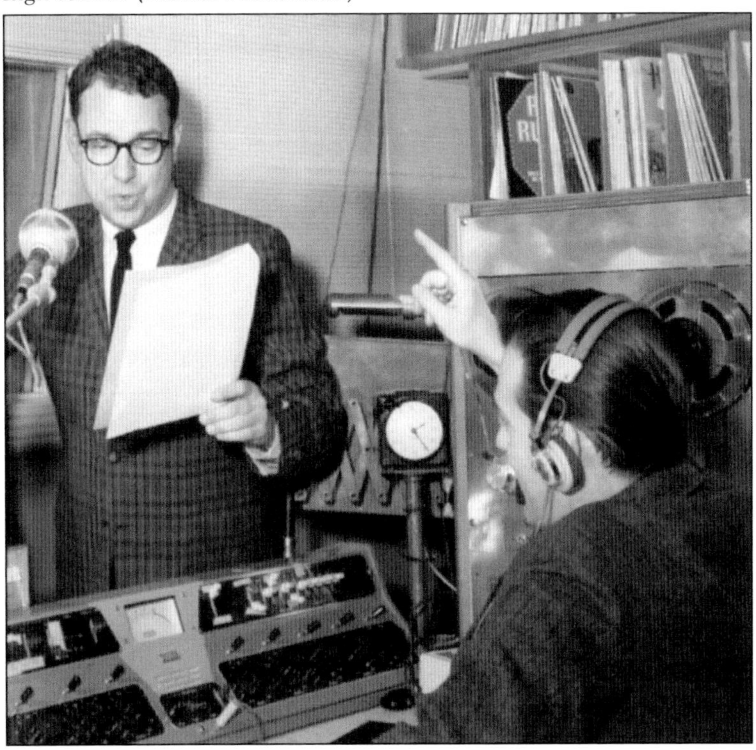

WCOL morning DJ Wes Hopkins prepares to read commercial copy as DJ Jerry Dean, seated, cues him to begin talking. Often the DJs worked with each other in the creation and recording of the commercials, the most important product of a station. By the 1960s, it was common to have prerecorded commercials with music and sound effects, ensuring consistency in the sound of the advertisement. (Author's collection.)

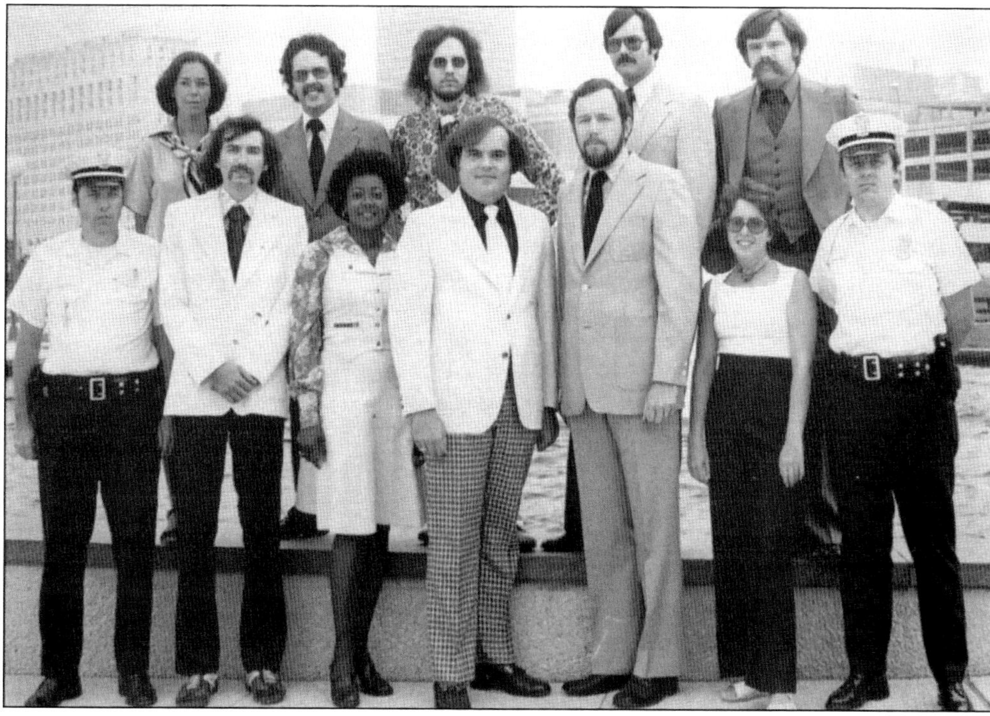

News director Jay Solomon, the tall bearded fellow third from right in the first row, is pictured with his WCOL news team in the late 1960s. It was a very large news staff for Columbus radio, but this was a time when the FCC required even the teen music stations to provide news. WCOL took it seriously and was very good at it. (Author's collection.)

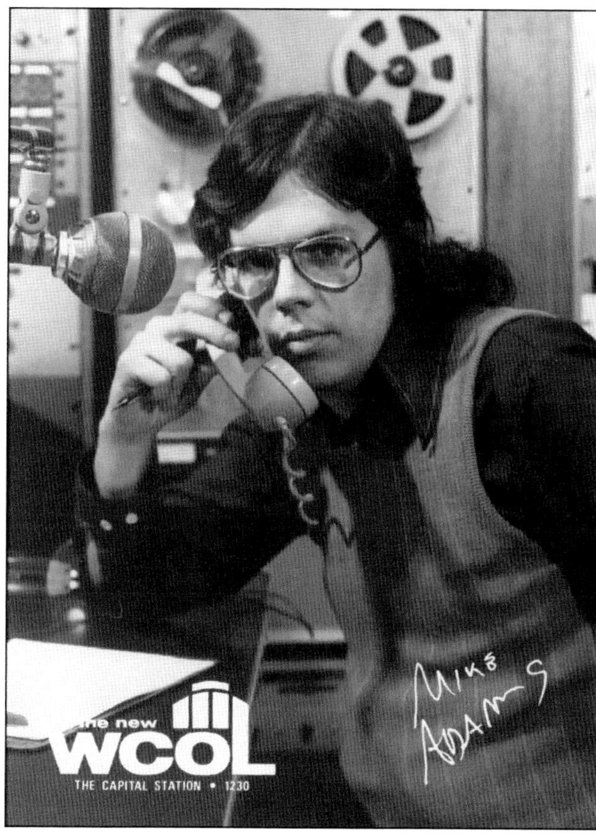

This is the author of this book, Mike Adams, who has been the WCOL historian since the 2003 reunion. Mike started at WCOL AM in 1963 at age 19 and worked as on-air DJ, music director, program director, and production director. After grad school at OSU, Mike went to California and became a professor of radio, television, and film, serving 30 years at San Jose State University, where he was the faculty advisor of the school's FM station, KSJS-90.5. (Neal Shapiro.)

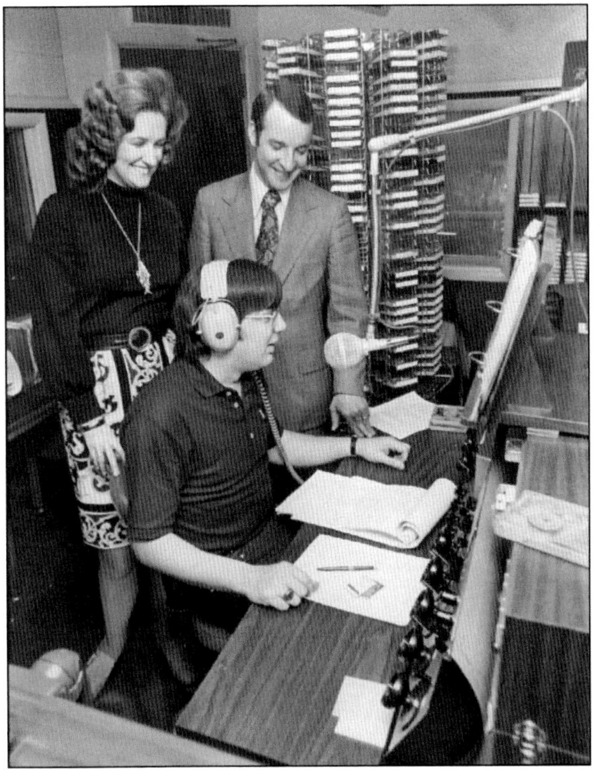

WCOL DJ Lou Henry, seated, is recording a commercial, and it must be very important, as standing and observing are program executive Sharon DuBord and general manager Dan Morris. Dan began as a DJ while an OSU student and rose to program director, then manager. He was a good boss and eventually became the head of WNCI and the Nationwide Communications–owned radio stations. (Author's collection.)

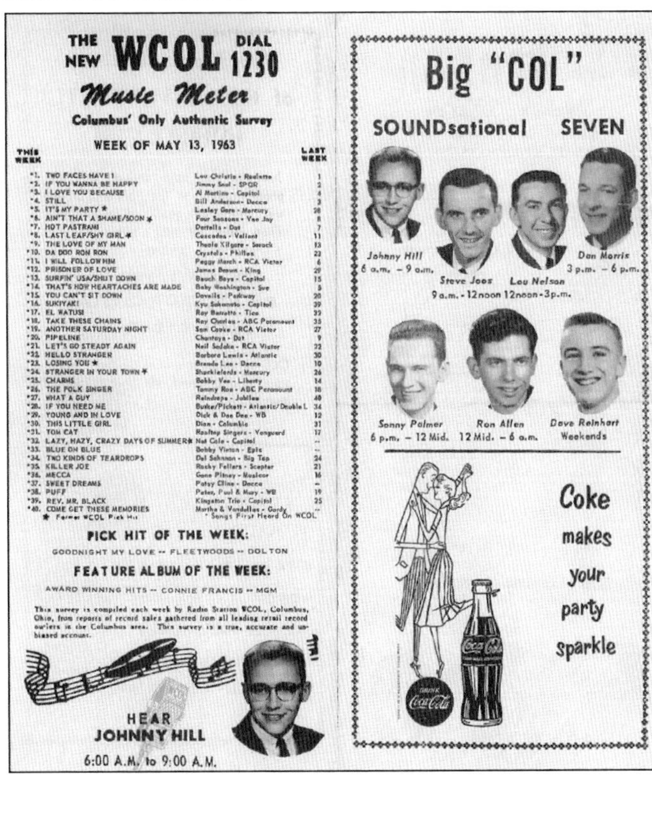

THE NEW WCOL DIAL 1230

Music Meter

Columbus' Only Authentic Survey

WEEK OF MAY 13, 1963

THIS WEEK			LAST WEEK
*1.	TWO FACES HAVE I	Lou Christie - Roulette	1
*2.	IF YOU WANNA BE HAPPY	Jimmy Soul - SPQR	2
*3.	I LOVE YOU BECAUSE	Al Martino - Capitol	4
*4.	STILL	Bill Anderson - Decca	3
*5.	IT'S MY PARTY ★	Lesley Gore - Mercury	28
*6.	AIN'T THAT A SHAME/SOON ★	Four Seasons - Vee Jay	8
*7.	HOT PASTRAMI	Dartells - Dot	7
*8.	LAST LEAF/SHY GIRL ★	Cascades - Valiant	11
*9.	THE LOVE OF MY MAN	Theola Kilgore - Serock	13
*10.	DA DOO RON RON	Crystals - Philles	23
*11.	I WILL FOLLOW HIM	Peggy March - RCA Victor	6
*12.	PRISONER OF LOVE	James Brown - King	29
*13.	SURFIN' USA/SHUT DOWN	Beach Boys - Capitol	15
*14.	THAT'S HOW HEARTACHES ARE MADE	Baby Washington - Sue	5
*15.	YOU CAN'T SIT DOWN	Dovells - Parkway	20
*16.	SUKIYAKI	Kyu Sakamoto - Capitol	39
*17.	EL WATUSI	Ray Barretto - Tico	32
*18.	TAKE THESE CHAINS	Ray Charles - ABC Paramount	35
*19.	ANOTHER SATURDAY NIGHT	Sam Cooke - RCA Victor	27
*20.	PIPELINE	Chantays - Dot	9
*21.	LET'S GO STEADY AGAIN	Neil Sedaka - RCA Victor	22
*22.	HELLO STRANGER	Barbara Lewis - Atlantic	30
*23.	LOSING YOU ★	Brenda Lee - Decca	10
*24.	STRANGER IN YOUR TOWN ★	Shacklefords - Mercury	26
*25.	CHARMS	Bobby Vee - Liberty	14
*26.	THE FOLK SINGER	Tommy Roe - ABC Paramount	18
*27.	WHAT A GUY	Raindrops - Jubilee	40
*28.	IF YOU NEED ME	Burke/Pickett - Atlantic/Double L	34
*29.	YOUNG AND IN LOVE	Dick & Dee Dee - WB	12
*30.	THIS LITTLE GIRL	Dion - Columbia	31
*31.	TOM CAT	Rooftop Singers - Vanguard	17
*32.	LAZY, HAZY, CRAZY DAYS OF SUMMER ★	Nat Cole - Capitol	--
*33.	BLUE ON BLUE	Bobby Vinton - Epic	--
*34.	TWO KINDS OF TEARDROPS	Del Shannon - Big Top	24
*35.	KILLER JOE	Rocky Fellers - Scepter	21
*36.	MECCA	Gene Pitney - Musicor	16
*37.	SWEET DREAMS	Patsy Cline - Decca	--
*38.	PUFF	Peter, Paul & Mary - WB	19
*39.	REV. MR. BLACK	Kingston Trio - Capitol	25
*40.	COME GET THESE MEMORIES	Martha & Vandellas - Gordy	--

★ Former WCOL Pick Hit

* Songs First Heard On WCOL

PICK HIT OF THE WEEK:

GOODNIGHT MY LOVE -- FLEETWOODS -- DOLTON

FEATURE ALBUM OF THE WEEK:

AWARD WINNING HITS -- CONNIE FRANCIS -- MGM

This survey is compiled each week by Radio Station WCOL, Columbus, Ohio, from reports of record sales gathered from all leading retail record outlets in the Columbus area. This survey is a true, accurate and unbiased account.

HEAR JOHNNY HILL

6:00 A.M. to 9:00 A.M.

Big "COL"

SOUNDsational SEVEN

Johnny Hill 6 a.m. – 9 a.m.

Steve Joos 9 a.m. - 12noon

Lou Nelson 12noon - 3p.m.

Dan Morris 3 p.m. – 6 p.m.

Sonny Palmer 6 p.m. – 12 Mid.

Ron Allen 12 Mid. – 6 a.m.

Dave Reinhart Weekends

Coke makes your party sparkle

The WCOL survey of records being played on the air went through several name changes. In 1960, it was called the rather generic "Hits of the Week," then "Music Meter," and finally it was the "Hitline Survey." Here is one from May 1963, with morning DJ Johnny Hill on the cover and the other DJs on the back. (Author's collection.)

A young Bryan McIntyre is on the air at WCOL in the 1960s. Like 95 percent of the WCOL DJs, Bryan was a communications major at Ohio State University. Bryan started as a DJ and then eventually became one of the station leaders as music director, program director, and operations manager into the 1970s and 1980s. (Bryan McIntyre.)

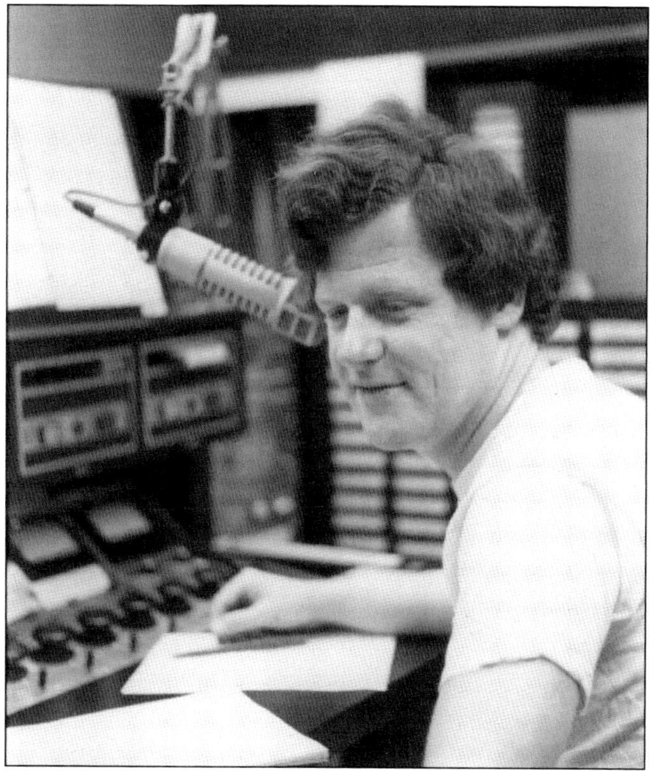

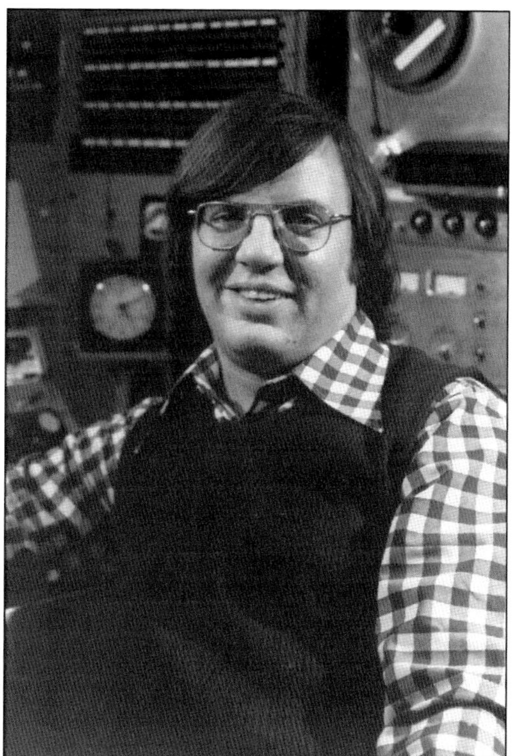

Lou Henry worked at WCOL for seven years, then went to Detroit to work at WCAR and CKLW. Like most of the WCOL air staff, he received his communications degree from OSU while in Columbus. Lou was wise to the fortunes of radio and while in Detroit graduated from law school, going from a DJ to a JD with his juris doctorate. (Lou Henry.)

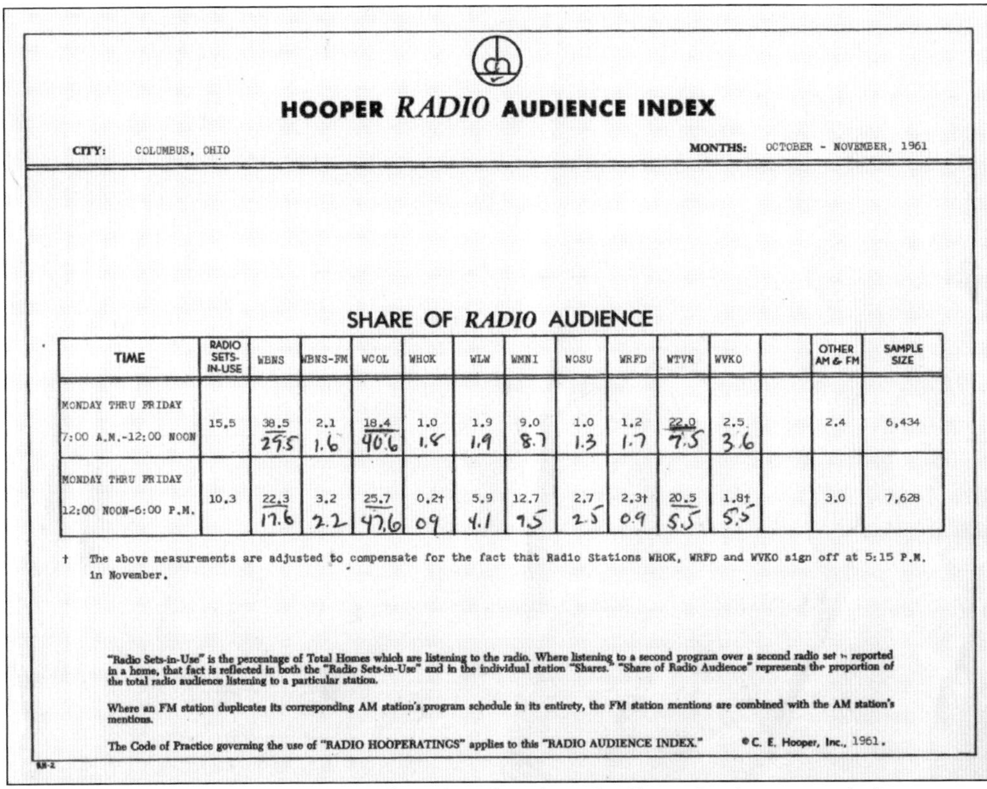

HOOPER *RADIO* AUDIENCE INDEX

CITY: COLUMBUS, OHIO

MONTHS: OCTOBER - NOVEMBER, 1961

SHARE OF *RADIO* AUDIENCE

TIME	RADIO SETS-IN-USE	WBNS	WBNS-FM	WCOL	WHOK	WLW	WMNI	WOSU	WRFD	WTVN	WVKO		OTHER AM & FM	SAMPLE SIZE
MONDAY THRU FRIDAY 7:00 A.M.-12:00 NOON	15.5	38.5 29.5	2.1 1.6	18.4 40.6	1.0 1.8	1.9 1.9	9.0 8.7	1.0 1.3	1.2 1.7	22.0 7.5	2.5 3.6		2.4	6,434
MONDAY THRU FRIDAY 12:00 NOON-6:00 P.M.	10.3	22.3 17.6	3.2 2.2	25.7 47.6	0.2† 09	5.9 4.1	12.7 7.5	2.7 2.5	2.3† 0.9	20.5 5.5	1.8† 5.5		3.0	7,628

† The above measurements are adjusted to compensate for the fact that Radio Stations WHOK, WRFD and WVKO sign off at 5:15 P.M. in November.

"Radio Sets-in-Use" is the percentage of Total Homes which are listening to the radio. Where listening to a second program over a second radio set is reported in a home, that fact is reflected in both the "Radio Sets-in-Use" and in the individual station "Shares." "Share of Radio Audience" represents the proportion of the total radio audience listening to a particular station.

Where an FM station duplicates its corresponding AM station's program schedule in its entirety, the FM station mentions are combined with the AM station's mentions.

The Code of Practice governing the use of "RADIO HOOPERATINGS" applies to this "RADIO AUDIENCE INDEX." ©C. E. Hooper, Inc., 1961.

In 1961, three Columbus stations either played rock and roll, made plans to end playing it, or were just beginning to play it. WCOL started late but stayed at it tenaciously, non-stop, 24 hours a day. These are the Hooper Ratings for the fall of 1961. Notice that WBNS is still highly rated, as are WTVN and WCOL. When WTVN ended its rock era, WVKO took over the format but quickly gave it up. (Jim Pidcock.)

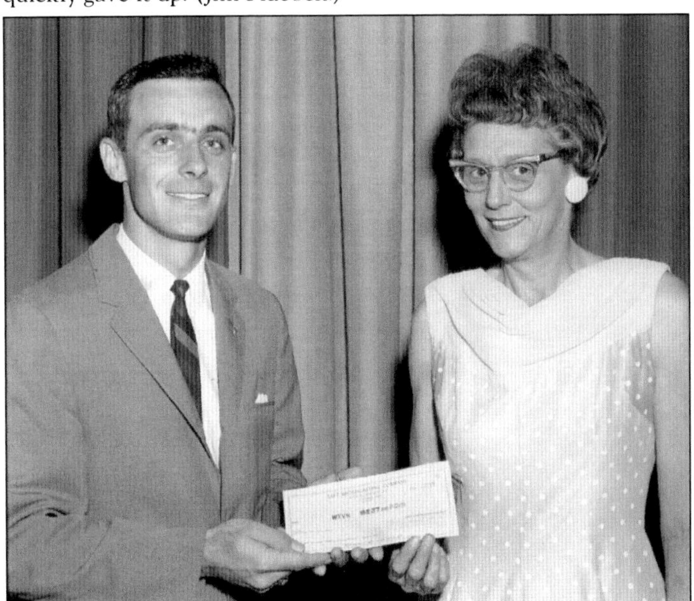

Pictured is WTVN in the early 1960s. Every pop music station had a "cash call" contest. The station would advertise a starting amount of money to be given at random to a listener who knew that correct amount. A station might begin with their frequency, say 610, and make the opening amount $6.10, then increase it each hour. In this photograph, Johnny Dollar presents a check for $237.90 to a lucky listener. That would roughly amount to $2,000 today. (Jim Pidcock.)

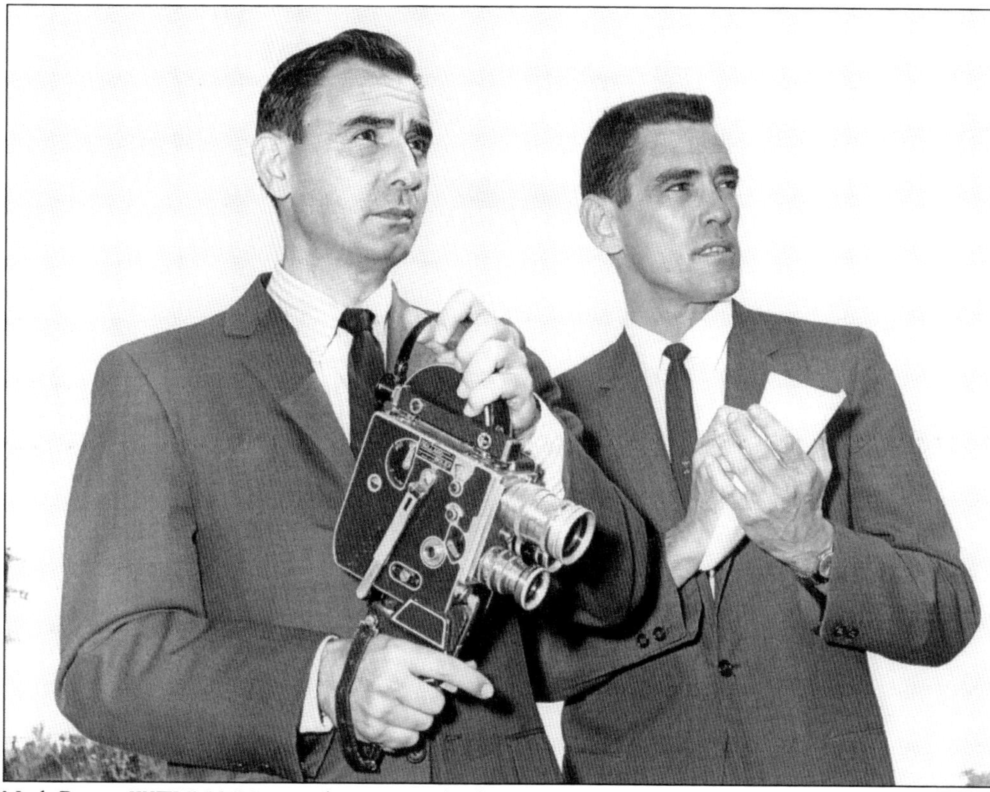

Nick Basso, WTVN TV news director, and John Fraim, WTVN radio news, pose in 1961 with a Bolex 16-millimeter film camera, one of the models used for local news until video replaced film in the 1970s. Several of the major Columbus radio stations went on the air in the 1950s with television. They began these broadcasts by using the talent from their radio stations. There were exceptions, and some with great voices were not liked by the camera. (*Columbus Citizen-Journal*/Photohio.org.)

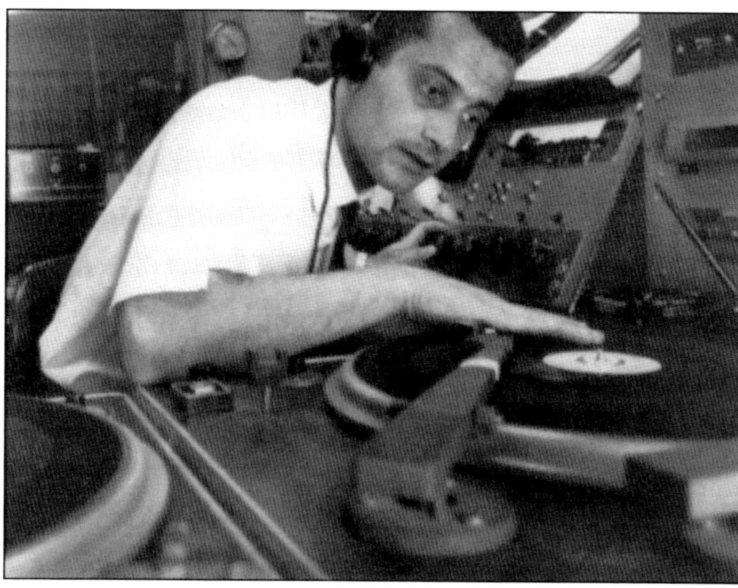

For a brief time in 1960, WTVN had some big market talent, including Dave Hull as the morning drive-time DJ. Dave went on to Los Angeles and KRLA for the remainder of his career and wrote a book about his radio experience. Here is DJ Dave Hull on the air. (Dave Hull.)

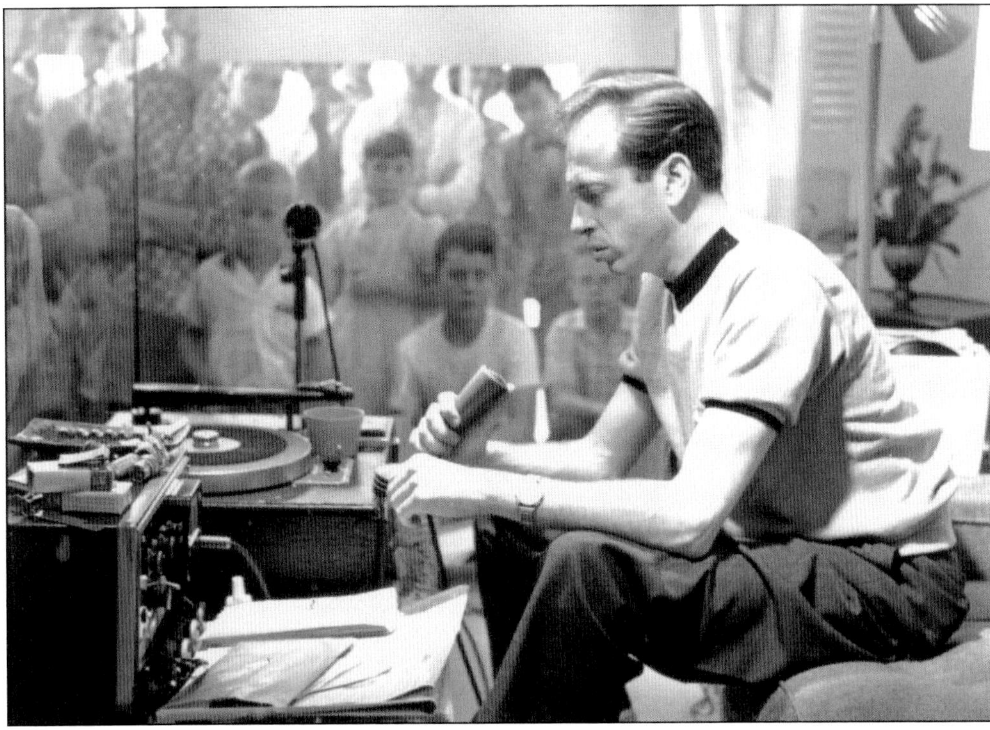

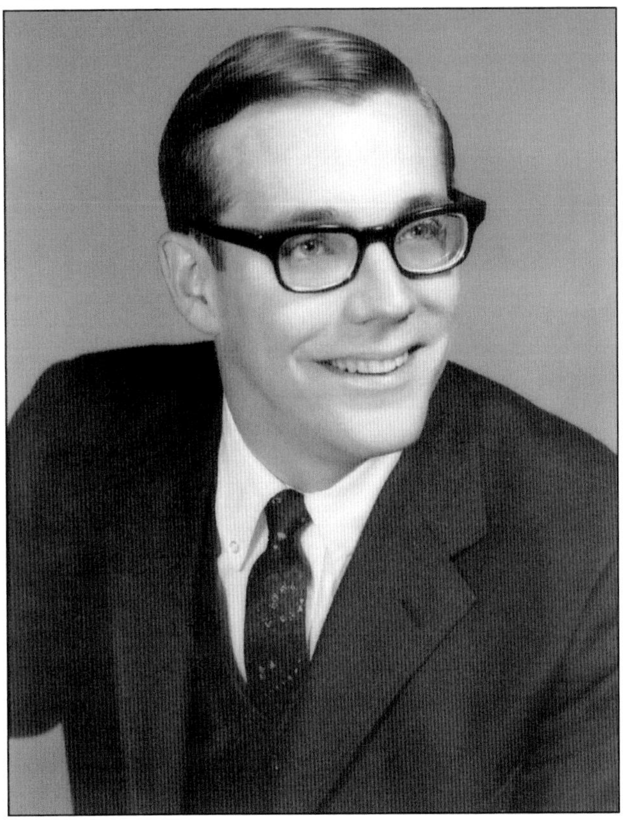

Another of the great voices briefly on WTVN was Jim Runyon, seen in this 1960 photograph at a live remote broadcast, adoring fans looking on in the background. Jim looks unhappy to be there. He left WTVN after a few years when the station abandoned the rock format. (Jim Pidcock.)

This is WTVN DJ Jim Lohse, who became program director in 1968. He was known locally for his earlier nighttime program, which he called Lohse's Lounge. Jim played the piano on his air shift and wrote many songs, one of which became a hit by singer Al Martino. (*Columbus Citizen-Journal*/Photohio.org.)

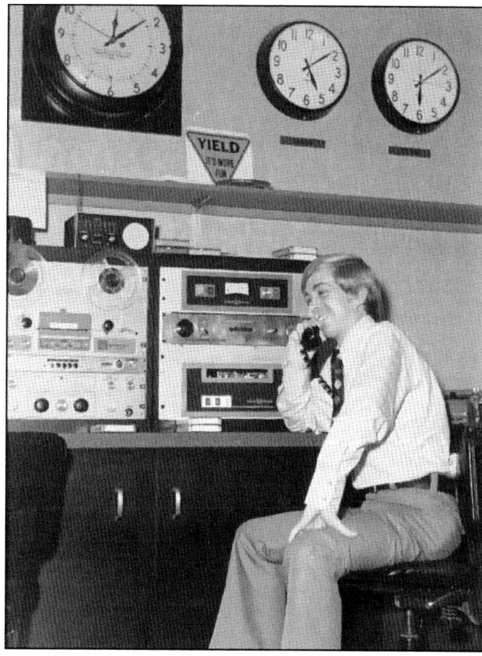

Newsman Tom Burris said, "As a kid right out of college, landing a job at WTVN was an incredible opportunity. I was told at the time that I was the youngest person ever to work full time at the station. They called me 'the kid.' It was intimidating at times, but always exciting." Later he became a television reporter. (Tom Burris.)

Here is a late-1960s or early-1970s image of the morning man and the boss. Seated is John Fraim during his time as morning DJ, and watching over him is program director Jim Pidcock, also known by his air name of Johnny Dollar. In the 1980s, Fraim was on WCOL AM and would broadcast his show live from a room high atop the Leveque-Lincoln Tower. (Jim Pidcock.)

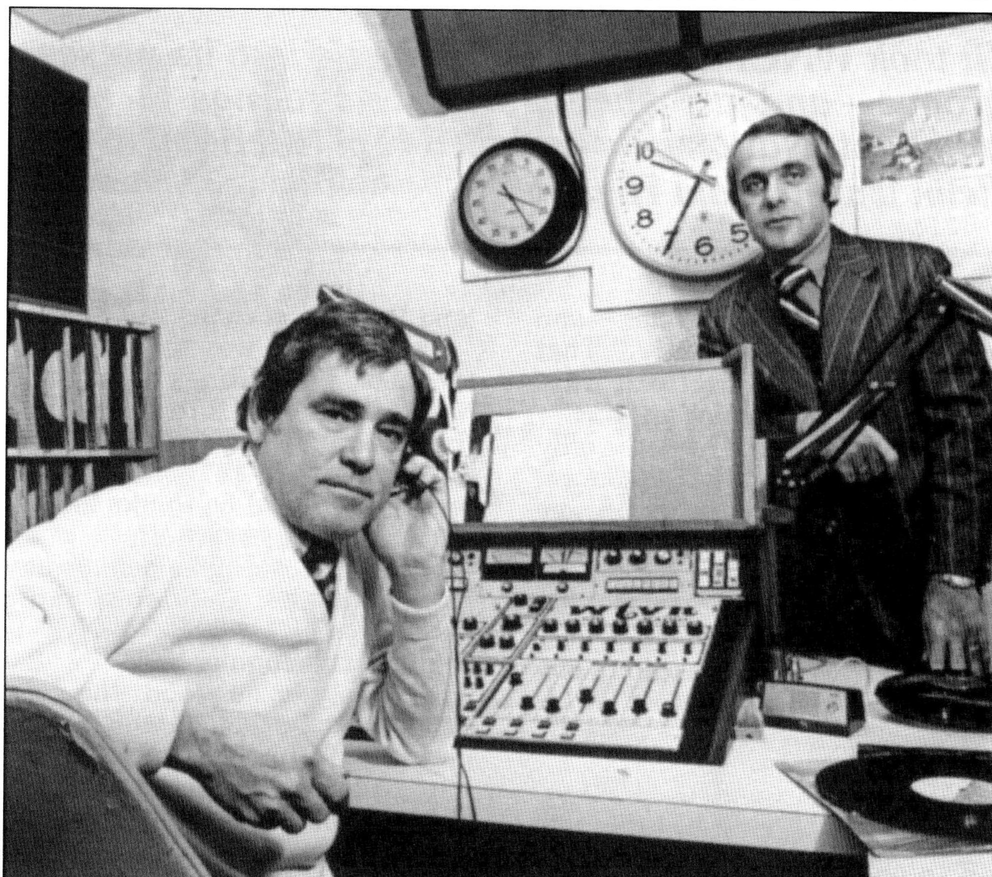

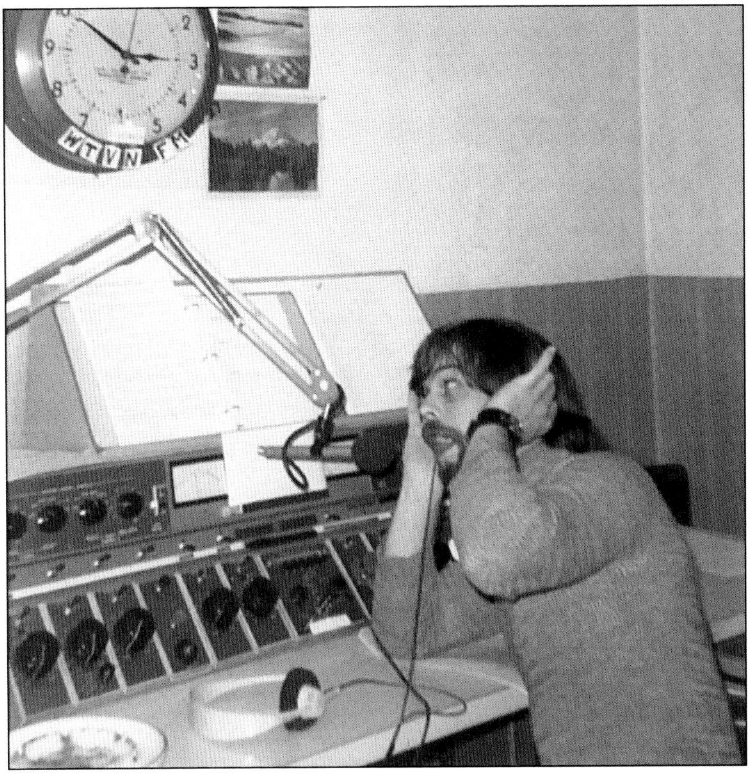

This is WTVN DJ Bill Smith on the air in 1972. According to Rick Minerd's book on Columbus radio, *Deputy in Disguise*, "Bill Smith was the most talented person I ever met in radio." He was apparently a production whiz: "Bill could do things back then with just a microphone and a tape recorder that even with today's technology it would be difficult to come close to in terms of style, delivery and technology," wrote Minerd. (Tom Burris.)

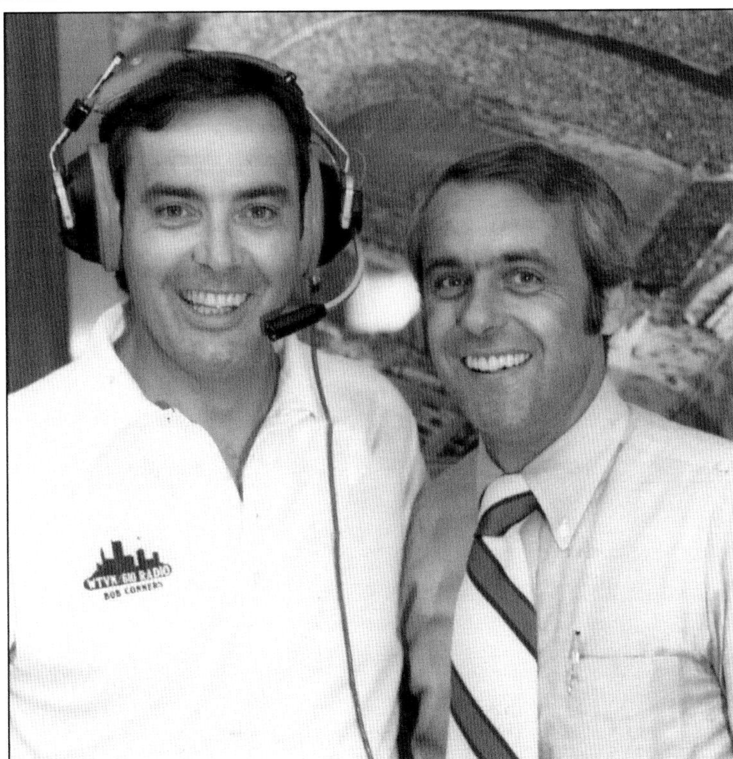

From 1978 until 2011, Bob Connors (left) was the morning DJ on WTVN AM, 33 years at the same station and at the same time, the longevity record for a Columbus DJ. Jim Pidcock (right), who was Johnny Dollar on WTVN and WVKO during their rock era, returned as program director of WTVN, later serving as sales manager and general manager. Pidcock provided most of the WTVN images used in this book. (Jim Pidcock.)

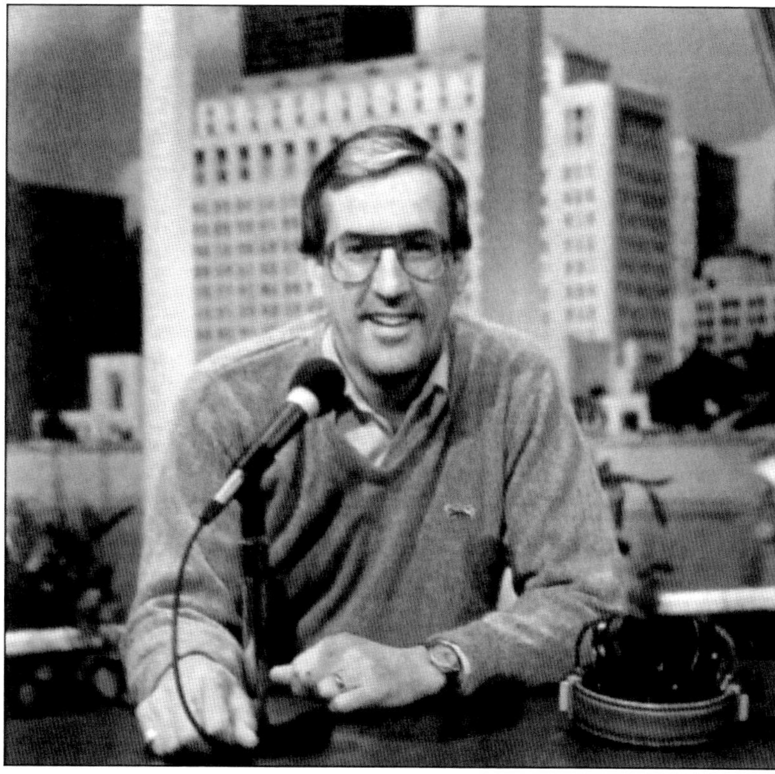

Longtime midday DJ Dave Logan was on WTVN for 30 years in the same shift. This would break the record of the Early Worm, Irwin Johnson, who was the morning voice on WBNS from 1940 until 1969, or 29 years. The Columbus radio market did have some areas of remarkable job stability, led by WBNS and WTVN. (Jim Pidcock.)

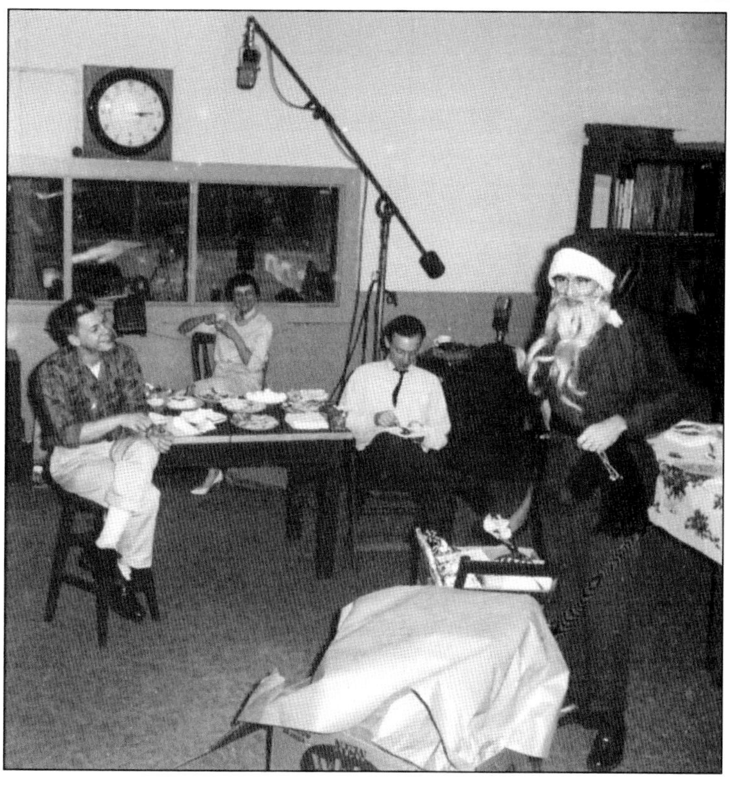

The year is 1962, and the WOSU staff is surprised by a visit by the real Santa Claus to the WOSU studios. Radio is sometimes fun and games. By the end of the 1960s, WOSU AM and FM would begin to offer different programming, the AM becoming news and talk, the FM classical music and NPR. (A.V. Shirk.)

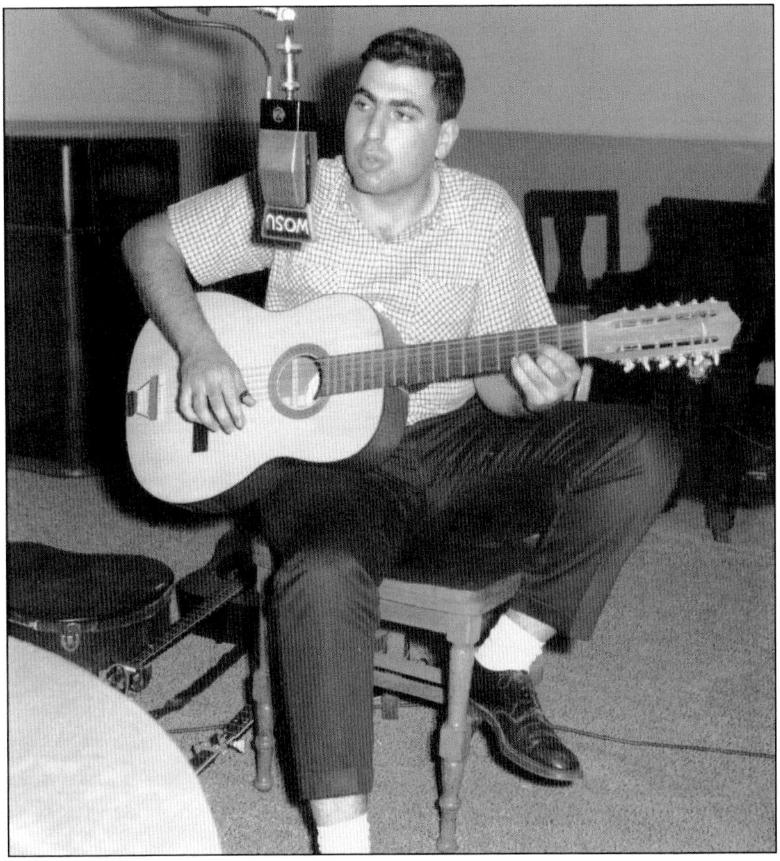

David Suchman records folk music in 1961 in the WOSU studios. A few professors were musicians, and many appeared on WOSU, one of the last stations to air traditional music, some of it live from the studio. (A.V. Shirk.)

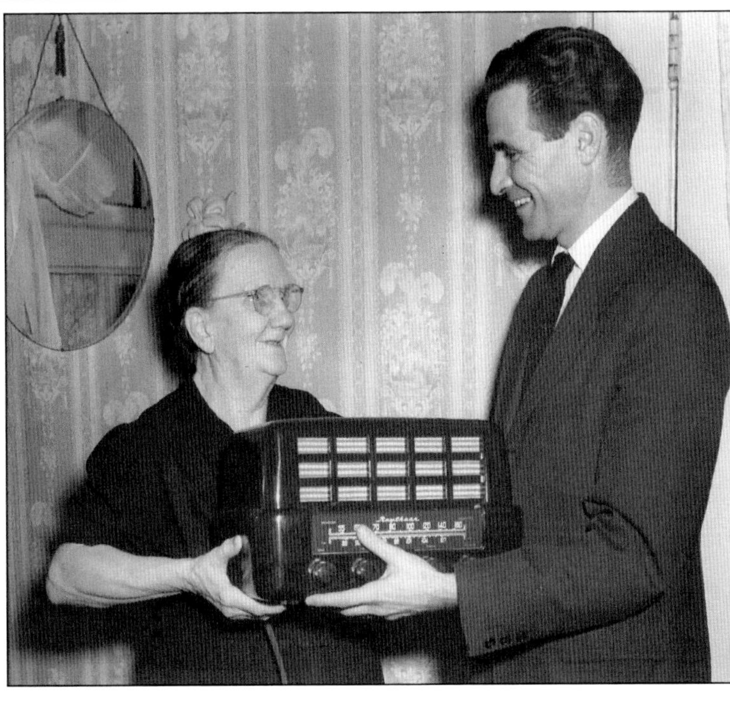

WVKO owner Bert Charles gives a prize to a contest winner, an AM-FM radio. WVKO began as a low-power, daytime-only station that went on the air in late 1951 but struggled to find an audience, trying rock for a year, then soul for several decades. Now it is gospel and religion. Bert Charles was also known in Columbus as the voice of Ohio State Buckeye football play-by-play. (*Columbus Citizen-Journal*/Photohio.org.)

When WTVN exited the rock-and-roll format, some of the DJs took the format to WVKO. It was not successful there, as, among other problems, WVKO was a daytime-only operation, and nights were when the rock listeners were most able to tune in. And they did, but to WCOL. In this 1962 photograph is the WVKO version of the hit chart, the "Fabulous 50 Tunedex." On the air there are former WTVN DJs Johnny Dollar and Dave Hull. (Author's collection.)

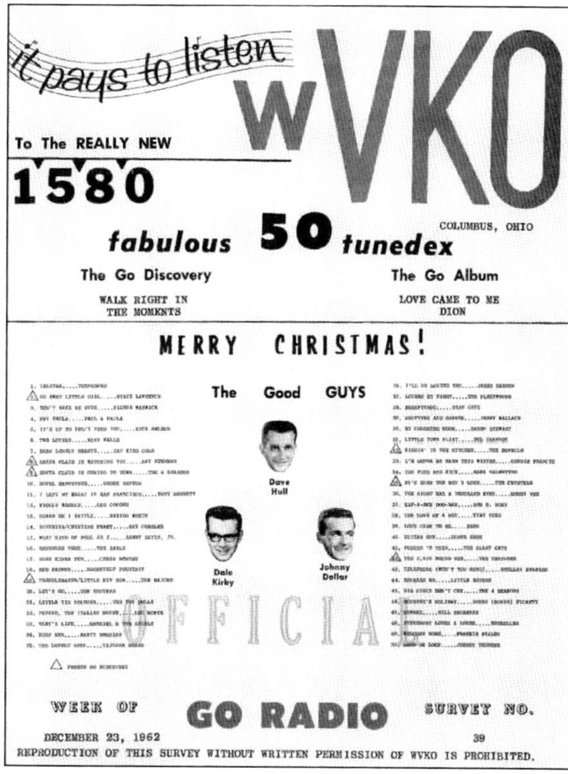
it pays to listen
To The REALLY NEW
WVKO
1580
fabulous 50 tunedex
COLUMBUS, OHIO
The Go Discovery
WALK RIGHT IN
THE MOMENTS
The Go Album
LOVE CAME TO ME
DION
MERRY CHRISTMAS!
The Good GUYS
Dave Hull
Dale Kirby
Johnny Dollar
OFFICIAL
WEEK OF
DECEMBER 23, 1962
GO RADIO
SURVEY NO.
39
REPRODUCTION OF THIS SURVEY WITHOUT WRITTEN PERMISSION OF WVKO IS PROHIBITED.

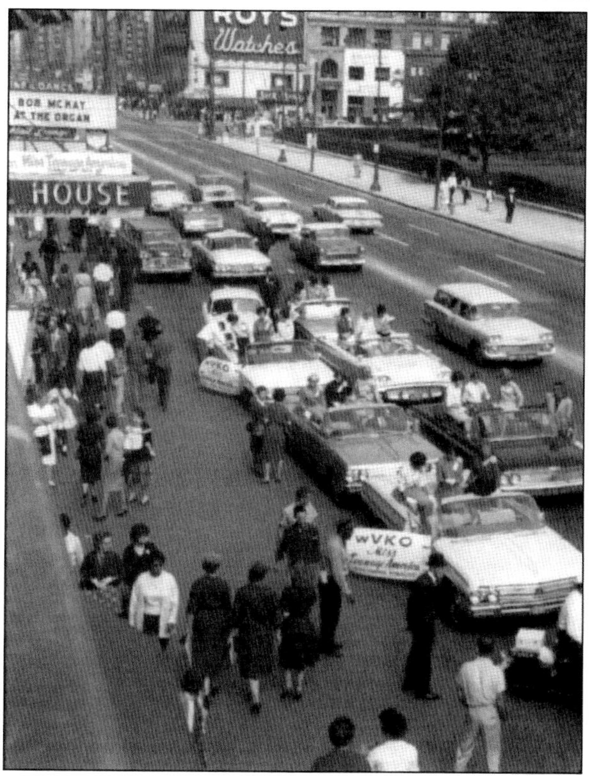

A major promotion involves WVKO morning DJ Dave Hull and Miss Teenage America. It looks like the purpose of this promotion was to tie up traffic in downtown Columbus in 1962. Major promotions like this one aimed at a teen audience could not save the format. (Dave Hull.)

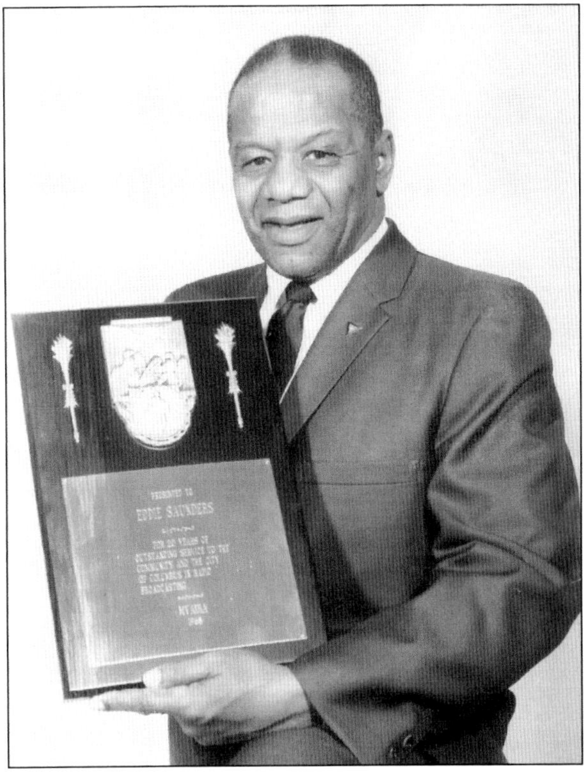

This is longtime WVKO personality Eddie Saunders receiving an award for his many contributions to Columbus civic life. Saunders is also to be thanked for his posthumous contribution to this book, as he saved many photographs and papers from his WVKO days and placed them with the Ohio History Connection. (*Columbus Citizen-Journal*/Photohio.org.)

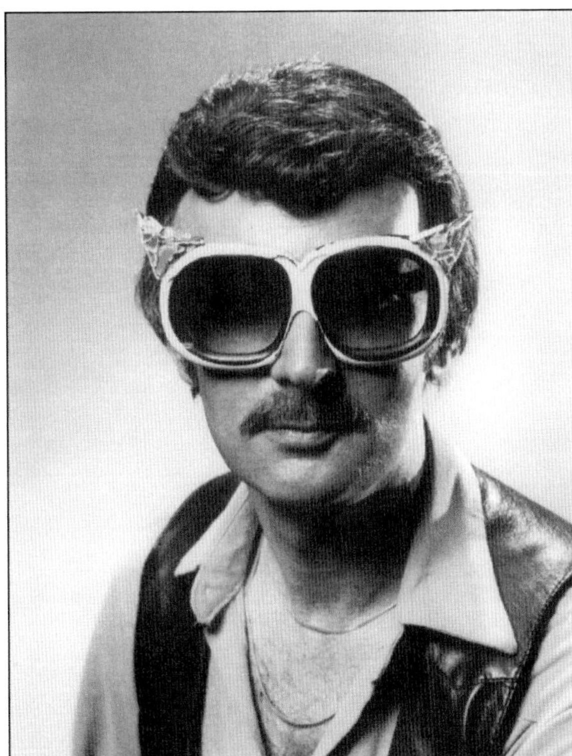

A radio renaissance man, Fritz Peerenboom is pictured in the 1970s wearing his trademark "Nite Owl" glasses. "Uncle Fritz" was on several area radio stations, including a jazz show over WBNS in the early days of stereo broadcasting, before 1960. For this early stereo, the left channel was broadcast on the AM frequency and the right channel by the WBNS FM transmitter. Listeners needed two radios, one AM, one FM. Later he moved his popular jazz program to FM 101, by then in so-called "multiplex" stereo. (Fritz Peerenboom.)

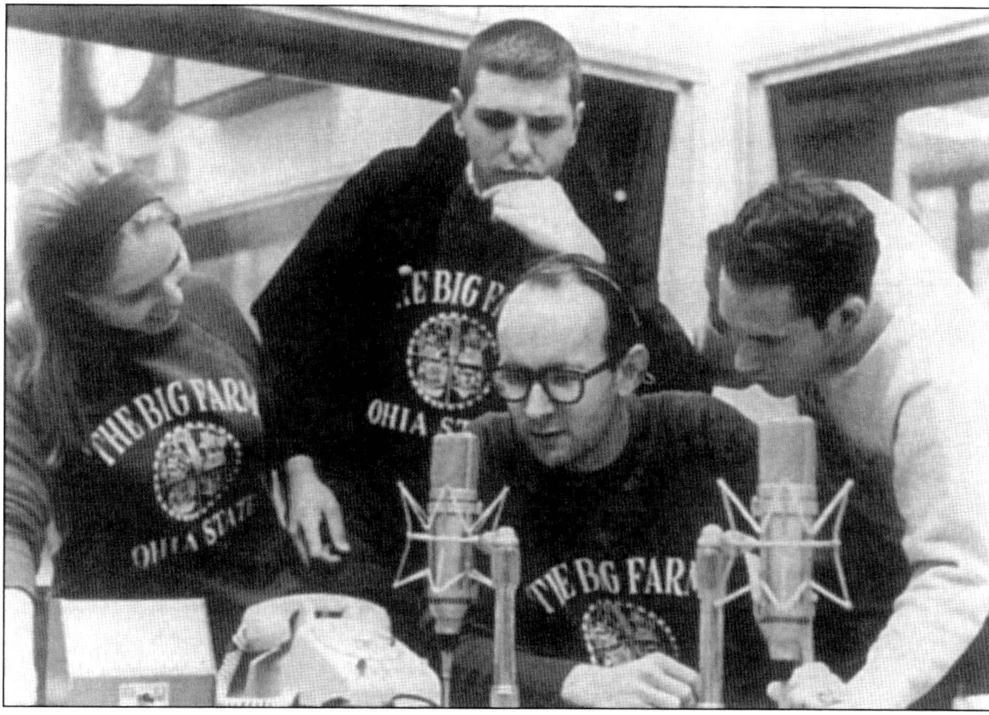

Fritz Peerenboom is pictured in the 1960s in his element, on the air with OSU students. College students listened to Fritz, and he reciprocated by wearing the "Big Farm" OSU sweatshirt. Fritz has several degrees from OSU, first as a teacher and then in cinema. He was a filmmaker along with his radio and television work. (Fritz Peerenboom.)

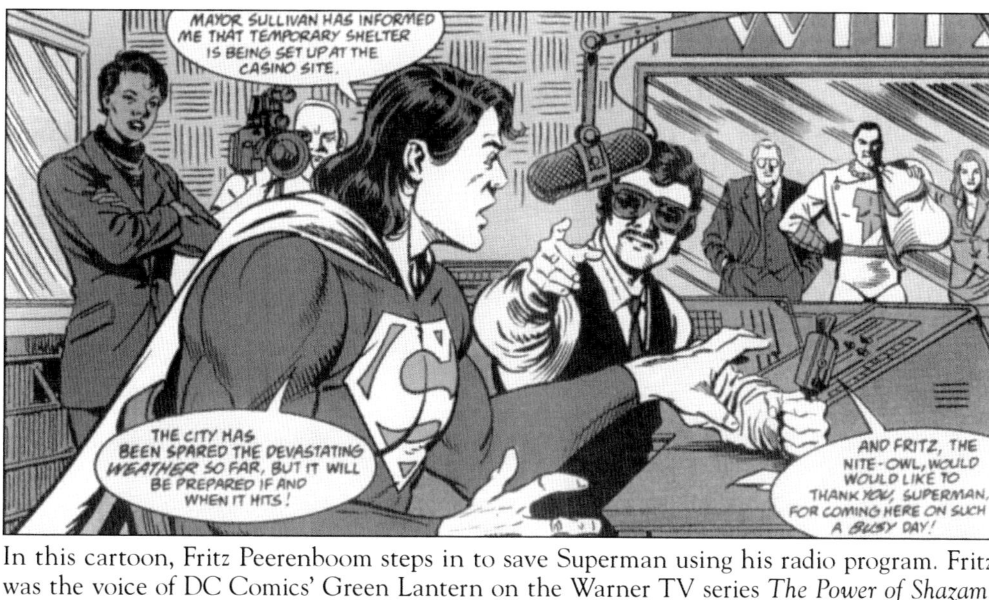

In this cartoon, Fritz Peerenboom steps in to save Superman using his radio program. Fritz was the voice of DC Comics' Green Lantern on the Warner TV series *The Power of Shazam*. Peerenboom hosted the late night "fright" movies on WBNS-TV, for which he won two Emmys. (Fritz Peerenboom.)

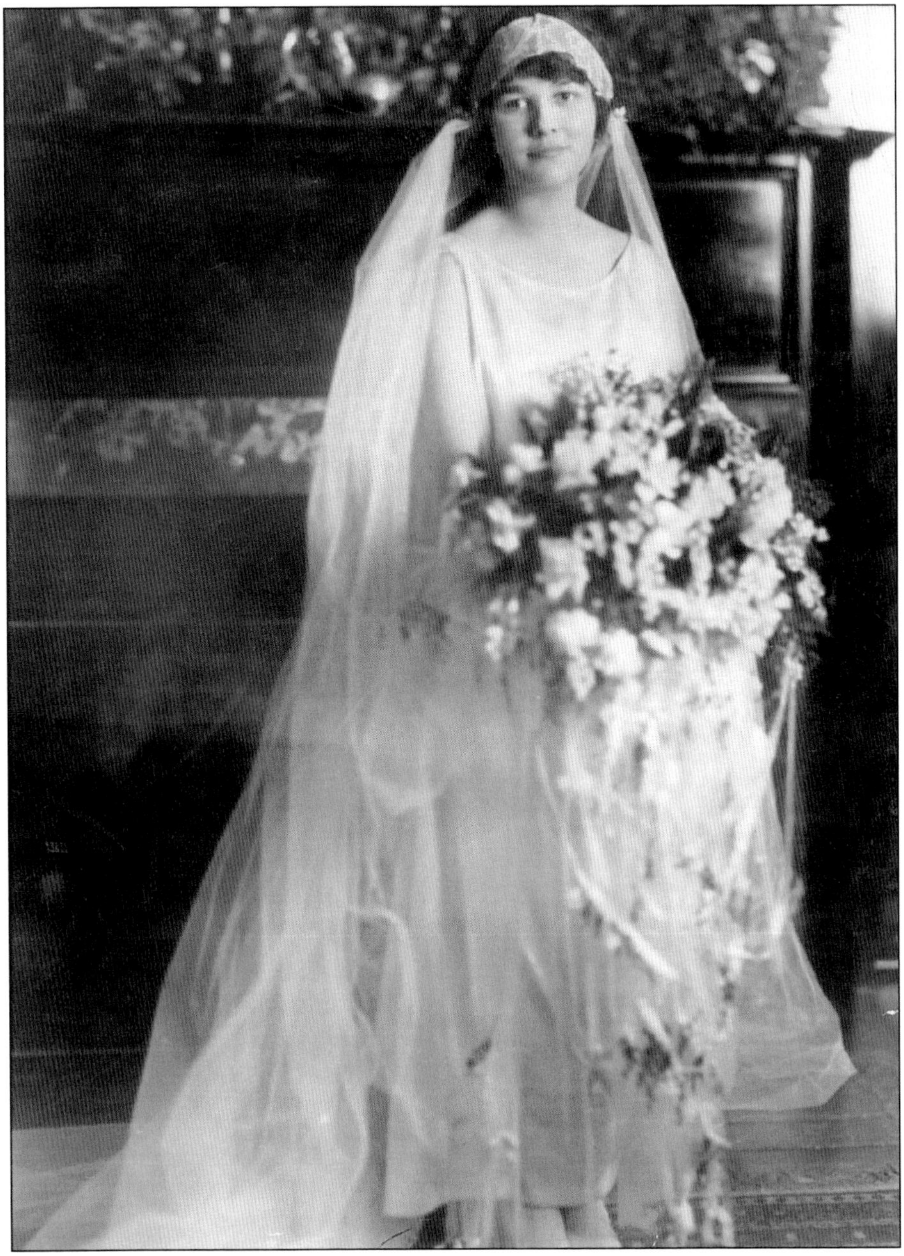

Everybody loves a bride. This is the 1924 wedding of Alice Kilgore Winters Bahman, who was the WIZE Springfield, Ohio, announcer for three decades. Her famous son, Jonathan Winters, was born and raised in Springfield and started his show business career in 1949 at WING in Dayton. Soon he moved to WBNS, leaving in 1953 for New York. Alice Bahman was also the host of a women's issues talk and call-in show and a news reporter. (Mike Adams was on the air at WIZE in 1967, and Alice was his news reporter.) In a 2006 *Springfield News-Sun* interview, the 80-year-old Jonathan said his mother gave him this advice for getting a liberal education: "First of all you get into the library and read all about Springfield and about the time of the Indians, the Shawnee. Next, the reading should turn to general knowledge about the state and the country." (Natalie Fritz, Curator of Library & Archives, Clark County Historical Society at the Heritage Center.)

This early-1970s photograph features Harry Valentine, who started in radio while an OSU student, answering phones at night at WCOL. Soon he was on the air. Harry graduated and eventually became the program director of KFRC in San Francisco. It paid to be a WCOL phone boy. (Neal Shapiro.)

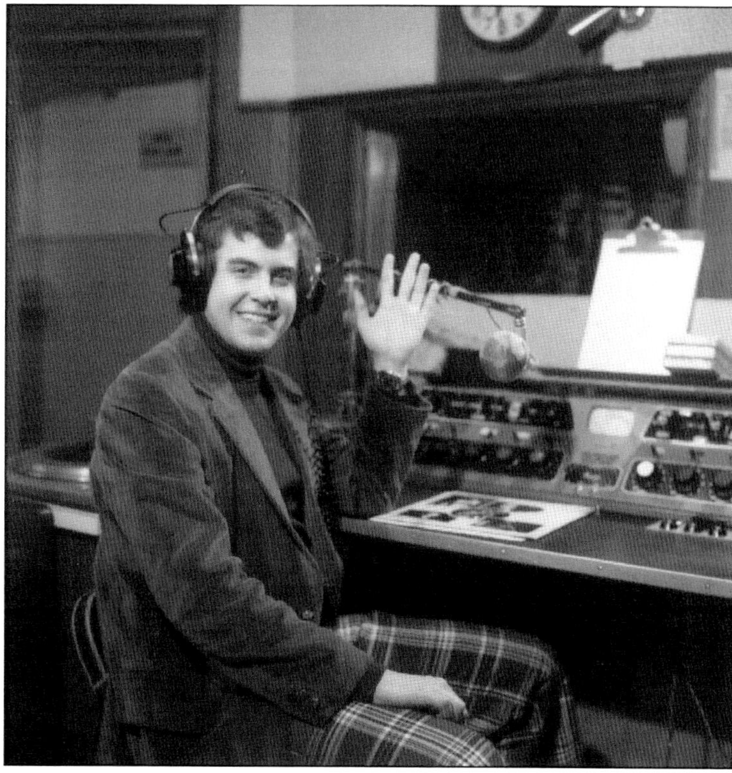

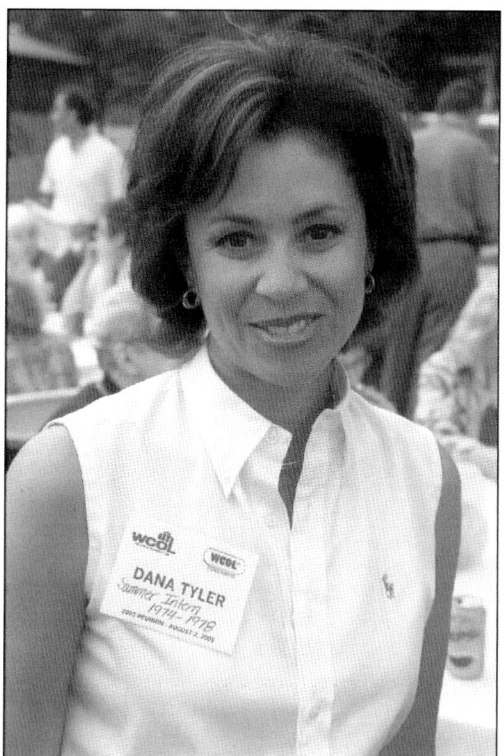

Another WCOL person who made good, this is Columbus-born Dana Tyler, who went from being a summer intern at WCOL in 1974 to a news reporter on WBNS-TV to a news anchor on WCBS-TV in New York. Who said WCOL was not a stepping stone to fame? (Author photograph.)

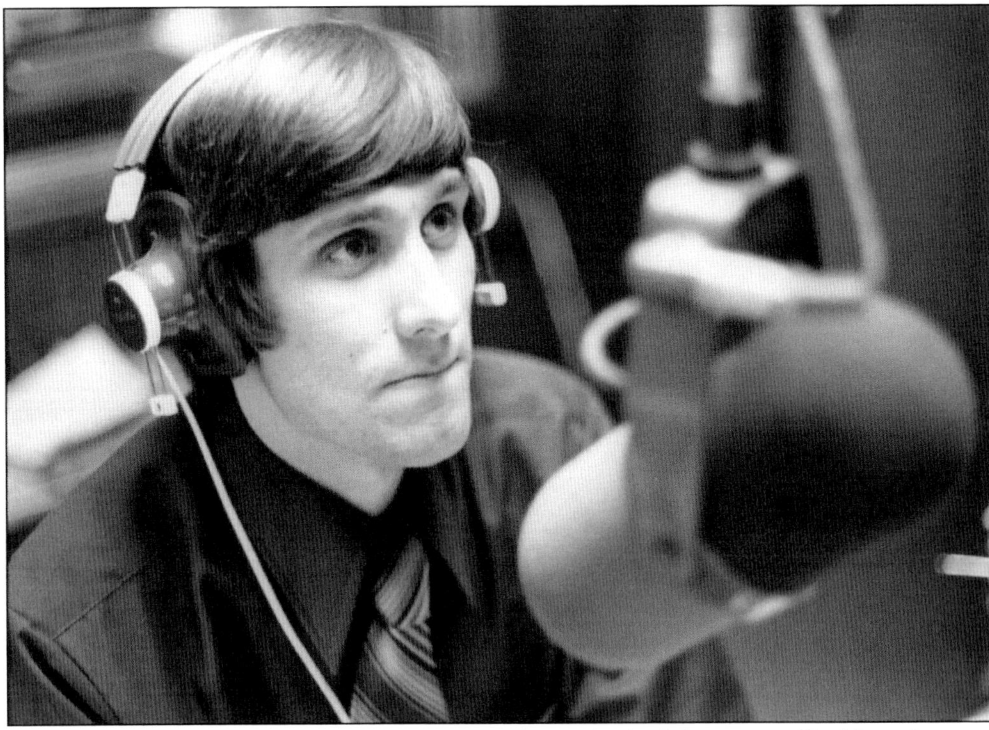

This is Bob Alan on the air in the late 1960s. Those who had the correct "look" might move beyond the job of the unseen and low-paid DJ into a public role on television. Bob went on to be a reporter for WTVN-TV. (Bob Alan.)

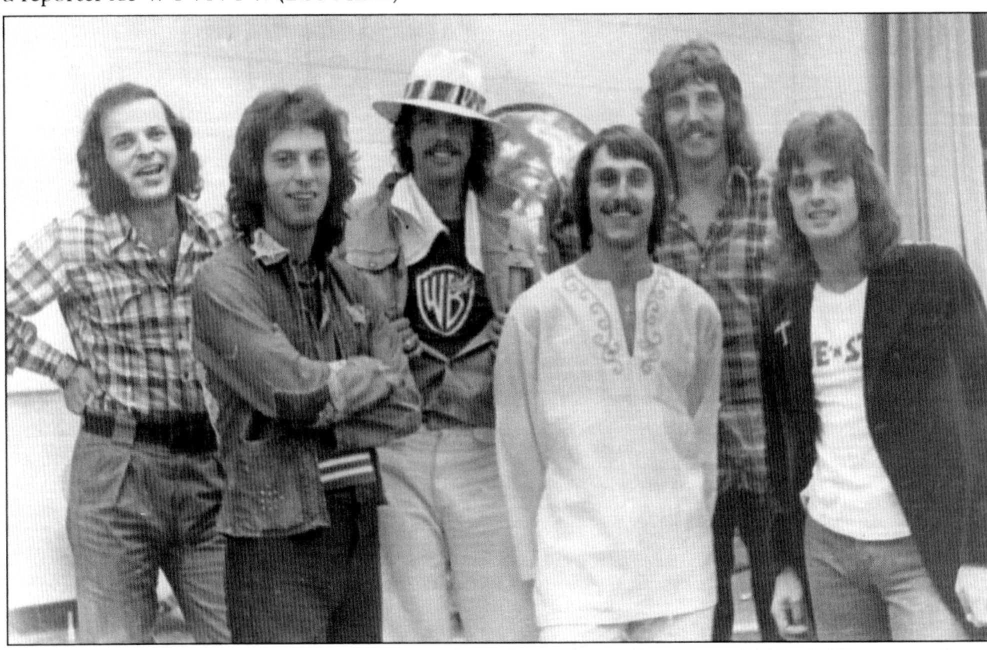

WCOL DJ Bob Alan, in front wearing a white shirt, does what Top 40 DJs did best, involving the radio audience with the actual groups who performed the music. This is Bob with the Grass Roots on the occasion of their appearance at the Ohio State Fair. (Bob Alan.)

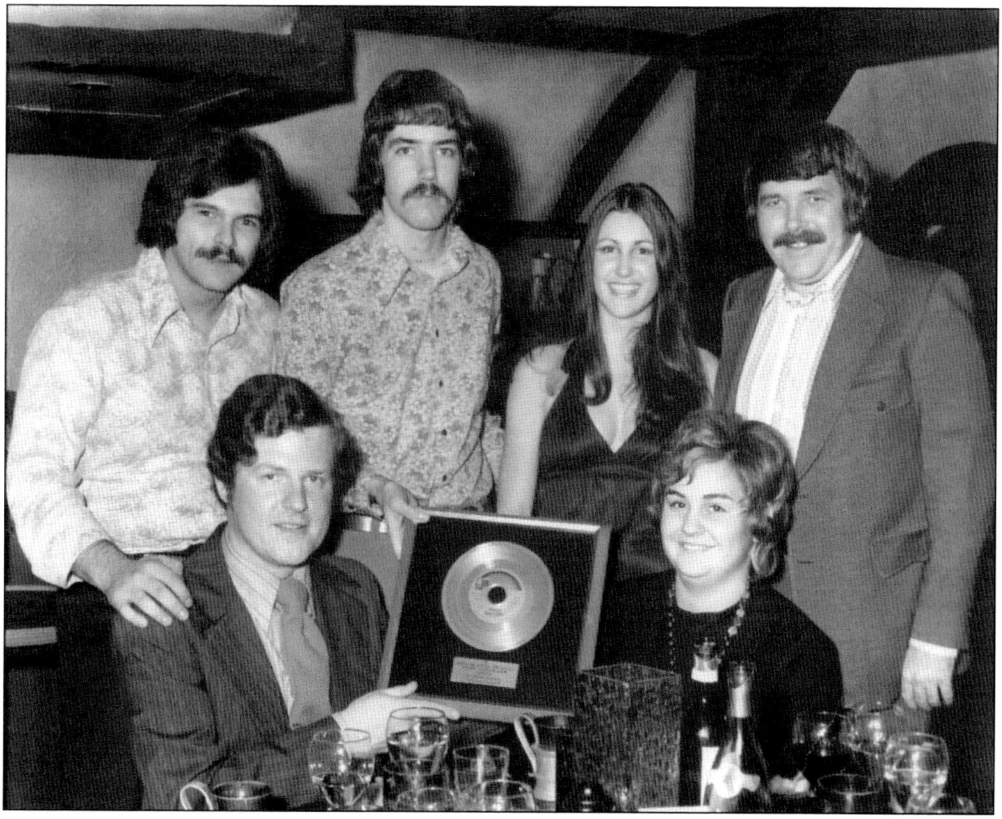

A gold record from the RIAA, the Recording Industry Association of America, was an award given to a station for being the first to recognize and play a song that because of its airing would be a hit nationwide. Seated wearing a tie and holding the gold record is WCOL music director Bryan McIntyre. Standing at right is DJ Bob Harrington, who probably was the first to play the record. This photograph was taken in 1972. (Bryan McIntyre.)

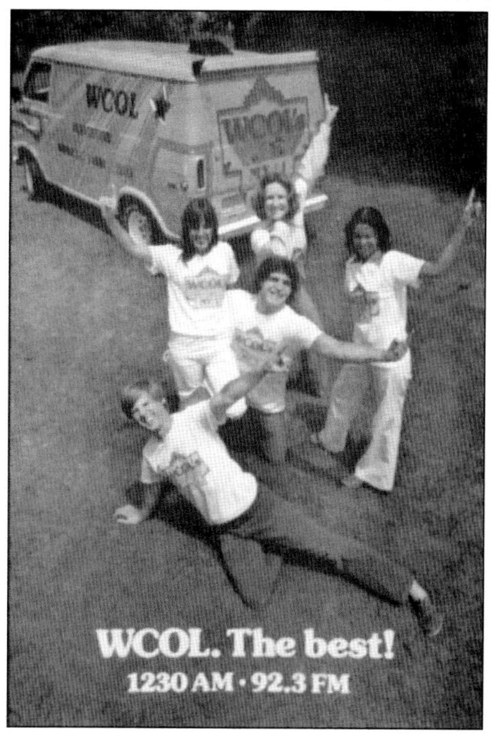

A typical publicity shot of WCOL on-air DJs in the mid-1970s includes the WCOL truck. Today, all manner of vehicles are branded with the logo of the station, and they are usually parked at the entrance to a concert or sporting event. The goal is to keep the brand in front of the radio listener. (Author's collection.)

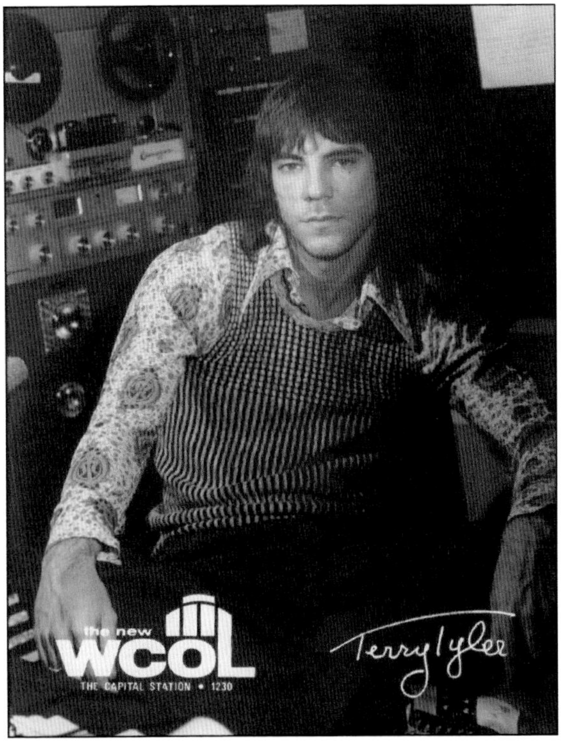

All of the on-air talent had their pictures taken for newspapers, fans, and overall promotion, including AM DJ Terry Tyler, seen here. WCOL had a full-time photographer on staff who also ran an offset press for producing the considerable print output of the station. Print promotion for radio was always important for keeping the brand in front of the public. (Neal Shapiro.)

As one of the best-known radio and television personalities in Columbus, Spook Beckman worked for practically every radio and television station in Columbus. Here is Spook on the air at WCOL AM in the 1970s. Columbus loved Spook. He was community-oriented and used radio to help the less fortunate. (Tracy Beckman.)

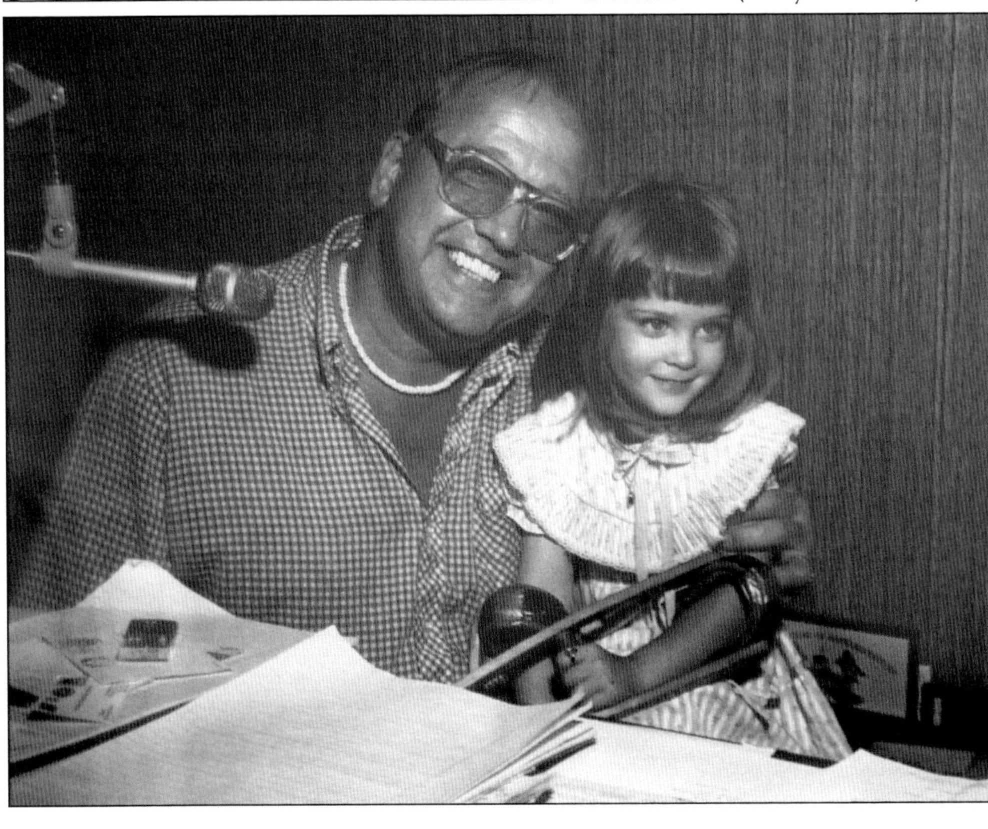

This is classic Spook Beckman, riding an elephant in a Columbus parade. During his long radio and television career in Columbus, Spook was one of the major entertainers in the market, beginning at WTVN in the 1950s and ending his career at WCOL AM in the 1970s. (Tracy Beckman.)

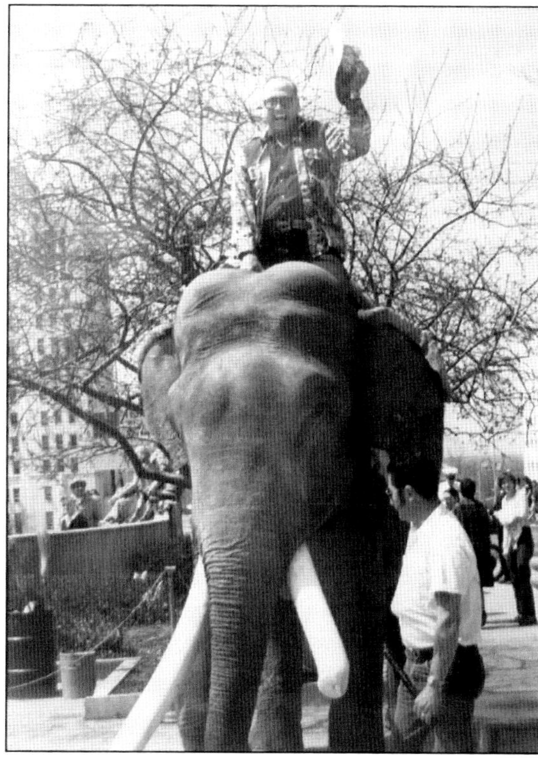

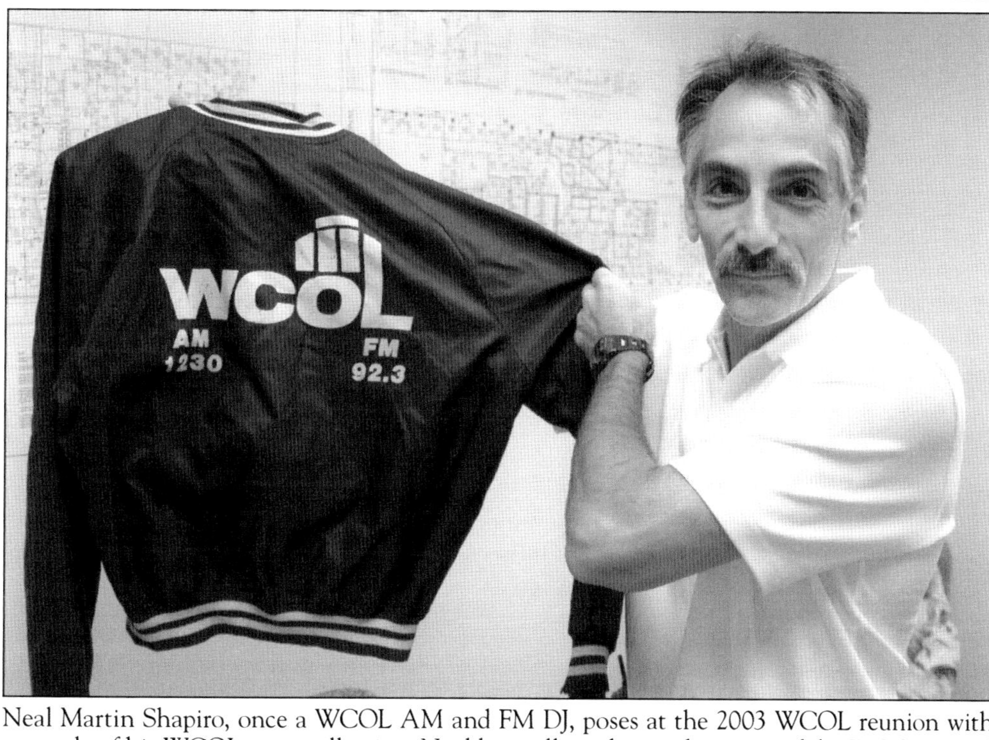

Neal Martin Shapiro, once a WCOL AM and FM DJ, poses at the 2003 WCOL reunion with a sample of his WCOL-wear collection. Neal has collected a good portion of the WCOL visual history and has been important in the production of this book. (Author photograph.)

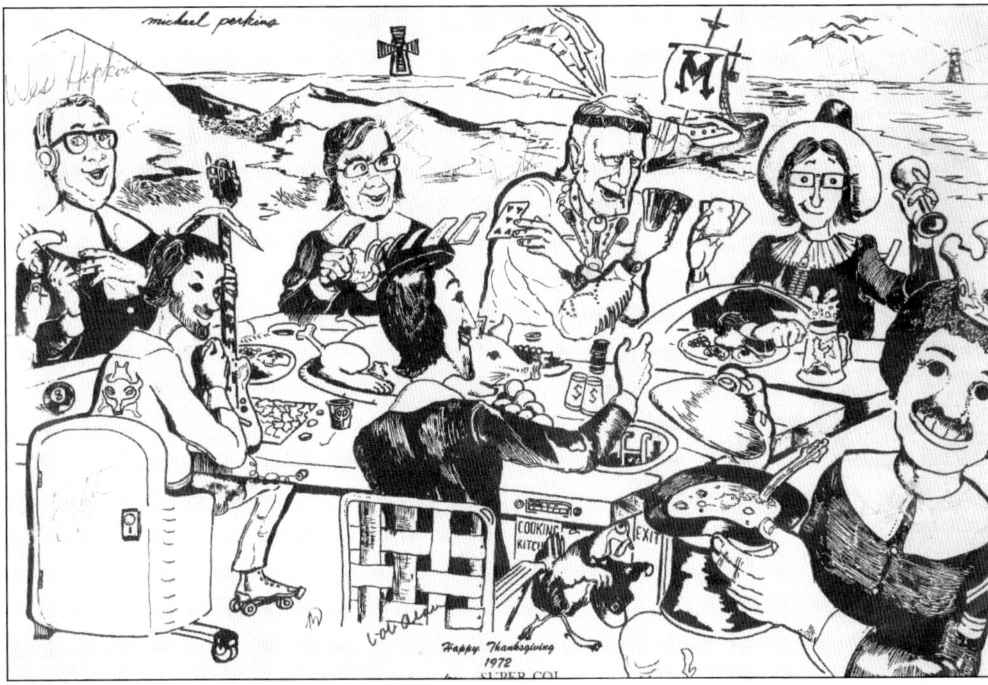

This is an original illustration by WCOL-FM morning DJ Mike Perkins. This is a tribute to Thanksgiving in 1972 featuring the WCOL-AM DJs, and their cartoon representations are all signed by the DJs themselves. From left to right are (first row) Terry Tyler, Bob Alan, and Duke Hobson; (second row) Wes Hopkins, Lou Henry, Jim Davis, and Dave Roberts. (Neal Shapiro.)

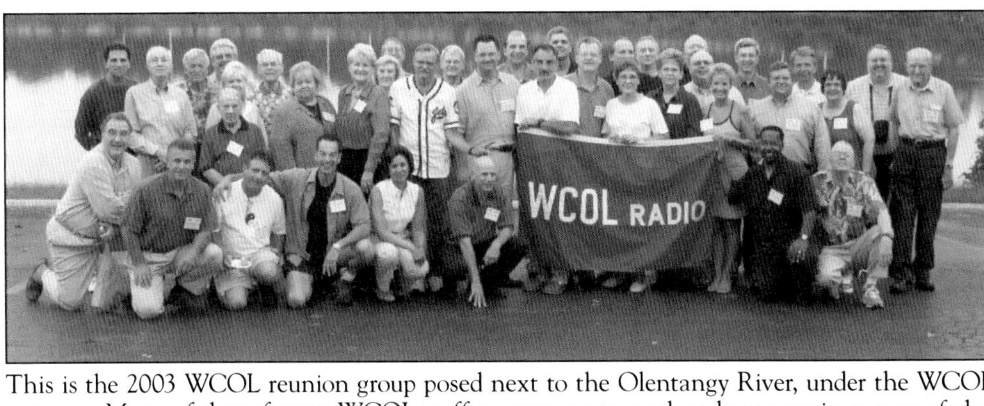

This is the 2003 WCOL reunion group posed next to the Olentangy River, under the WCOL antenna. Many of these former WCOL staffers went on to work at larger stations, some faded into obscurity, and a number have passed on since this event. What happened to WCOL-AM? In the later 1970s, the station moved toward adult contemporary. It flipped to news/talk, then oldies, and now carries a sports talk format as WYTS. (Author's collection.)

Six

The Rise of FM Changes Everything

Radio adapted as FM began its dominance in the 1970s. The audio fidelity of AM cannot be improved as a medium for high-quality music. WCOL spun off its FM to air progressive rock, a format often called "free form," or no format at all, as knowledgeable DJs played what they believed their listeners wanted to hear. The popularity of the highly structured Top 40 format once popular on AM was waning, and the new album music was now in stereo for those with an FM radio, soon the majority of the audience. Other stations emerged in the 1970s, notably WNCI-FM, music formats proliferated, and as the 1970s ended, news, talk, and sports kept AM afloat. WOSU-FM and WCBE moved from "educational" to National Public Radio. Once known as a source of "beautiful music" for discerning listeners, FM would go mainstream.

FM was a separate technology from AM with advantages that were now obvious. Radio stations were originally AM because everyone had an AM radio. But while the aural superiority of FM was demonstrated by Maj. Edwin Armstrong as early as the mid-1930s, broadcasters were not interested in changing the receiving standards of their very successful programming, which had been AM since the beginning. Such a standards conversion would make millions of radios obsolete. For this reason, FM would have to wait until the 1970s, when it would become the preferred set of channels. The broadcast engineers were always aware of the advantages of FM, but it was the owners that had to sell the airtime.

Into the 1980s and beyond, there was competition for audiences from television, movies, and finally the Internet. It can be said that the success of FM in the 1970s was the result of more and higher-quality music in stereo. The low fidelity of AM and its limited nighttime signal was just not good enough to retain those listeners who had FM in their cars and homes. The late 1960s also introduced cultural changes, with much of the accompanying new music protesting the Vietnam War, parents, schools, politicians, capitalism, and authority in general. WCOL-FM was the Columbus station that first spoke to this increasingly liberal, educated, and influential audience. But while the 1970s belonged to FM, it really began in 1940 for Columbus. Just a few stations would take a chance in the 1940s.

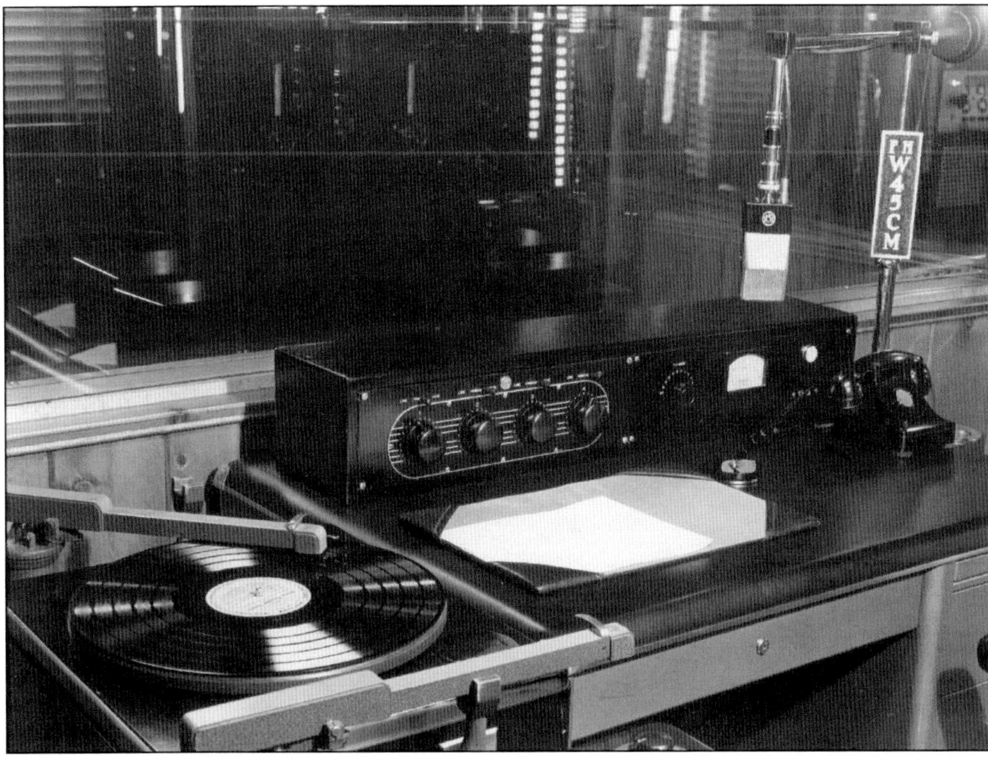

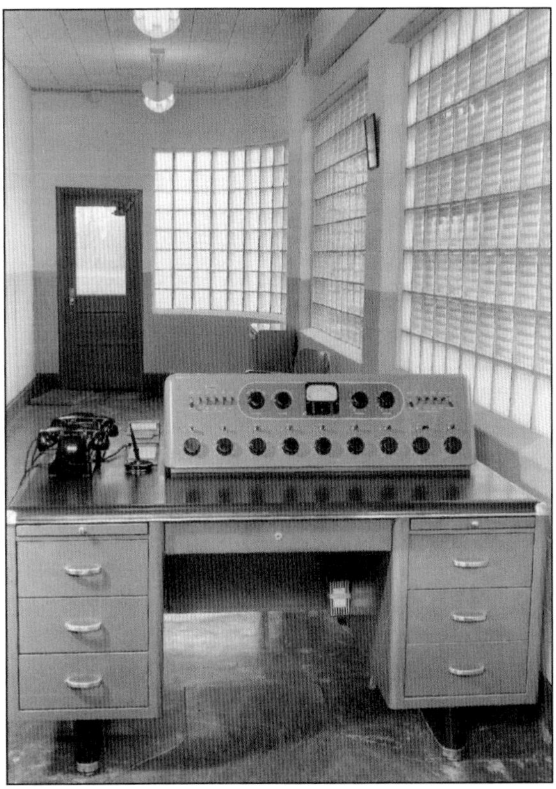

Only four FM stations were licensed to the Columbus radio market in the 1940s: WCLT-FM, WCOL-FM, WELD-FM (WBNS), and WOSU-FM. In 1940, WBNS had the first FM station in Ohio, licensed as W8XVH, an experimental call sign. After the war, it became W45CM. In this image, the control board of that first FM station is installed at the WBNS-AM transmitter building. (Greg Armstrong, Radio Ohio, WBNS.)

Pictured is a later WBNS-FM audio board. By 1941, the FCC had granted the experimental FM service of WBNS a power increase to 6,000 watts, and the FM was moved to the AM transmitter location. The programming consisted of CBS programs not carried on AM and music from the World Transcription Library. Some live programs were aired on FM, and these originated at the main WBNS studios. In a few years, the FM station received the call letters WELD. (Greg Armstrong, Radio Ohio, WBNS.)

Oddly, and due to a belief that FM would not survive and prosper, WELD-FM went off the air in 1953 but returned in 1957 as WBNS-FM to simulcast the AM programming. Its antenna and transmitter site is with WBNS-TV, Channel 10. (Greg Armstrong, Radio Ohio, WBNS.)

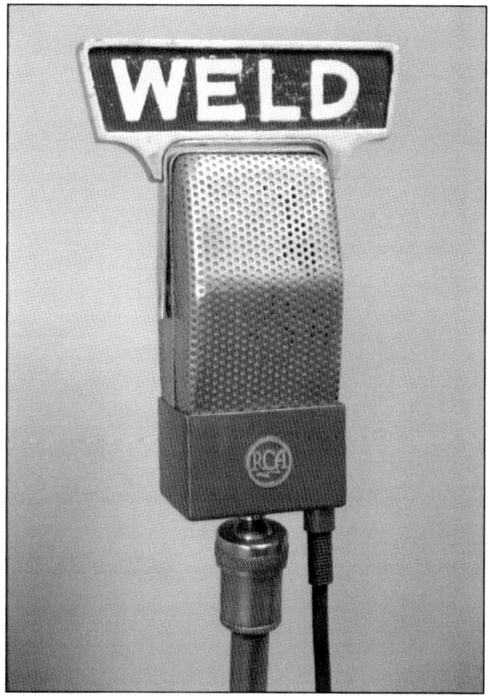

Suburban WCLT did just the opposite of most stations: it went on the air first with an FM signal and did not get the AM license until three years later. This is its basic FM control room in 1947. The large record on the turntable is a 16-inch transcription disc, thus the 1940s phrase "This program is transcribed." (Douglas Pricer, WCLT.)

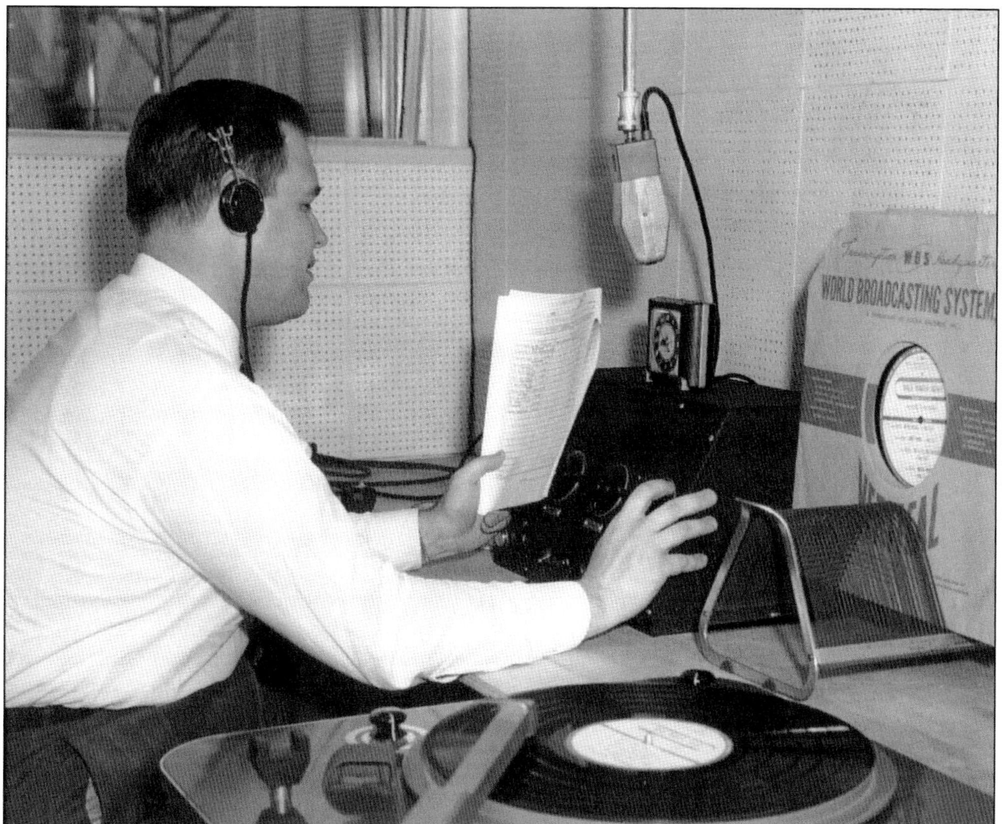

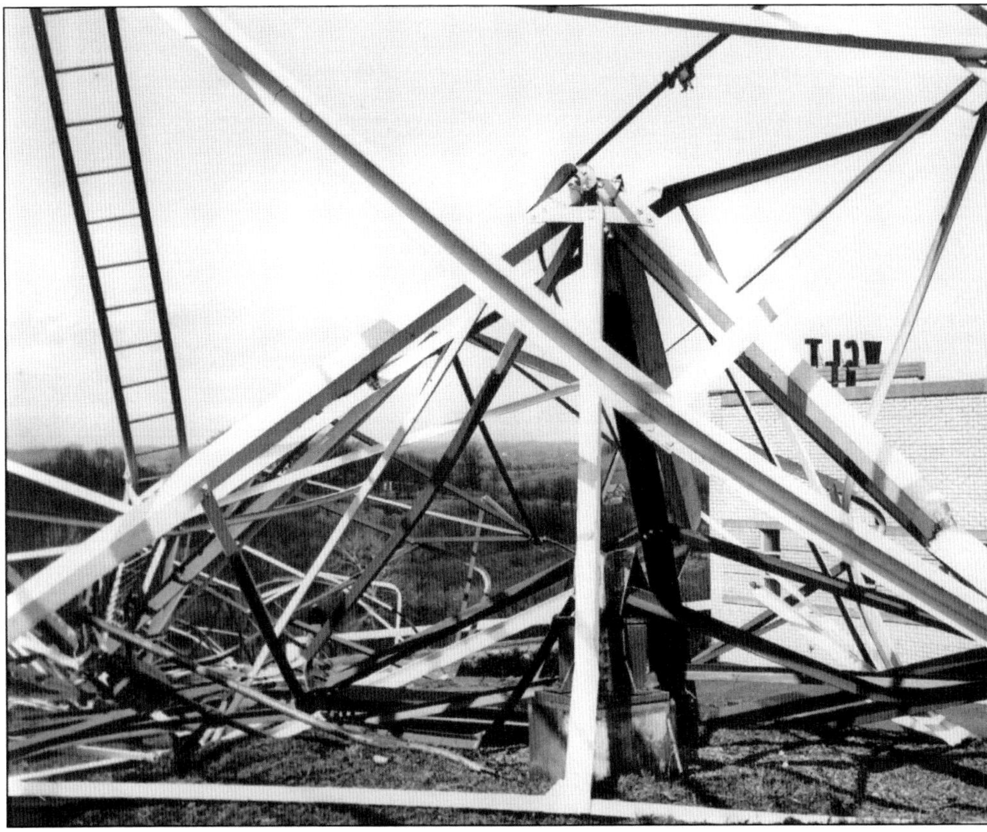

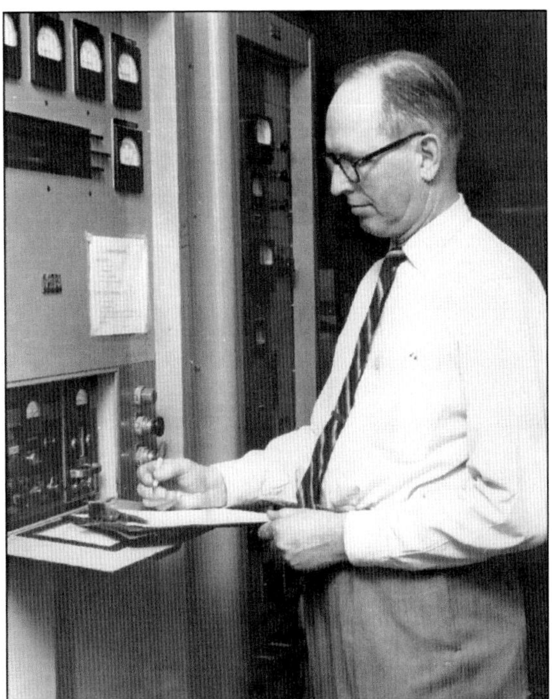

WCLT-FM went on the air in July 1947 with 8,500 watts of power. Because FM receivers were so scarce, the station owner, the *Newark Advocate* newspaper, offered free print advertising to stores that would sell FM radios. After just a few years on the air, a powerful storm knocked down the tower. No one was injured. (Douglas Pricer, WCLT.)

Here is Ben Windle, WCLT chief engineer, monitoring the FM transmitter. Under his direction, the FM antenna was unbolted from the top of the fallen tower and strapped to the chimney on the roof of the station. WCLT was back on the air in six hours. (Douglas Pricer, WCLT.)

WOSU-FM signed on in 1949 and joined WCOL, WCLT, and WELD with the mysterious and seldom-listened-to new high-fidelity service. For the first several decades, WCOL and WOSU carried a single program on both AM and FM transmitters. In this image, one of the very first voices on the new WOSU FM, Dana Vibberts, is broadcasting his program *Folk Trails*. (Thomas Rieland, WOSU Public Media.)

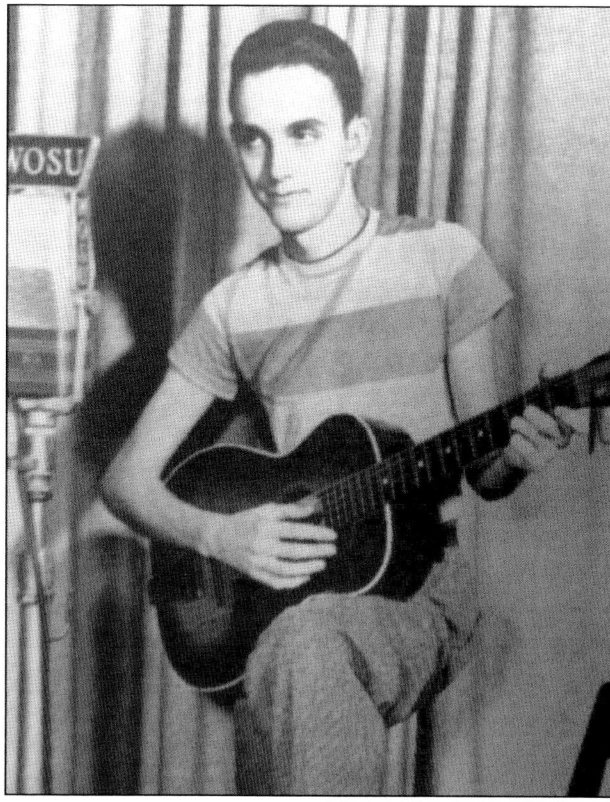

WOSU-AM and FM have programmed separately since 1968, the AM carrying news and talk while the FM carries National Public Radio and classical music. In this 1981 image are Jody Williams, midday host, and John McGrody, classical music programmer. (Thomas Rieland, WOSU Public Media.)

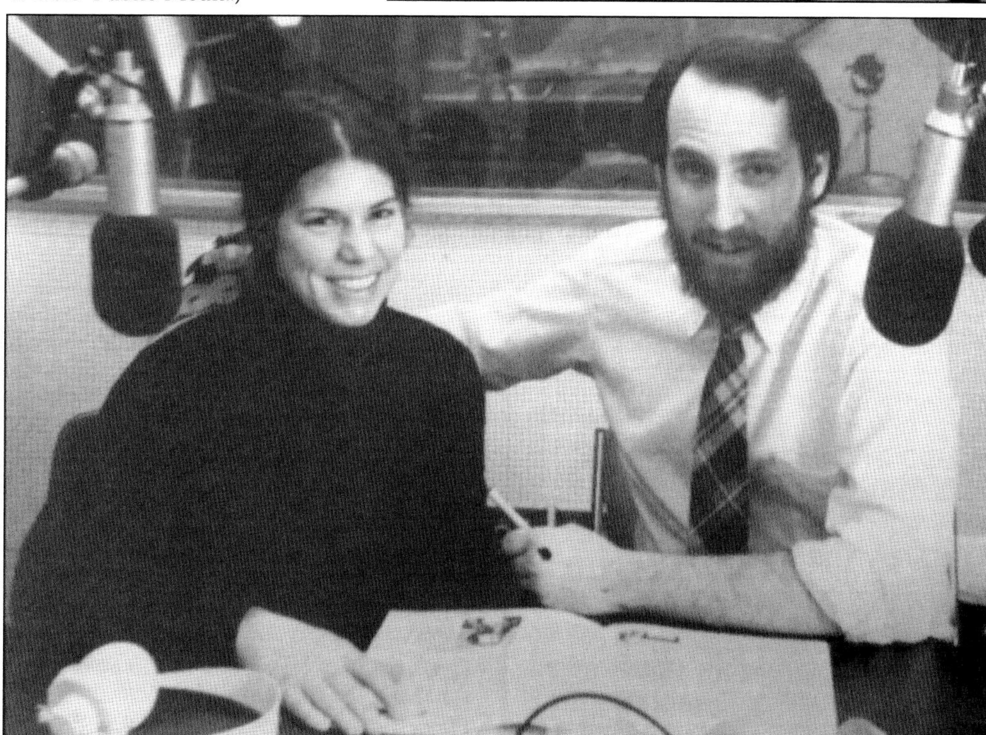

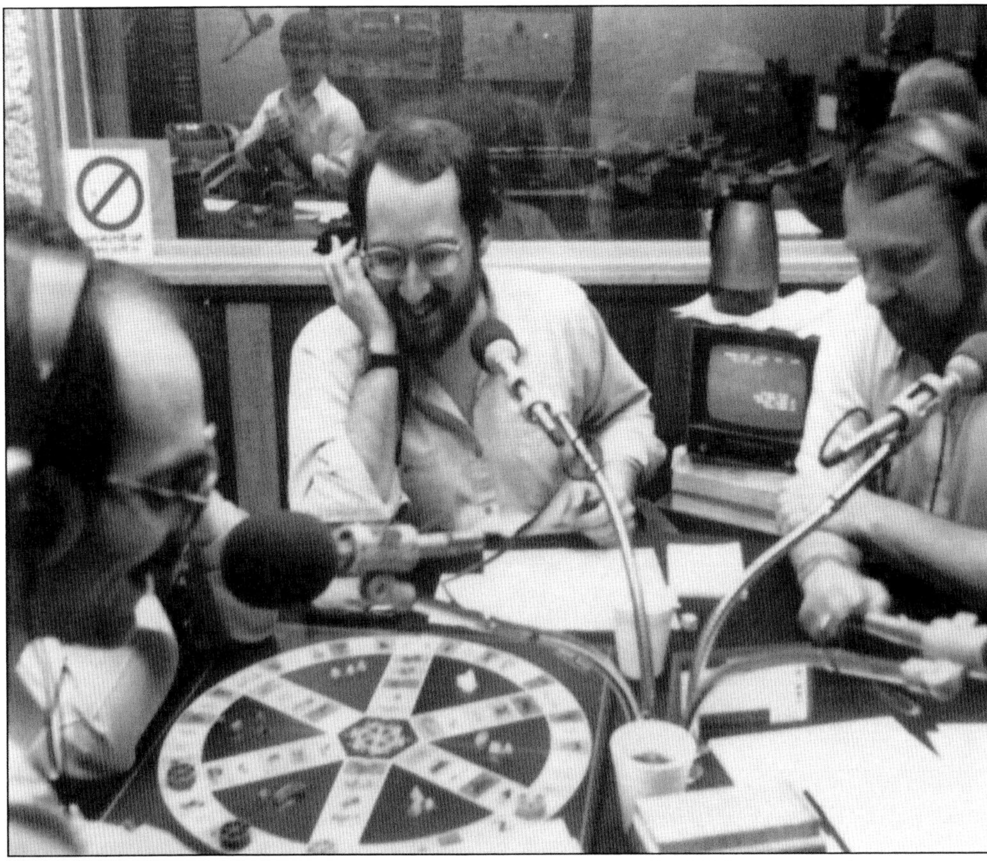

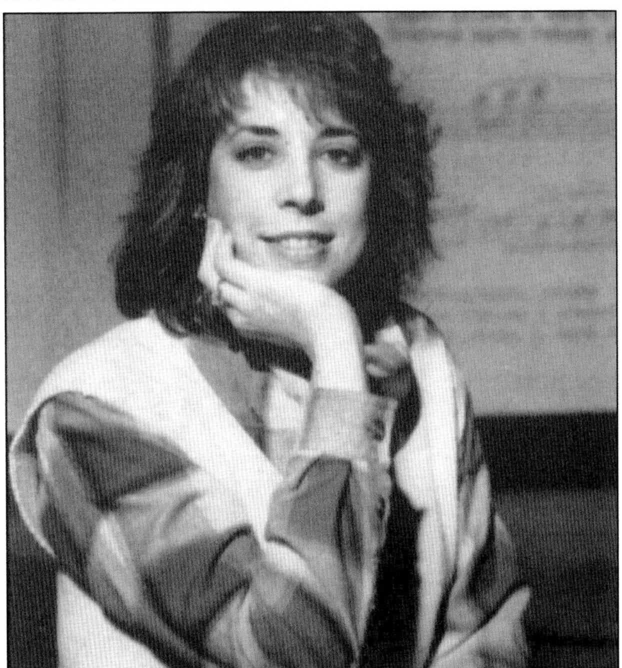

In 1984, an on-air fundraiser called the Trivial Pursuit Fest raised over $90,000 for WOSU-AM and FM. The high-quality public stations like WOSU always find new ways to engage their audience. (Thomas Rieland, WOSU Public Media.)

WOSU-FM music director and station supervisor Beverly Ervine is pictured in 1986. By then, the WOSU stations were totally separate, and in 2011, the AM station was sold to a religious broadcaster. The FM added an all-classical station now called WOSA, leaving the original WOSU-FM as primarily NPR. (Thomas Rieland, WOSU Public Media.)

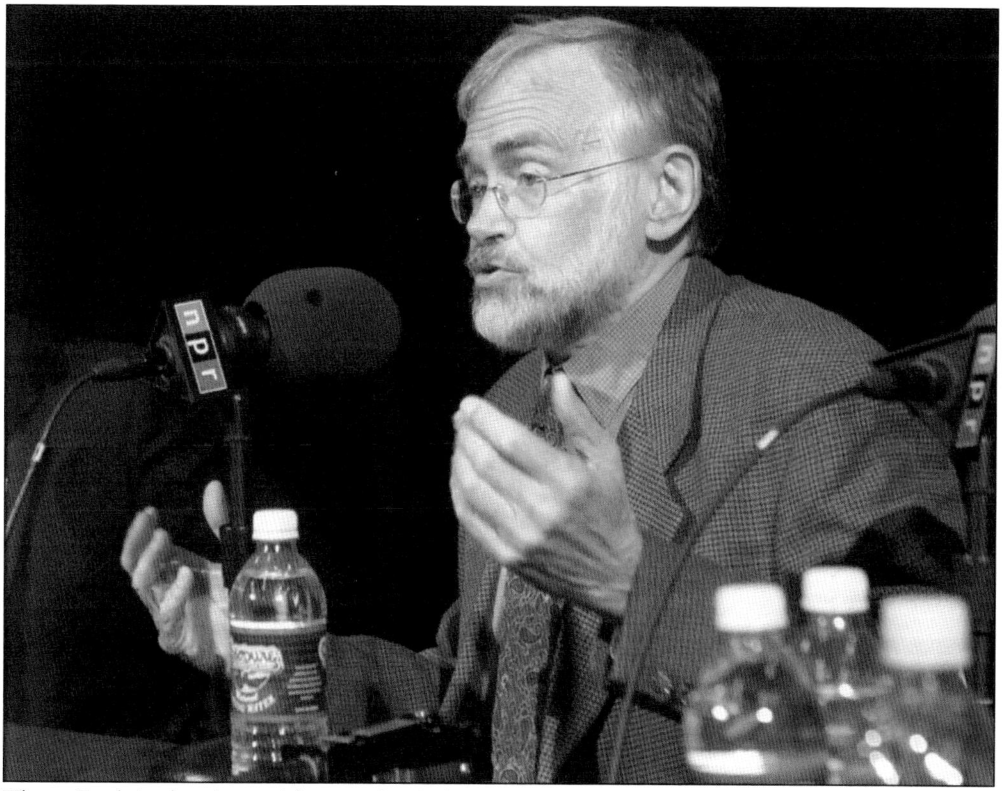

This is Fred Andrie, host of the popular WOSU-FM Open Line radio talk show for three decades, originally a four-hour show. (Thomas Rieland, WOSU Public Media.)

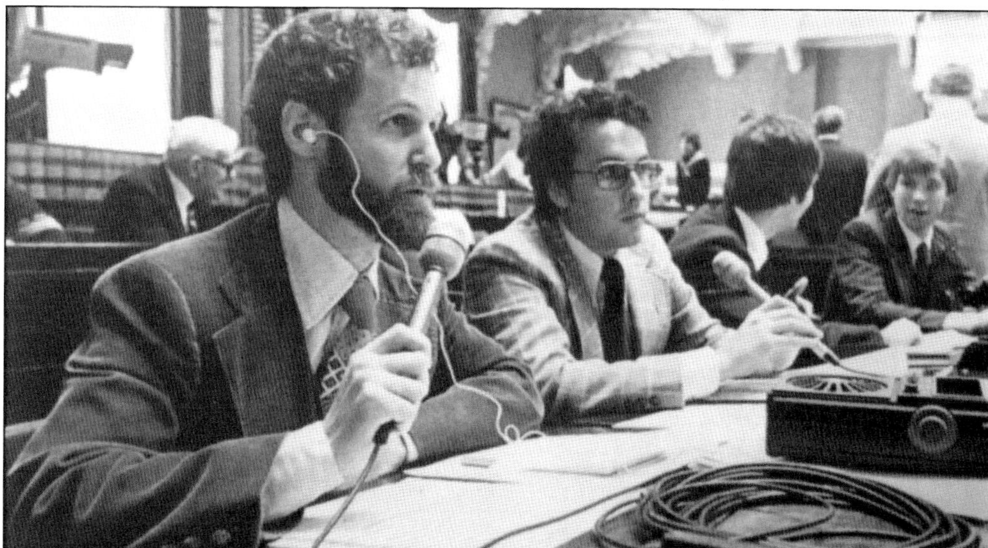

In 1979, WOSU covers the Ohio governor's state of the state address. This is reported live by news reporters Bill Cohen and Larry Hudson. In the 1970s, the WOSU-AM signal began an all-news format, leaving the FM for classical music and other programming. (Thomas Rieland, WOSU Public Media.)

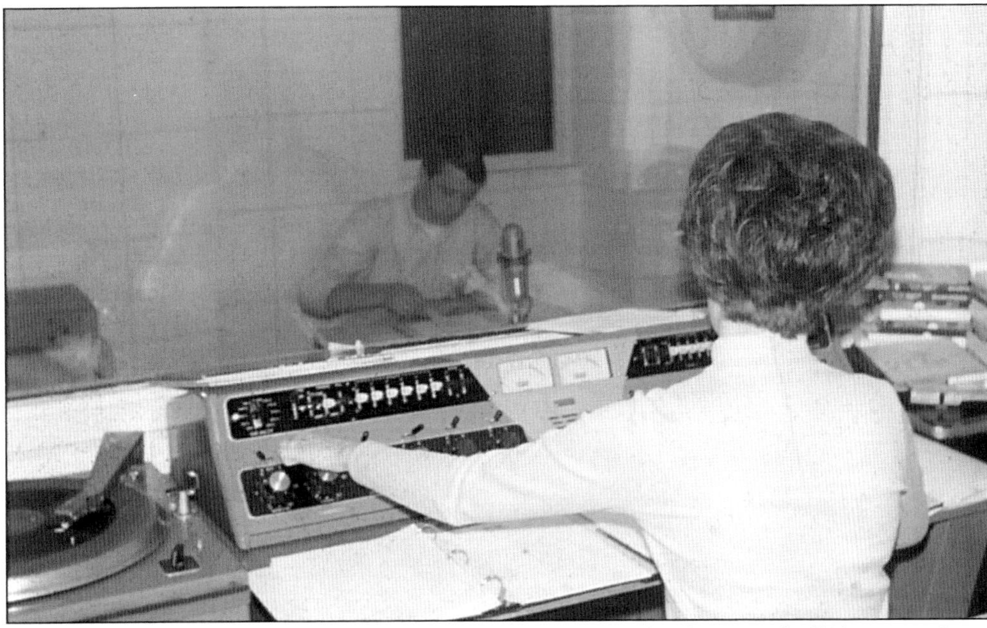

WCBE began in 1956 as the educational FM station of the Columbus Board of Education. It was designed to broadcast into classrooms in the school district, an early gambit in educational radio for K-12 students. Then, classrooms were equipped with FM radios. Today, it is an important Columbus NPR and eclectic music station, a community voice, but still licensed to the Columbus Board of Education. (Dan Mushalko, WCBE.)

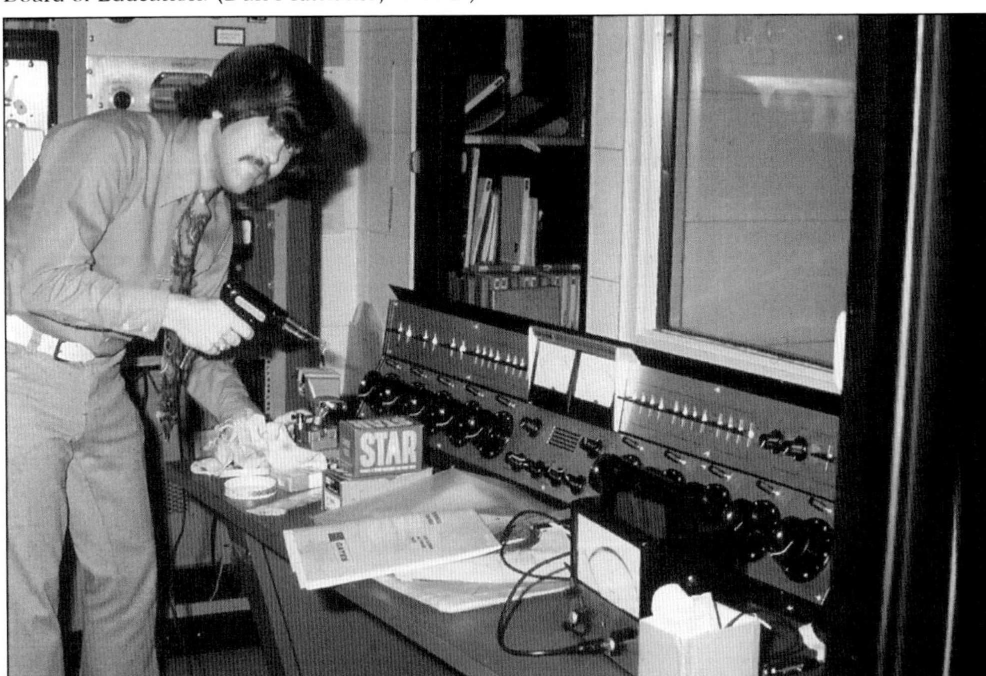

The station signed on with a message from school superintendent Harold Eibling. The director of the station was John Sittig. Here, an engineer works on part of the audio equipment, probably in the 1960s. (Dan Mushalko, WCBE.)

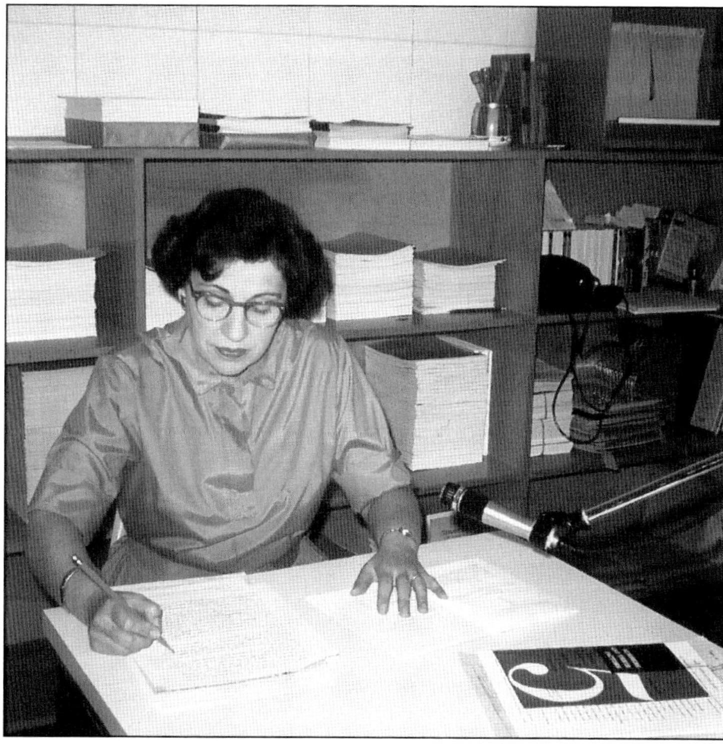

Here is a teacher presenting an audio lecture. When the station first went on the air, it was only for an hour a day, and sample programs included *Adventures in Research* for seventh through ninth grades and *Our Neighbors*, interviews with students from different countries. (Dan Mushalko, WCBE.)

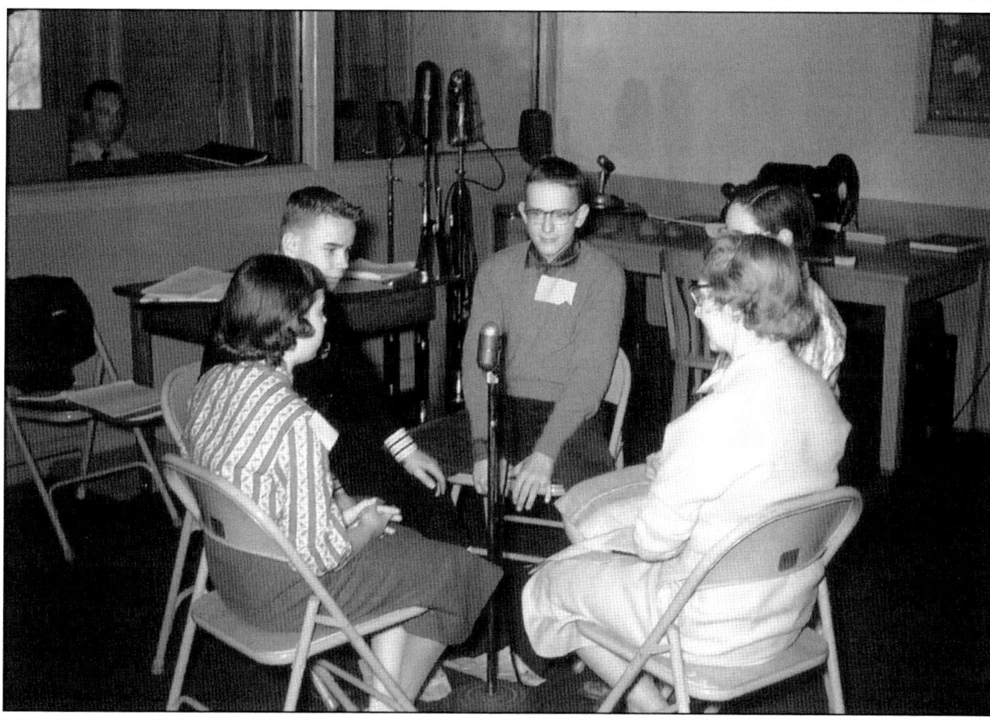

This is a typical class involved in a radio lecture. Other programs included *Music Can Be Fun*, *The Ohio Story*, and *Stories about Columbus*. As with early educational film and slides, radio in 1956 was a novel way to deliver knowledge to large groups of students. (Dan Mushalko, WCBE.)

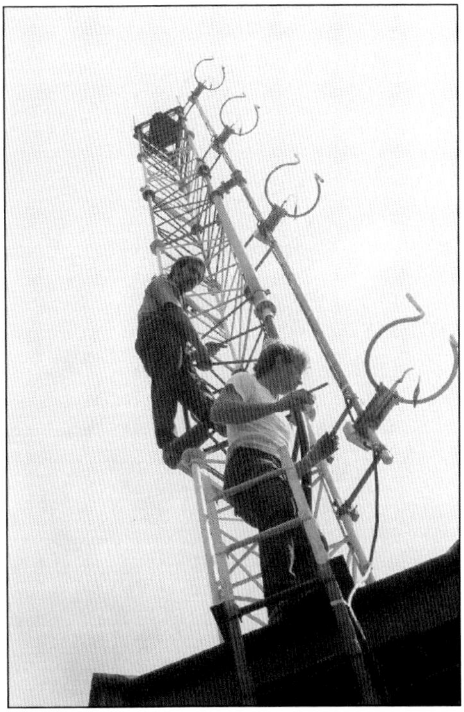

The 1950s news headline "Parents Soon May 'Tune in' City Schools" suggested that parents anywhere could listen to the same lectures as their children and thus know what they were learning. The 3,000-watt signal was beamed from the top of the Leveque-Lincoln Tower. The first transmitter used at WCBE was donated by the WBNS stations. (Dan Mushalko, WCBE.)

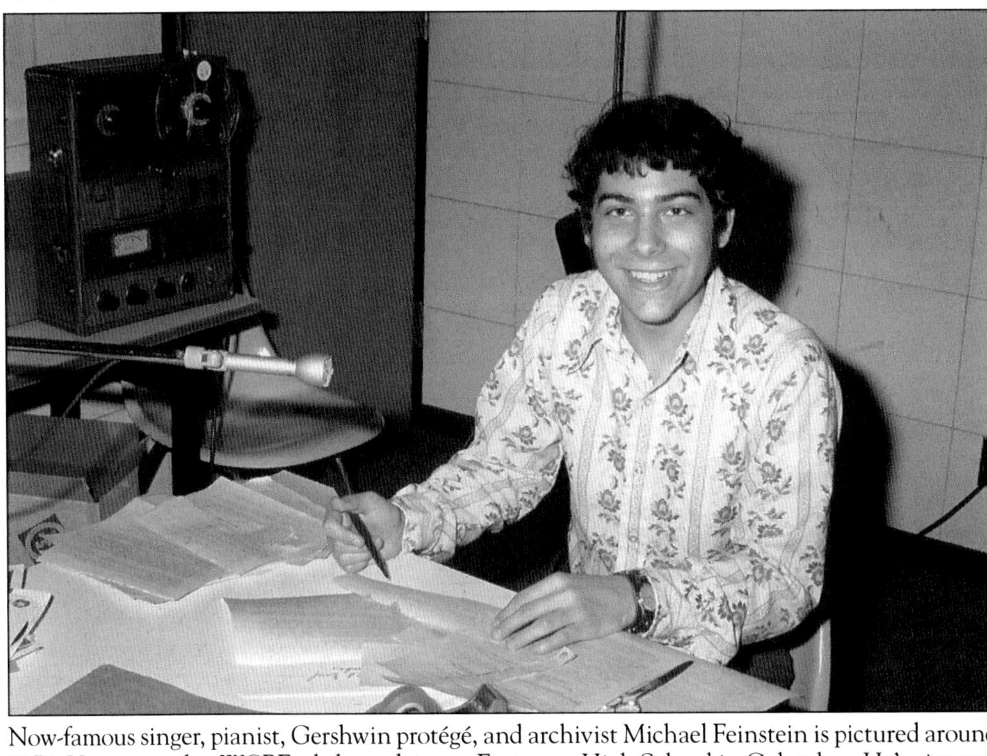

Now-famous singer, pianist, Gershwin protégé, and archivist Michael Feinstein is pictured around 1971. He interned at WCBE while studying at Eastmoor High School in Columbus. He's pictured in the station's old facilities in the basement of Columbus City Schools headquarters at 270 East State Street. (Dan Mushalko, WCBE.)

He called himself "Bill Moss, the boss with the red hot sauce" in his WVKO days, which was most of the 1960s and the first half of the 1970s. But unlike many who began and ended their careers in radio, Moss became a politician. He was restless. He was passionate about serving his community. In this 1968 photograph he enters the Chest X-Ray cruiser, one of WVKO's public service efforts. (The Columbus Metropolitan Library.)

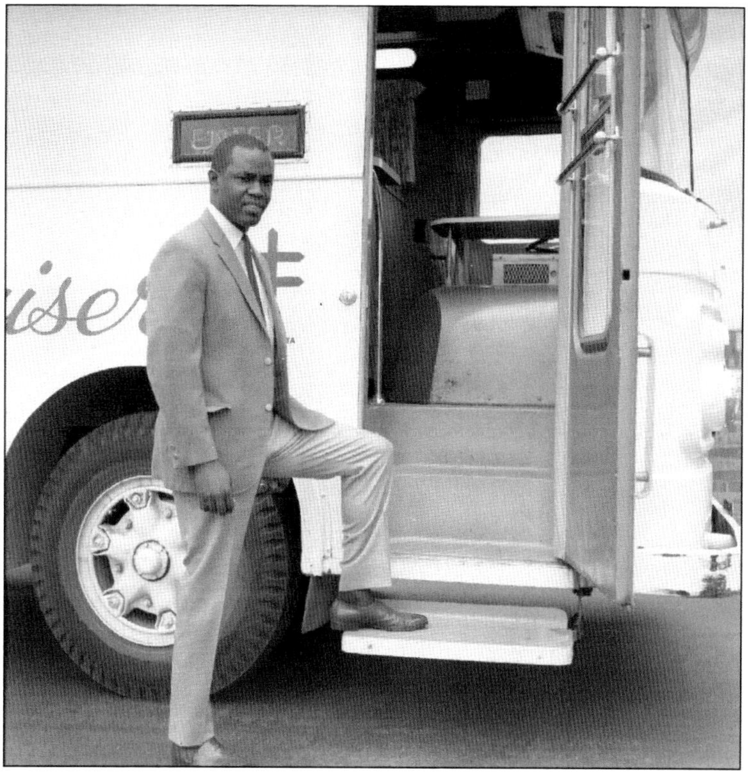

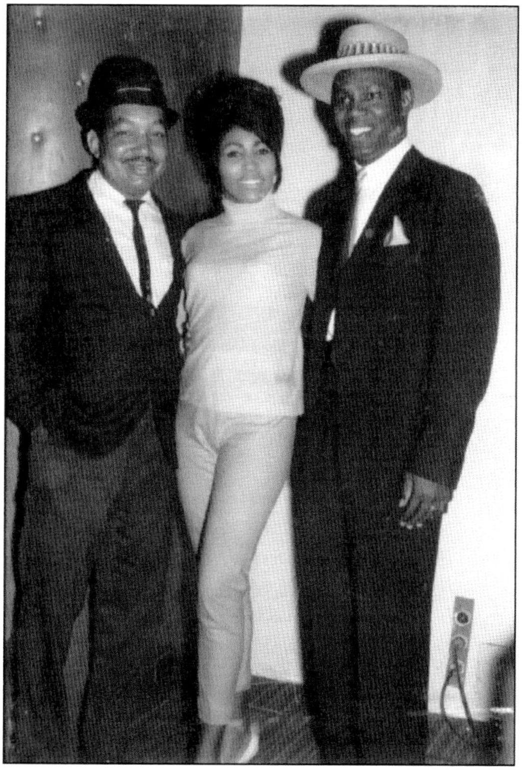

Picturd in 1964 from left to right are WVKO DJ Eddie Castleberry, singer Tina Turner, and Bill Moss. Music groups wanted their records played on the radio, and they were more than happy to appear in person. (The Columbus Metropolitan Library.)

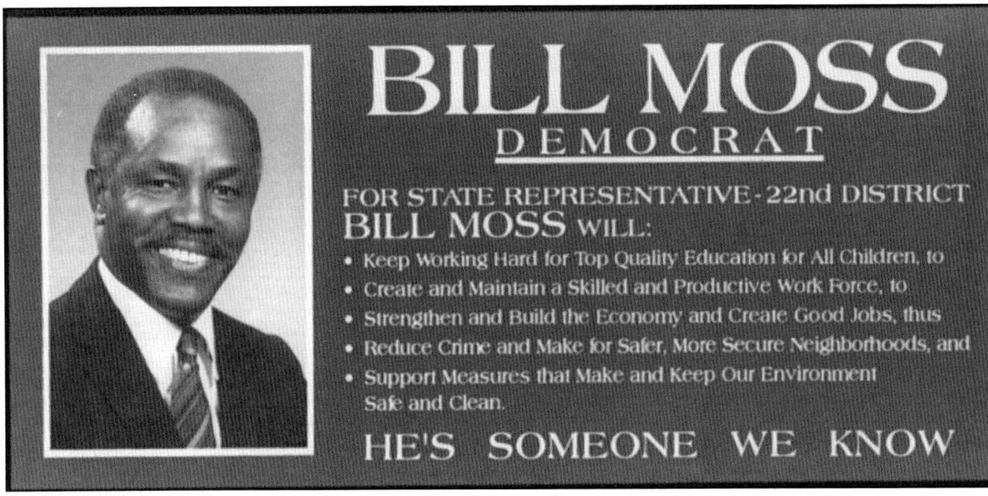

In this campaign flyer, Moss promises to "Keep working hard for education, create good jobs, reduce crime, and support measures that keep our environment safe and clean." Moss cared about Columbus and ran for many positions where he could help his community. He was most effective as a member of the Columbus School Board. (The Columbus Metropolitan Library.)

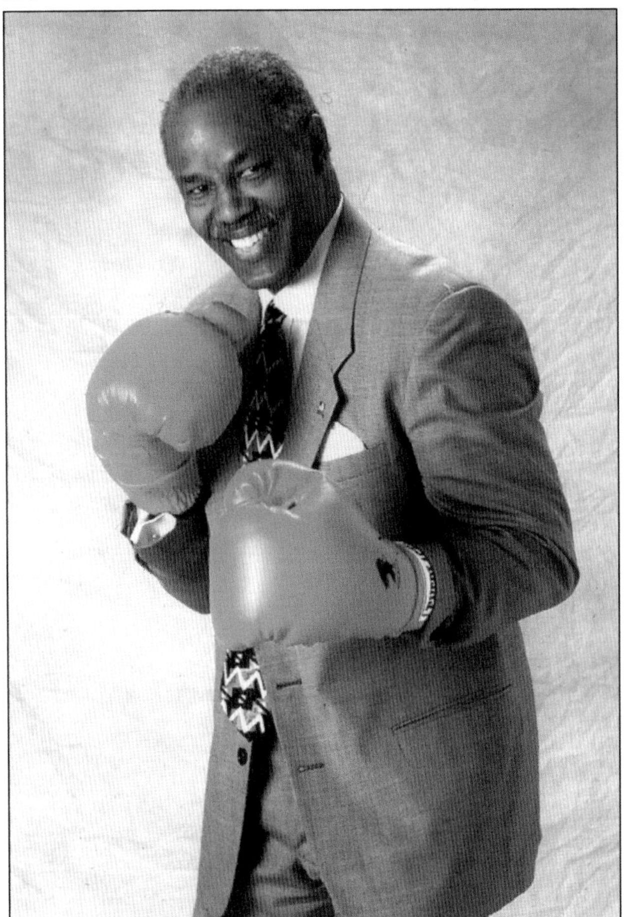

This is what DJ, recording artist, and politician Bill Moss would like to have people remember about him: he was always fighting for citizens at the local school board, for his community, his city, his state, and for his thousands of WVKO listeners. (The Columbus Metropolitan Library.)

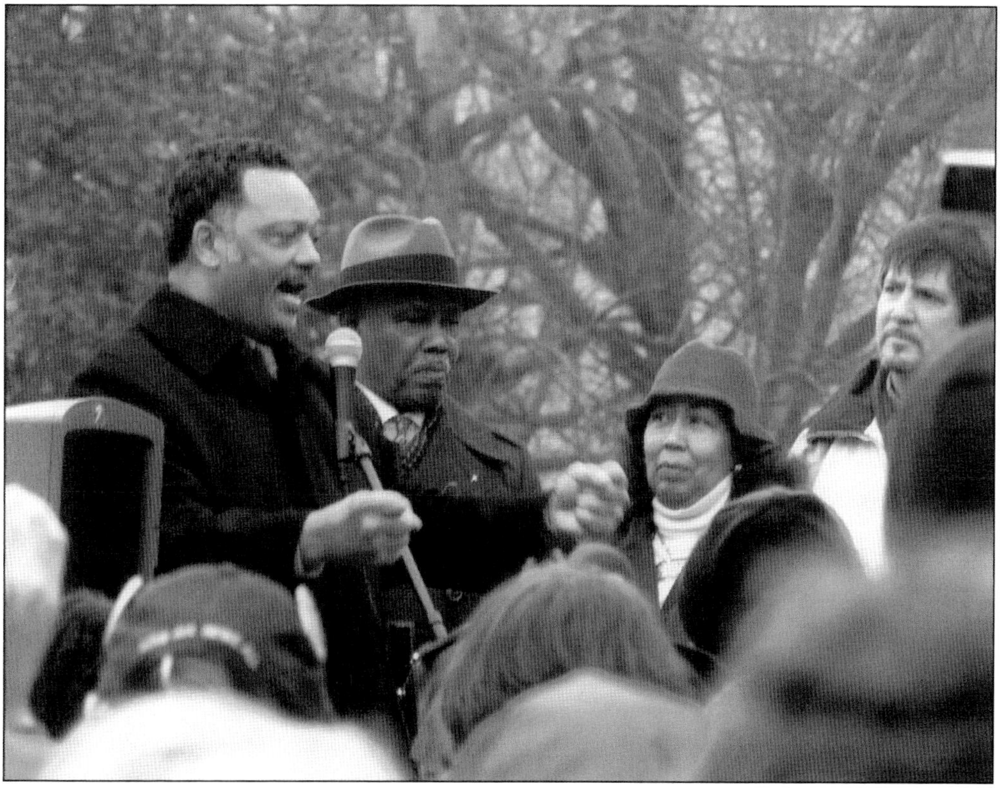

A year before his death in 2005, Moss is seen at an address with the Reverend Jesse Jackson several years after Jackson's unsuccessful run for president. Moss campaigned in Ohio for Eugene McCarthy and was a delegate for Jerry Brown during his presidential campaign. (The Columbus Metropolitan Library.)

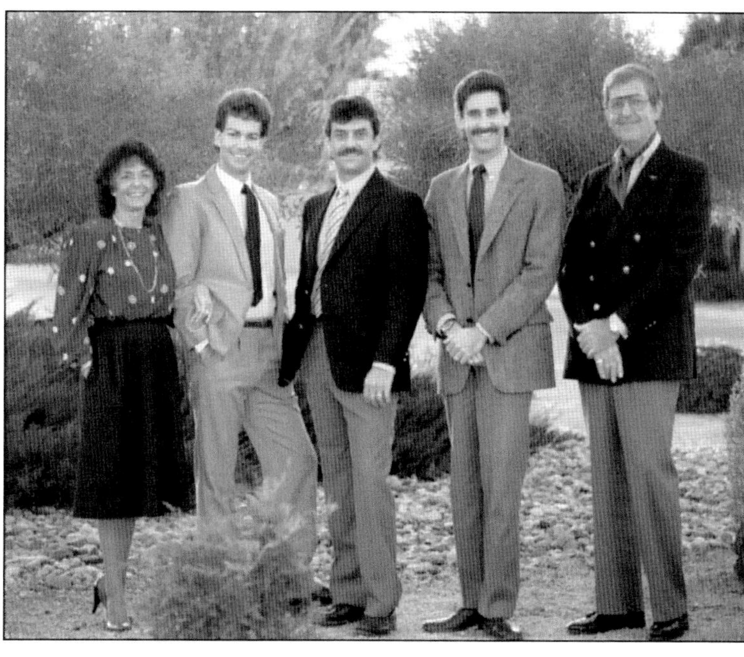

It must be something in the water, but these three young men from the Columbus suburb of Upper Arlington would all begin their radio careers in Columbus, and all were successful. From left to right, Steve, Bruce, and John Sinton all started at WCOL. (Sinton brothers.)

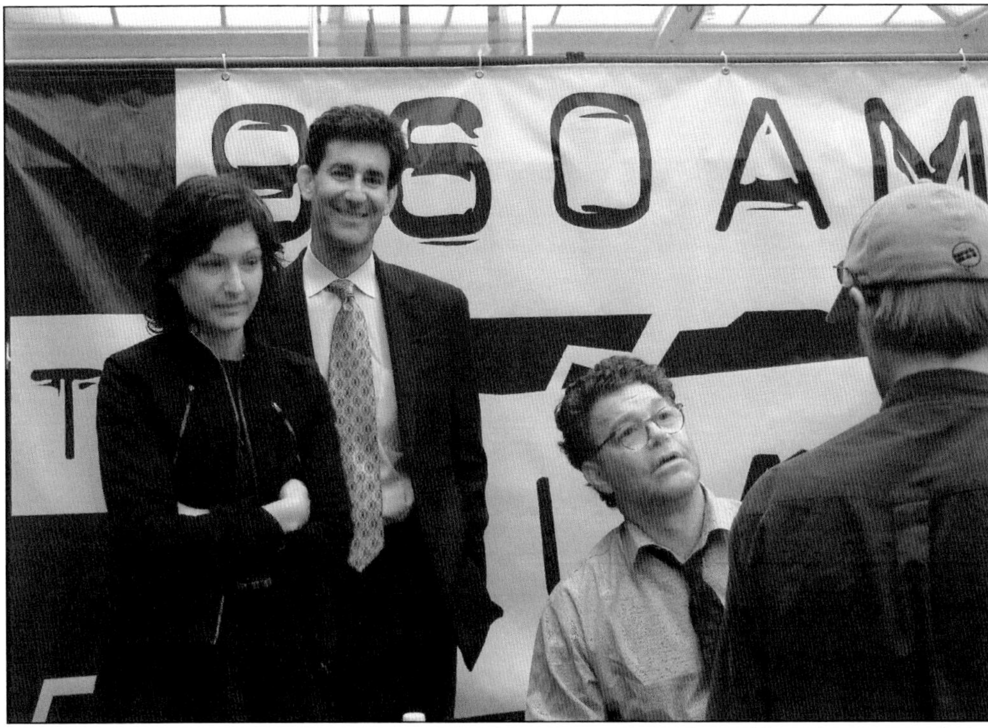

John Sinton, standing, wearing a tie, founded the progressive syndicated broadcast network Air America. This was to be a liberal alternative to the plethora of right-wing talk shows on AM radio. One of its main talk hosts was Al Franken, seated in this image. Franken is a former *Saturday Night Live* comedian, now a US senator from Minnesota. (Sinton brothers.)

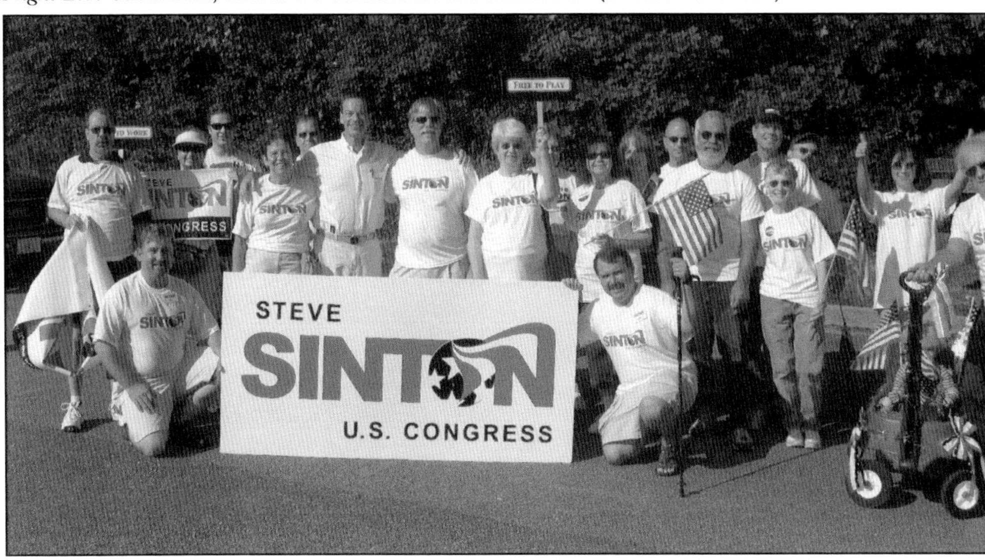

Steve Sinton ran for the US House of Representatives. A radio personality in Atlanta, Steve was asked to run for office by the local Democratic Party. This is a parade of his voters, designed like a radio promotion. He was running against a gerrymandered Republican incumbent, so one can guess the result. He is standing directly behind the "e" in "Steve." After the election, he went back to real life as a radio programmer. (Sinton brothers.)

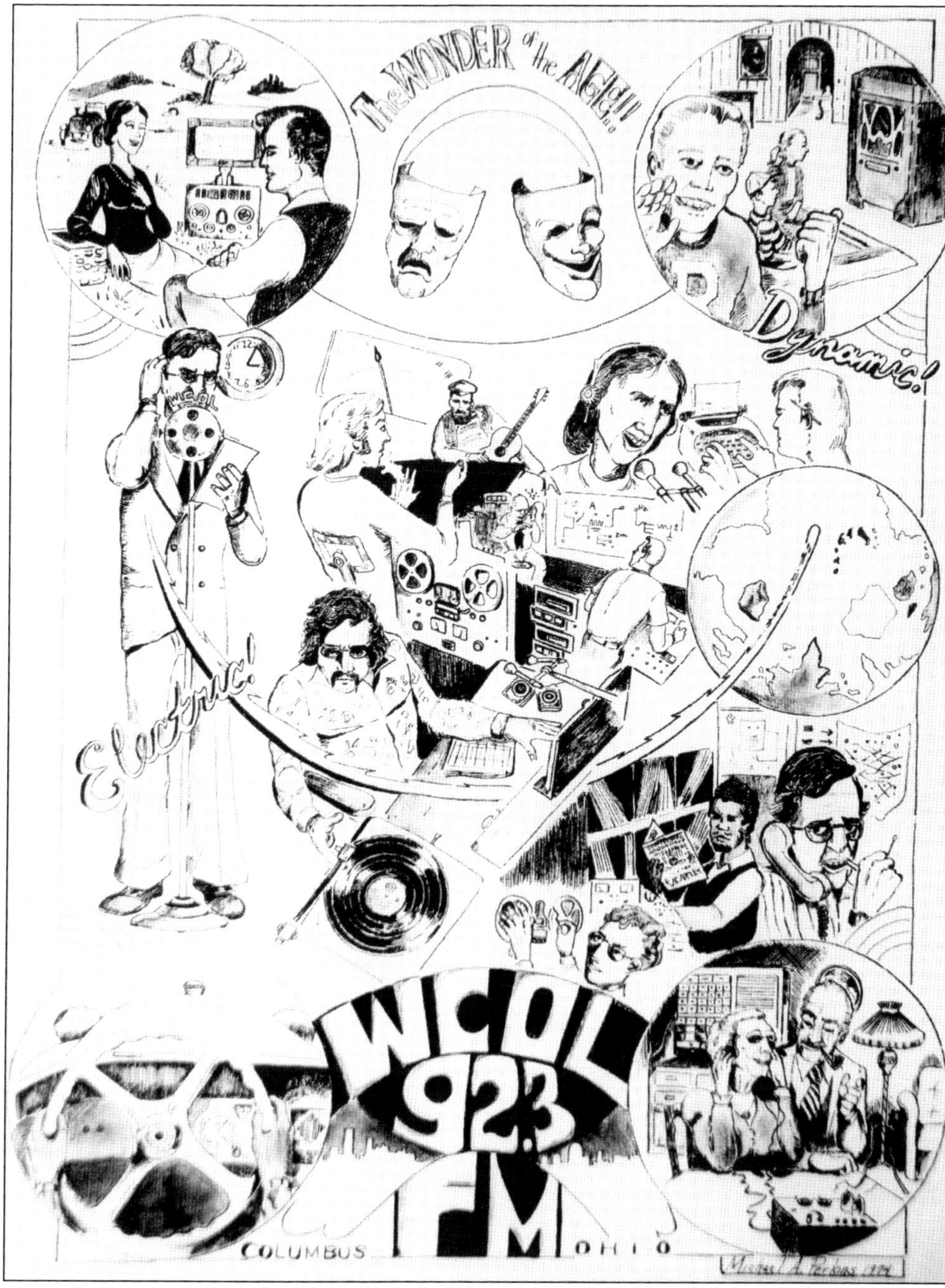

This is the history of broadcasting as imagined by WCOL-FM morning DJ and illustrator Mike Perkins in 1974. In the four corners of the image, clockwise, are a couple listening to a 1920s portable radio while seated at a picnic table; students listening to a 1930s console radio; grandma and grandpa with their crystal set; and a car radio from the 1920s. In the center of the image, the WCOL-FM DJs go about their daily work of broadcasting, surrounded by a collage of equipment. Perkins did a number of WCOL illustrations, many of which were used on the back of the Music Survey listings. He was a gifted illustrator who made many inspired drawings, all featuring a radio theme, to promote the WCOL-FM brand. (Neal Shapiro.)

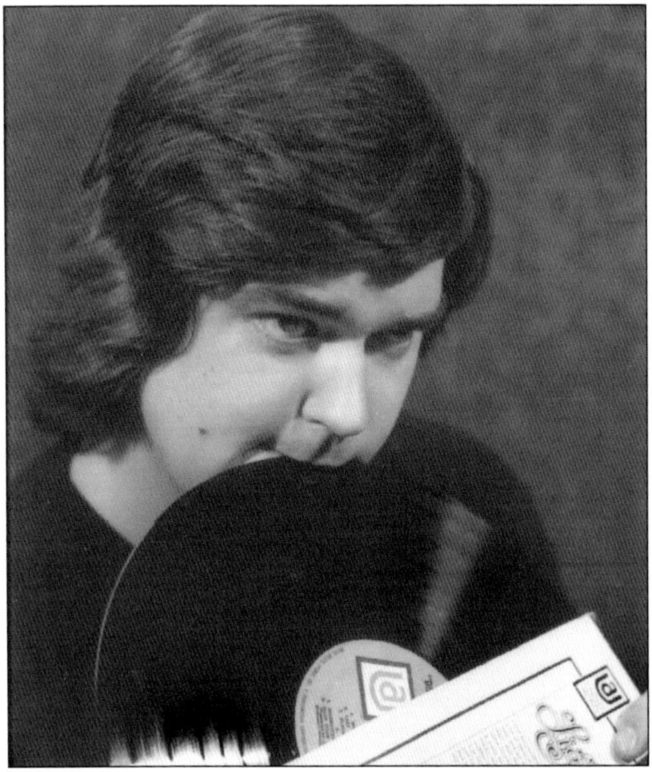

The artist of many WCOL-FM graphic stories, comics, and radio-themed posters was WCOL-FM "Morning Man" Mike Perkins. He is the creator of the "Wonder of the Age" radio history poster on the previous page. Perkins was the DJ from 6:00 to 10:00 a.m. in the 1970s. He is pictured doing a common DJ task: holding a record in his mouth while opening the cover with his two hands. (Neal Shapiro.)

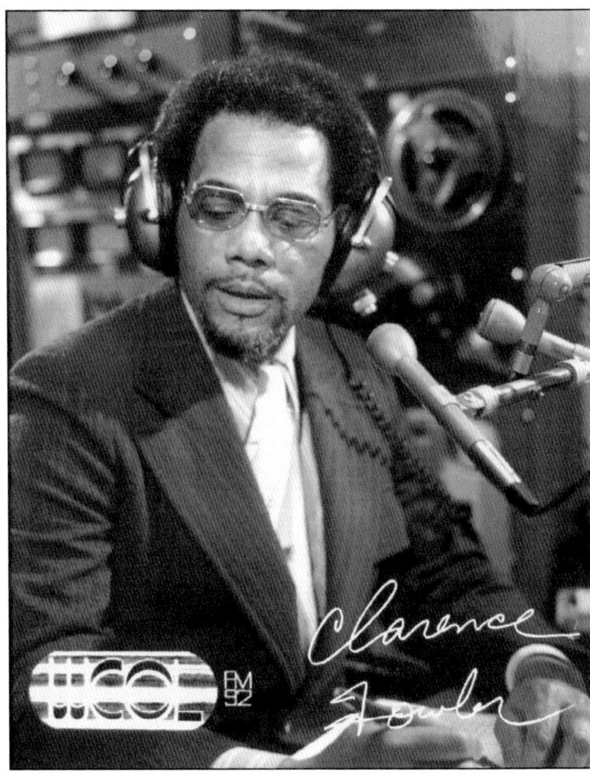

In the 1960s, Clarence Fowler began as the public service director of the WCOL stations, and he later became a part of the gospel programming on the FM station. Since the 1940s, WCOL-AM and FM carried the same programming, called a simulcast. In the later 1960s, the FCC required stations to split their programming and carry a different set of programs on FM. This was supposed to add diversity to radio. (Author's collection.)

When WCOL-FM became a separate station, its first format was 24 hours a day of gospel and religion. At that time, there were no other religious radio stations in the market. This is Bob Cunningham, one of the early FM gospel DJs. (Neal Shapiro.)

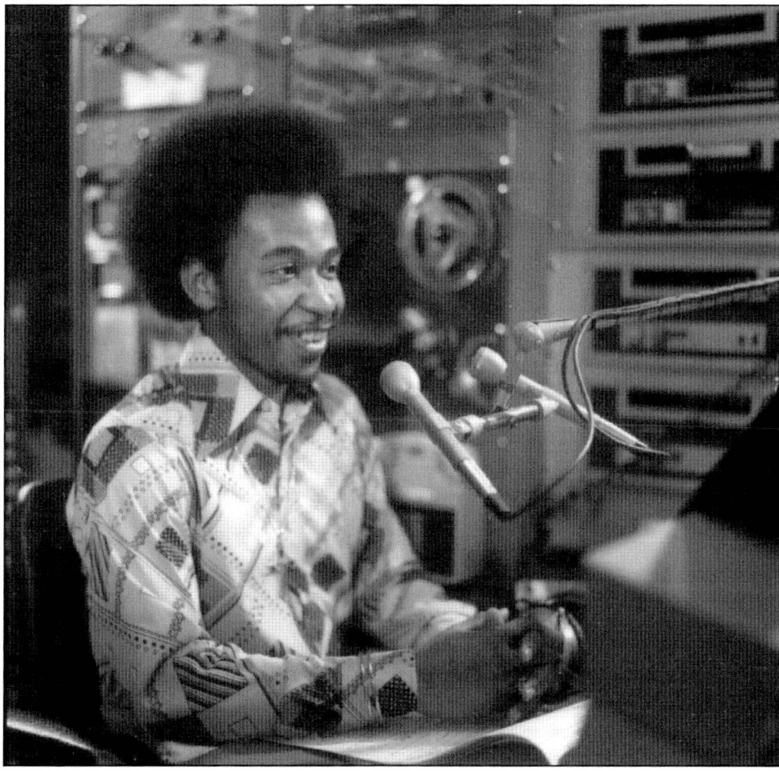

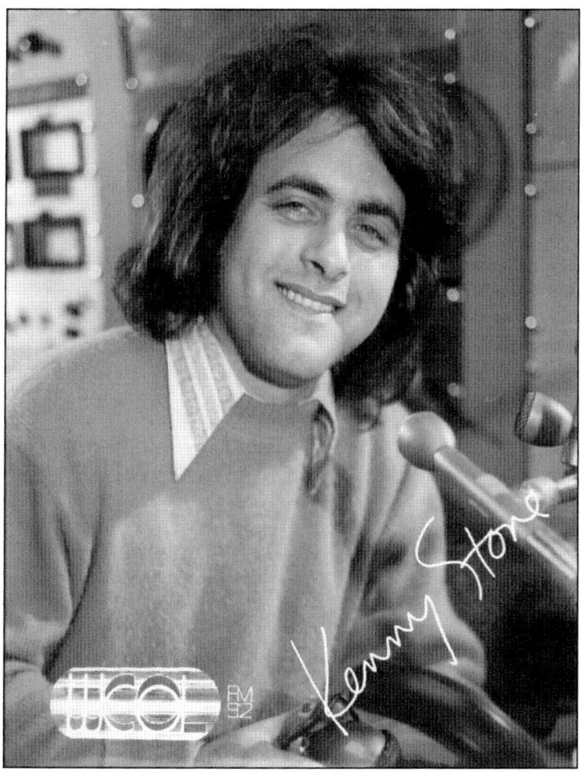

Within a few years, gospel gave way to progressive rock. Kenny Stone was one of the original WCOL-FM DJs around 1969. Following Ken Stone on the air was Jim Roach. The average listener in 1969 would surely chuckle when they learned that there was a Stone and a Roach on a station playing music of the so-called "underground format," and the two would seem to be named for references to the illegal weed. Not so—these were their real names. (Author's collection.)

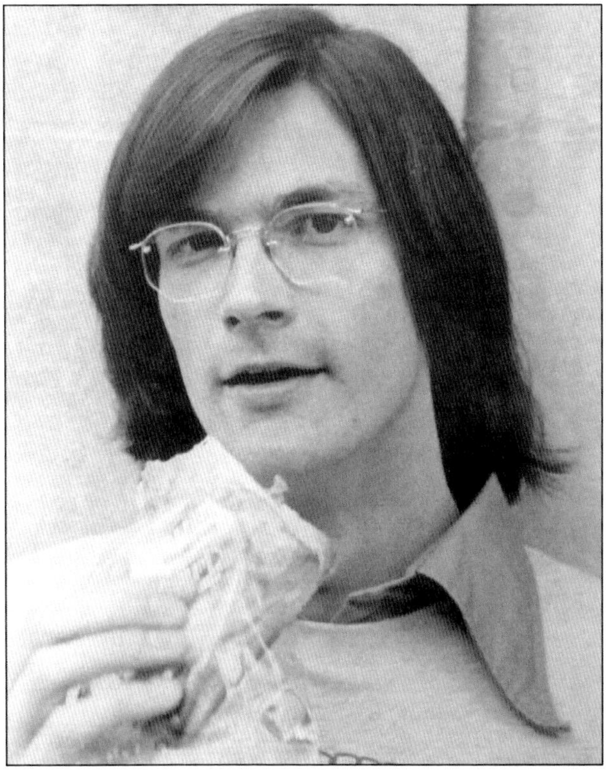

FM DJ Jim Roach is pictured in the early 1970s. Says Jim: "I was a true novice when I was asked by Dan Morris [the general manager] if I could handle a daily rock show. My only experience was introducing an occasional gospel song as filler between sermons. And since the format was entirely new, I had no role models to pattern my style after. WCOL FM was an incredible training ground." (Jim Roach.)

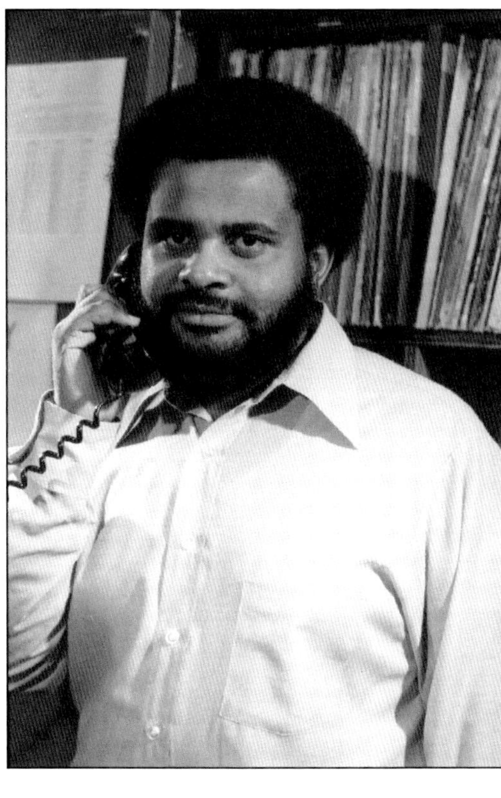

This is Bob Gooding, an FM DJ who later became the program director of WCOL-FM. He was a smart guy, and as the WCOL community outreach and public service person, he created some public service shows, such as the weekly *Listen Here*. (Neal Shapiro.)

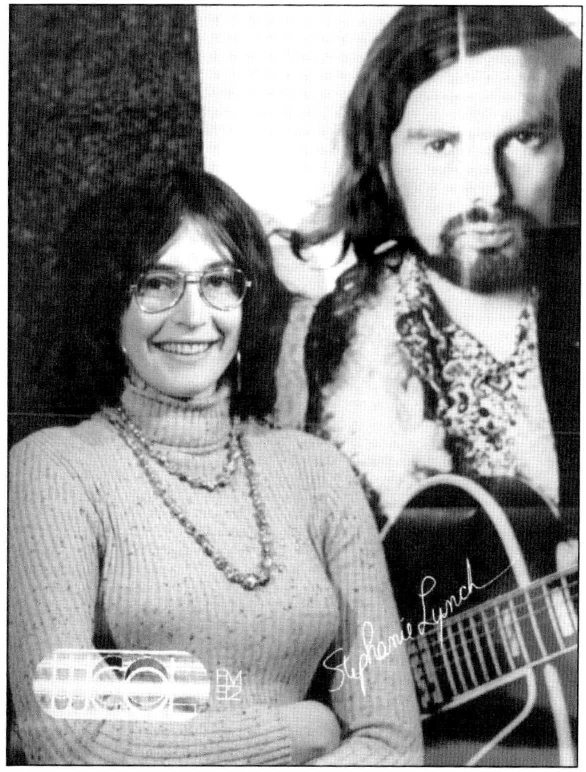

Stephanie Lynch, WCOL FM DJ, 1970. After decades of Top-40 hits on AM, the free form, non-format nature of the FM progressive rock service was hard for management to get used to. Imagine in today's radio environment just being handed an air shift and told to play what you wanted. Today it's called "college radio" and you don't get paid! (Author's collection.)

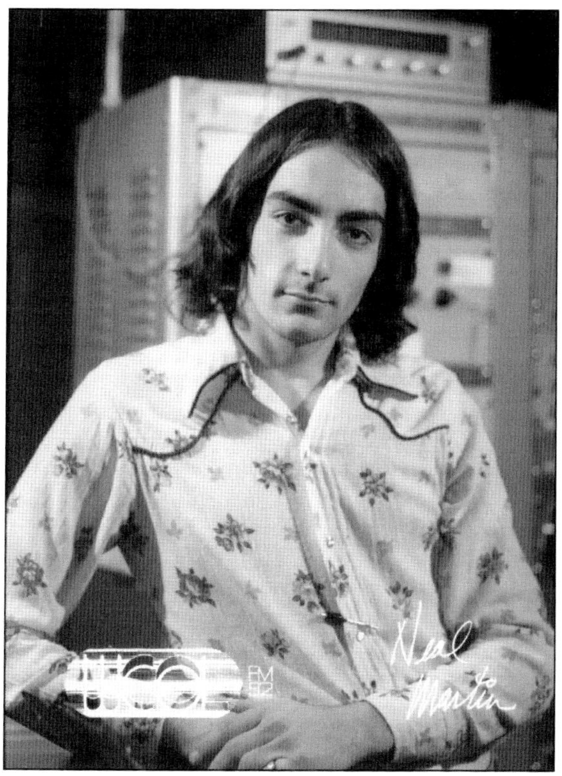

This is Neal Shapiro in the early 1970s. Neal helped the author of this book in many ways. Mostly, Neal has been collecting WCOL-branded clothing, hit sheets, and photographs, many of which appear in this book. Neal called himself "Neal Martin" while on WCOL-AM and FM. Like most of the WCOL air staff, he is an OSU communications graduate. (Neal Shapiro.)

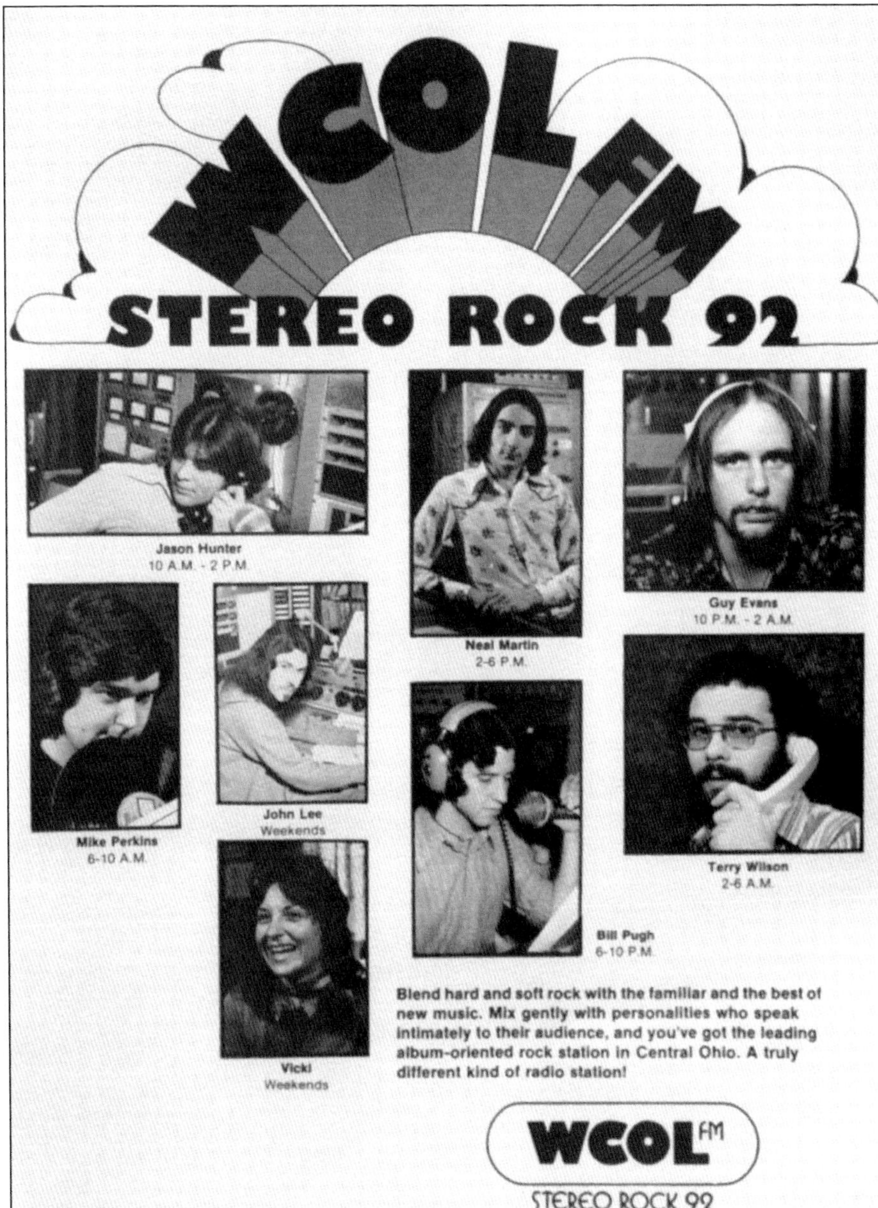

This is the promotional page announcing the WCOL-FM DJ lineup in the mid-1970s. The format is described as such: "Blend hard and soft rock with the familiar and the best of new music." It was popular, but were there too many commercials? Program director Bryan McIntyre wrote a paper for a graduate school class in the form of a memo to the station manager called "Commercial Limit on WCOL FM" in 1977. His argument was that because WCOL-FM has the largest number of commercials per hour in the market, it might have competition from the newcomer in the market, WLVQ, an FM station that was formerly WTVN-FM. He argued that WCOL's 12 minutes of commercial time per hour could not compete with WLVQ, which had half that much. He argued that short-term profits would lead to long-term losses. He suggested to management and sales that they lower their commercial load to eight minutes an hour, promote it, and go head-to-head with the new WLVQ. As McIntyre said, "The future of this building is on FM." (Neal Shapiro.)

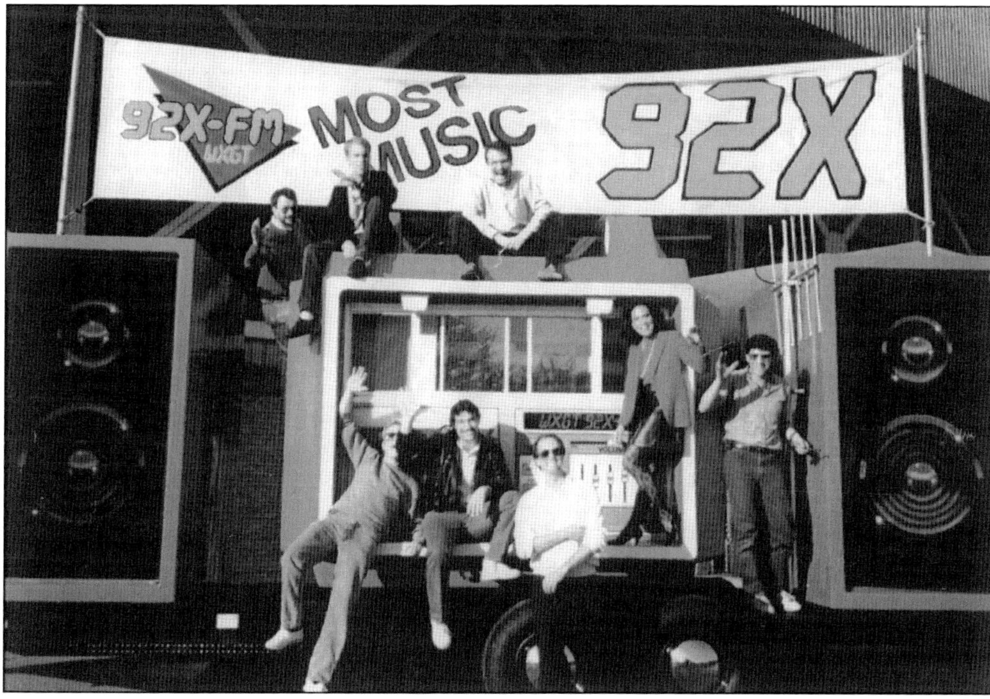

The 1970s were experimental years for many FM channels. WCOL-FM became WGXT by 1980, and the format, while rock, was tightly controlled. The era of free-form formats was over. Pictured is a mobile unit in the mid-1980s. Today, WCOL-FM is number one in the Columbus ratings as a country music station owned by iHeart Media. (Neal Shapiro.)

Mike Eiland explains this photograph: "It is the fall of 1979 and WLVQ was number one in the Columbus ratings." Mike, wearing a tie, is the man on the right, together with fellow announcers from what was called Q-FM 96. In the background is a significant symbol of Columbus, the Leveque-Lincoln Tower, home to several FM antennas. (Mike Eiland, iHeart Media.)

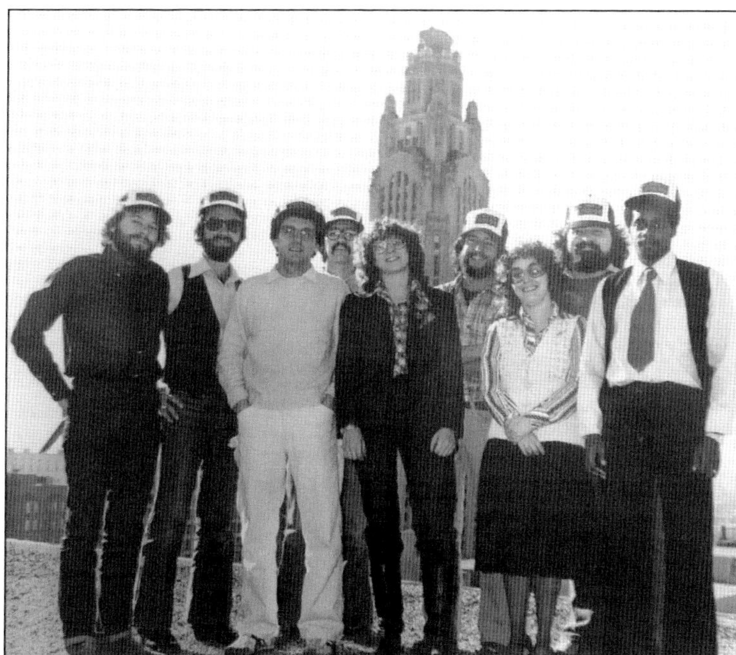

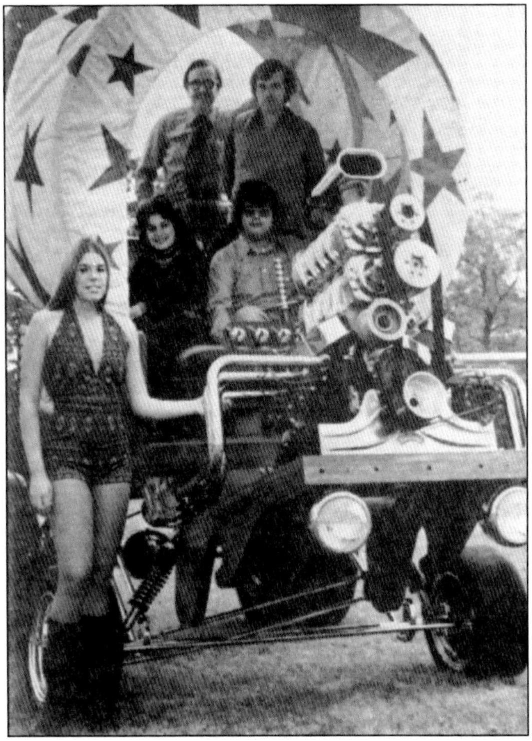

The top-rated station for much of the 1970s was WNCI-FM, and one thing it did well was involvement in local events, what contemporary stations call "promotion." Here are several WNCI DJs posing with Miss Autorama 1971. The promotion read, "Autorama 71 comes to Columbus and WNCI will be there." Counterclockwise from bottom left, the DJs are Cynthia Robins, Charlie Pickard, Bob North, and Steve Mountjoy. (Mike Eiland, iHeart Media.)

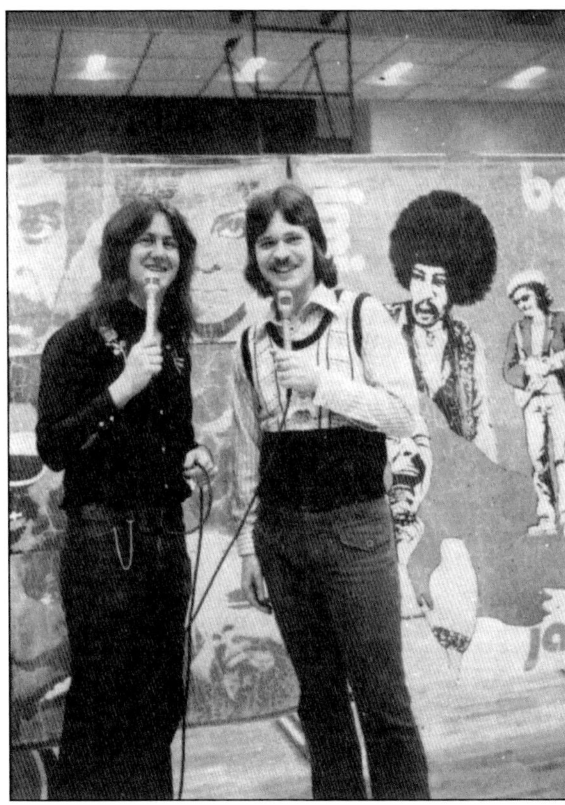

Another promotion, also a teaching moment as WNCI presented to high school assemblies, was "The Continuing History of Rock Music." Pictured left to right is the program's narrator, Mike Herman, with WNCI program director E. Karl. This event was photographed at suburban Dublin High School. It beats study hall any day. (Mike Eiland, iHeart Media)

In 1974, the WNCI weekly publication, *Record Rap*, announced the coming of Wolfman Jack, syndicated from Los Angeles and airing over WNCI on the weekends. Wolfman was on WNCI every Friday and Saturday night from 9:00 to midnight. In this cover photograph, the Wolfman poses with then WNCI program director Tom Mills. (Mike Eiland, iHeart Media.)

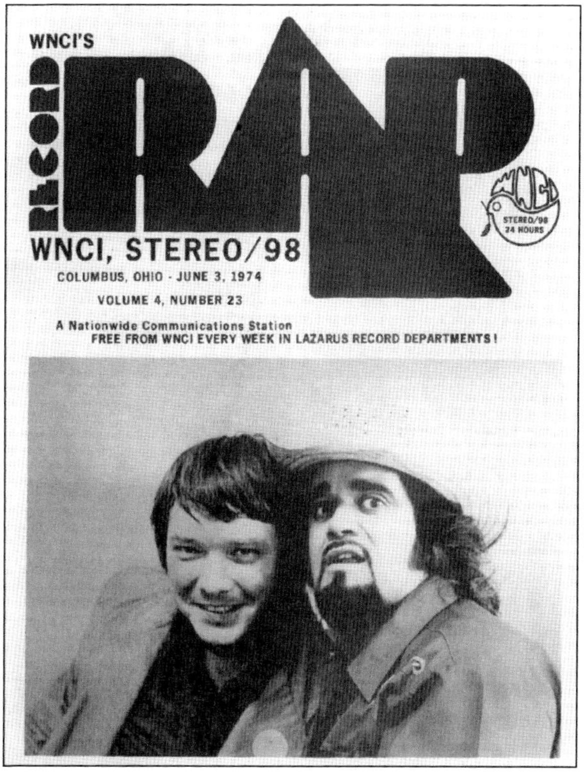

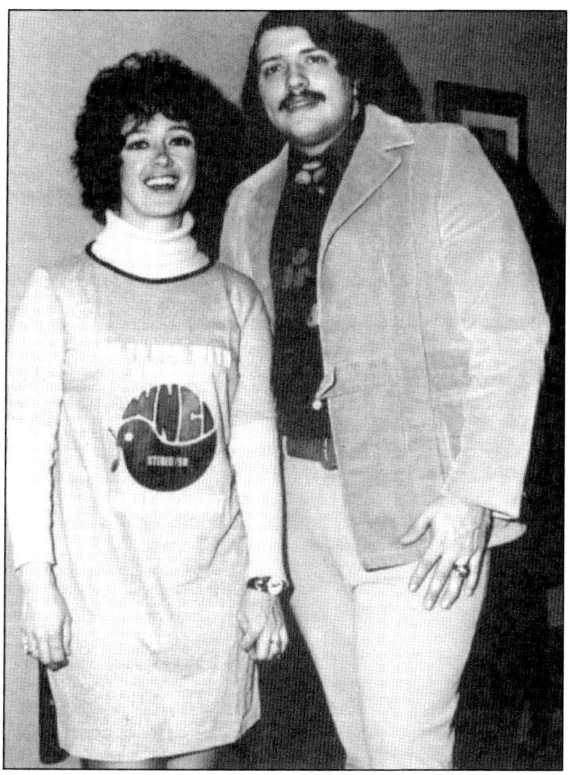

The *Record Rap* reads, "Proudly wearing her WNCI nightshirt is Donna Jean Young, the sex symbol of East McKeesport. The *Laugh-In* star was in Columbus recently to promote Junior Achievement." It is for charity. Posed with her is DJ John B. Canterbury. (Mike Eiland, iHeart Media.)

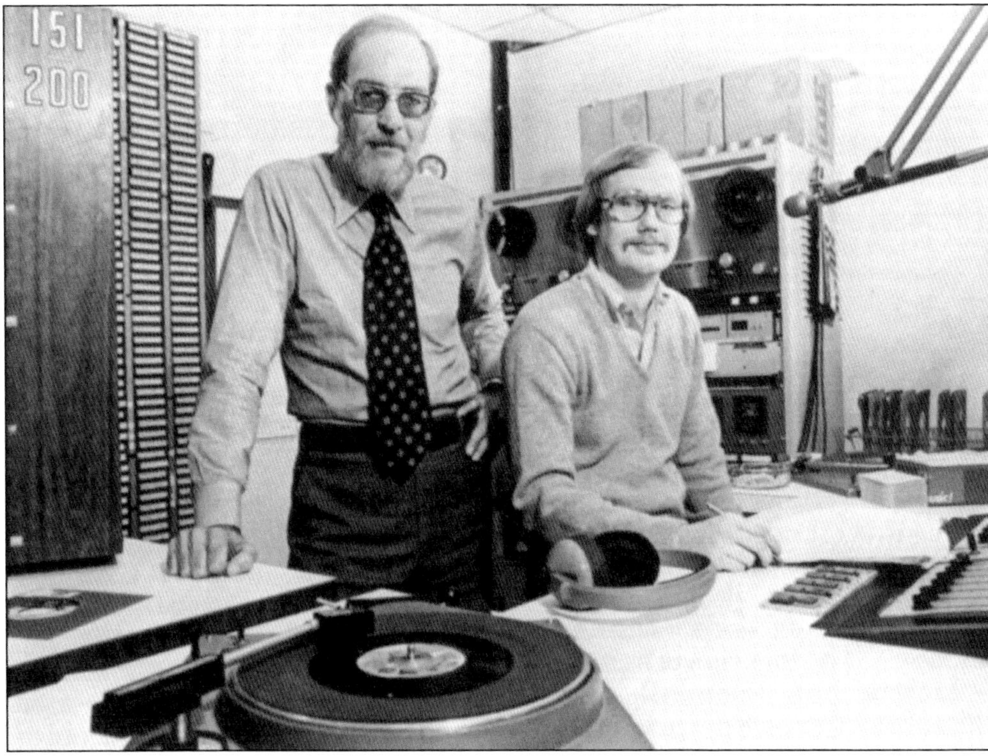

An undated photograph shows WNCI general manager Harold Hinson with DJ Mike Metzger. It is believed that Hinson is offering Metzger (the normally underpaid talent) a generous raise, health benefits, and a paid Hawaiian vacation. (Mike Eiland, iHeart Media.)

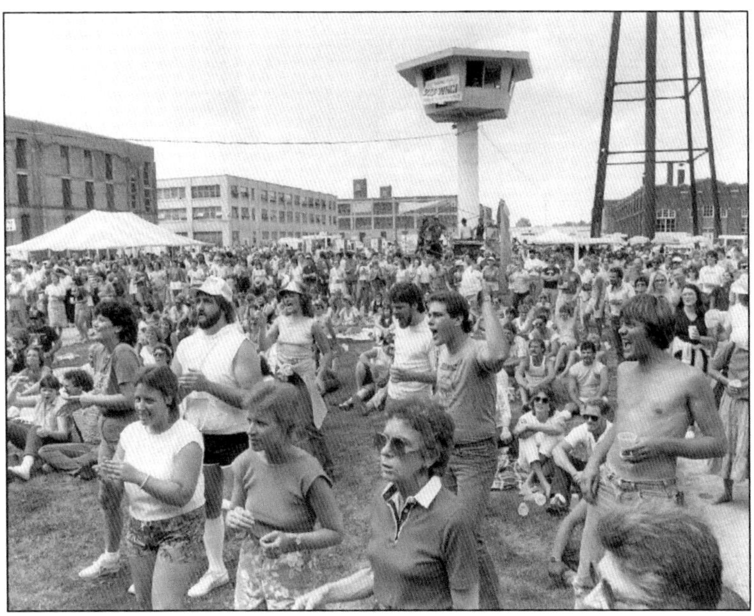

This is a large promotion sponsored by WNCI featuring live music and lots of armed men. It is "Party at the Penitentiary" in the early 1980s, and judging by the crowd, a good time was had by all—at least all those who could go home. (*Columbus Citizen-Journal*/Photohio.org.)

Conclusion

In the end, like the biblical "ashes to ashes," Columbus radio moved from the 10-watt WMAN Baptist church station in 1922 to WOSU-AM selling to a religious broadcaster in 2011. Obviously, radio has changed. Former AM giant WCOL is barely viable, the FMs pay the bills, and radio as it was once imagined by a hardy group of professors and preachers continues to be challenged by the likes of SiriusXM and streaming radio, which are taking over the last bastion of traditional radio listening: the car. And while the old order has changed, it is still radio, often with news, sports, music, and DJs, but less local for a new age. We will never experience radio in the same way as in those exciting times of discovery and promise. As always, we will adapt. We will live with it just fine.